39
TRAN.

PARIS PASSIONS

Watching the French Being Brilliant and Bizarre

By
Keith Spicer

D1053797

BookSurge

Copyright © 2009
by KSTransmedia Inc.
85 Montgomery Avenue
Toronto, Ontario
Canada M4R 1E1
Tel. (416) 485-4435
Fax (416) 485-5228

Spicer, Keith, 1934
All rights reserved.

ISBN: 1-4392-1392-5
ISBN-13: 9781439213926

To order additional copies, visit:
Your local bookstore
www.booksurge.com
www.amazon.com
www.parispassions.com

To contact author:
paris.passions@yahoo.com.

Cover photo with permission of the
Paris theater troupe Compagnie Jolie Môme:
www.cie-joliemome.org
Front-cover photographer: Paddy Sherman

OTHER BOOKS BY KEITH SPICER

A Samaritan State?
External Aid in Canada's Foreign Policy
University of Toronto Press

Cher péquiste...et néanmoins ami:
propos pré-référendaires dans un esprit post-référendaire
Les Éditions La Presse

Winging It
Doubleday

Think on Your Feet
Doubleday

Life Sentences
Memoirs of an Incorrigible Canadian
McClelland & Stewart

DEDICATIONS
*In memory of my great Francophile
friend Hamilton Southam,
In gratitude to my wise and generous
accomplice Paddy Sherman,
With love to my three half-French,
half-Canadian, but never half-
hearted, children:
Dag, Geneviève and Nick – all
offspring of
my "amie de toujours" and inspiring
first
French girl-friend, Thérèse*

CONTENTS

PART II:
PEOPLE FACING THEIR MUSIC

PART III:
A COUNTRY IN FAST-FORWARD

∽

Preface

She seduced me when I was twenty. Half a century later, I'm still her head-over-heels love-addict. Over the centuries, Paris has snared countless lovers, but she always seems to have room for one or two more. To love Paris is to share her with thousands of rivals: Don't get involved with her unless you agree a little jealousy adds piquancy to passion.

Like every admirer, I yearned to shout my joy, my rooftop being a computer keyboard. Agape at the shelves of books about Paris, I wondered how to say anything new. Every cliché, proverb and story, every tree, fountain, museum, monument, park, square, alley, bar and restaurant claims fans worldwide. But Paris is everybody's private garden. To each Paris-lover, the city is a cherished secret. And as writers from Thomas Paine to Gertrude Stein, from Sigmund Freud to Pablo Neruda and Ernest Hemingway, have admitted, Paris easily becomes a second homeland. Even occasional visitors feel they own a unique Paris to which they'll always return. They learn there's Paris – then the rest of the world.

Here you feel a citizen of the world, even more so than in other fabled capitals. For Paris seduces not by money or power, but by culture, history, respect for individuality, and an unfailing faith in romance. The French do their PR brilliantly: "French *chic*" and "French lovers" make an enviable (and exploitable) reputation. And on top of these gallant myths the French all pass for inspired cooks. This book doesn't strive hard to dismiss any of that. There's a bit of truth in the legends, and besides, it's fun to believe.

Unlike some foreigners who profess that they "love France but can't stand the French," I suffer the great weakness of loving France *and* liking the French – indeed, a sure sign of infatuation? – right down to their egregious faults. The seventy-two mini-essays here convey anything but uncritical praise or blind sentimentality. Some are caustic, even borderline vicious, about certain aspects of French society and customs.

That's usually because these shortcomings illustrate some grand national illusion or (as I see it when impatient) hypocrisy – and every nation has its own versions of both. With regret, I'm hard on certain French faults – because I think they keep France from achieving its extraordinary potential as an intelligent, creative and humane nation. Making no excuses, I take refuge in the saying *Qui aime bien, châtie bien* – translatable, tongue in cheek, as in the old song, *You Only Hurt the One You Love.*

To advertise "Paris passions" is to betray a passion for all France, as well as for the French people. French customs, culture, reflexes, politics, aspirations – all claim space here. For Paris is not 'just' Paris; it's the capital, and in every sense heart, of France. (Well, Lyon claims it's France's apostolic and gastronomic capital.). Paris has been my observation post not only for Paris as a city, but inevitably for everything French.

This book is *not* a museum-by-museum Paris travel guide. It's a personal, highly idiosyncratic, survey of French people and institutions – of 'curiosities' that I hope may help you understand how the French think, feel, and look at the world. Drawing on fifteen years of living in Paris – "watching" from a metaphorical sidewalk café – I touch on wildly different topics. Their common thread: I found them all interesting. In some way fascinating, troubling, absurd, inspiring, infuriating, touching, or hilarious. Or just – hence our subtitle – bizarre.

I group the vignettes here by broad category, and link them with brief words of introduction and context. In most, I recall how history plays a huge and unavoidable role. For in France it is everywhere. To understand almost anything here, you need to look for its roots, often centuries-old. In these unpredictable, sometimes quirky, subjects, I've tried to identify whatever helps reveal French character and dreams. And the enchantment that is Paris.

The first eight chapters tend to look at longstanding realities of Paris and France. The last six, while still anchored in the past, weave in many of the startling changes now underway in French society and politics. In both cases, I try to pace reading by deliberately leaping from serious to satirical, from philosophy to frivolity, from hard-core analysis to softer glances at Parisian life.

Whether you're visiting Paris or just dreaming about it, I hope this book can give you something of a long-term resident's feel for Paris and France. Naturally, it looks up-close at Paris itself. But it moves on to intriguing French people and French activities – whether within France or in Europe, indeed farther afield.

Confession: I remain a dyed-in-the wool Anglo, Canadian-style. I am, as we Canucks are, a diffident, undemonstrative patriot of the Great White North. We are decaffeinated Americans – or Europeans in a hurry. No flag-waving or hand on heart for us. We are just quietly wild about our own gigantic Invisible Country – one of the world's most complex yet unknown societies.

France, of course, is anything but quiet, diffident, decaffeinated and undemonstrative. It refuses on principle to be boring. It's delighted to be thought crazy, as long as by that you mean brilliant, original, infinitely creative, and look-at-me amusing. That's why there will be room for *your* book about Paris too, plus countless others.

K.S.

Paris, November 2008

P.S. Suggestion: The book's memories and observations, if they please at all, may work best as a dip-in, drop-out read. As a menu of *apéritifs*, a sampler for browsing, daydreaming or dozing off, with a snack or two to feed some real dreaming. If they induce sleep too soon, ask for your money back.

Acknowledgments

Many thanks first to my newspaper, the *Ottawa Citizen*. Scott Anderson, its former editor-in-chief (and now editorial boss of Canwest Newspapers), got me back into ink-stained wretchery as the *Citizen*'s Paris columnist. Thanks to him, the *Citizen* subsidized cherished gastronomic vices as I wrote earlier versions of many of the vignettes here. The paper's op-ed editors – Graham Green, Leonard Stern, David Watson and Peter Robb offered encouragement, strong editing and much-valued friendship.

As the Dedications revealed, I owe a huge debt of inspiration to my dear Paris-loving friend Hamilton Southam – who, with a patriotic smile, left this world on Canada Day, July 1, 2008. My other extraordinary debt is to my old *Citizen* publisher, Paddy Sherman, an astonishing man who still climbs mountains at an age the French call 'four-times-twenty' – citing "twenty" being the only proper way to think of him. Paddy egged me on from the start, and critiqued every word of my first draft with kindly, but hawk-eyed bluntness – then casually pulled off a delightful cover photo. I consider him virtually a co-author, royalties being shared in fine restaurants.

The manuscript had the great benefit of scrutiny by four other astute readers, all media professionals as well as loyal friends: Vanessa Dylyn, Muriel Locker, Pat McKinna and Blanca Turcott. Blanca slogged through the text twice – both times spotting embarrassing errors. Each reader brought a fresh perspective that I treasure. I thank them all warmly for their always pertinent comments. As I do Mihaela Palela, who brought *her* passion for Paris to bear with clever photo-editing advice. Major thanks to Pat McKinna for helping design the cover, and for managing, with her usual brio, production and delivery of the final manuscript.

A special thank-you to Douglas Gibson, my former McClelland & Stewart publisher. From decades in the traditional publishing industry, he offered encouragement and practical advice – including the opinion that it may no longer be heretical for authors to take their own books in hand, from writer's computer to bookstore computer.

Merci, also, to my friend Brian Spence, the most informed and dedicated bookstore-owner in Paris. His encouragement, and tips on bookselling, from his Abbey Bookshop vantage-point give hope that our book won't reach the remainder shelves too soon. Brian gets a good bottle for suggesting a title that sums up my passion for Paris in two words.

A final word of thanks to the skilful and attentive professionals at BookSurge, my partners in publication. I am especially indebted to April Bogdon for assembling a first-rate team of professionals – Jason Ruhf, Jenny Parnow, Lauren Woolley and cover designer Jeremy Mace – to get this book out the door in good time and in such good shape.

∾

PART I

A FESTIVAL OF PLEASURES

Chapter One /

A TASTE OF MONTPARNASSE

The French don't live to eat, as detractors claim. Nor do they eat merely to live. They eat to taste, meet and mate. They cherish all opportunities to match tasting and talking, and, especially when flirting, they weave reassuring rituals around them. The theory: fast-food is fine on the run, but it's by definition barbaric and no way to carry on either business or a love affair.

The same goes for alcohol: quality, elegance and moderation are all. Frenchmen's cross-Channel cousins have earned a valiant reputation for binge boozing, for getting blotto on a bottle instead of glowing with a glass. Presumably, they believe this can serve romance with some mythic *mademoiselle* or – Albion's women are just as wild to carouse – devilish French lover. "Candy is dandy," they must have read in Ogden Nash, "but liquor is quicker." The French, wiser in love, tend to heed Shakespeare's famous caution more than do the Brits: Drink "provokes the desire, but it takes away the performance."

Sadly, fine dining in France, with or without romance, has now become such an endangered custom that the Ministry of Education makes schools teach children how to eat *à la française.* How? By teaching the joys of 'slow food,' punctuated by convivial talk. Fresh products, fresh ideas, fresh tastes aim to thrill Macdonalized palates. But freshness itself is now debatable: Many good cooks, even in decent restaurants, are caught nuking frozen food. In France, it must be said, this is often delicious stuff, not the perma-frost horrors you find in Anglo-Saxon lands. Still, Arctic temperatures do not improve Arctic char.

Tolerable food with a nip of the fermented grape certainly facilitates friendship. And for decent grub irrigated with plausible plonk, you can usually make friends by relying on a close-to-home Paris bistro. Once you make one place a habit, you'll soon get a neighborly buzz with your Bordeaux or beer.

Let's report first from such an emporium, then move up the food-chain of good taste from great to wonderful to sublime in food, drink and imagination. Sublimity, you'll not be surprised, comes with bubbles.

"Cheers"...for ma cantine

Lonely in Paris? A little reaching out will bring you neighbors, acquaintances, colleagues, allies, then friends and even, as the love-ads tease, "more if affinities." Meet them all in a nearby café or bistro. Make it a familiar and beloved haunt.

Call it your pub, your local, your watering-hole. It's a family for loners, an extended, cocooned identity. It's comforting, recharging, informal, embracing. It's a place for irony, even cynicism, about the trials and follies of society. It's a refuge for good times and bad. It's the center of your village, a welcome-home hideout where a smile and a handshake can open many doors. Speaking of opening doors, read on as we set some context.

Belying boxer's broken nose and beefy build, Fred Chevallier glides around his namesake bistro like a ballet-dancer. He serves up cognac, *petits rouges* and rum *grogs*

with darting handshake, grin and hearty *Comment ça va?*
He and his crew are the soul of rue d'Assas – well, between
rue de Fleurus and rue Vavin. His beautiful young wife
Virginie charms clients with easy grace and patient ear. His
Tamil chef Siva is the Escoffier of grilled salmon, *steak-frites*
and thick, runny omelets.

Au Chevallier, our handy neighborhood pub, is a real-
McCoy *cantine* – a favorite local eatery and drinking-shop,
a place where coziness, complicity and value for money
conspire to make you happy.

Localness in this ever-walkable city is all. Paris may be
a great world city, a fantasy of beauty and romance. But for
Parisians it's a loose confederation of villages. Each covers
maybe four or five streets. Each covers inhabitants and admirers with a cloak of hominess.

Fred Chevallier's (and my) village snuggles between
Montparnasse and the Luxembourg Garden. It shelters
trendies, bureaucrats, politicians, actors, artists, doctors,
spies, and a rich sprinkling of riff-raff like scribblers for foreign newspapers. It's also full of folks just making a living.
They may camp in a small loft or "maid's room" (from days
when people had servants). But they're part of our village
cosmos, the handful of streets that make up our *quartier.*
You can be poor in space here (my cleaning-lady lives in
seven square meters), yet when you step outside you're rich,
for you're in the heart of Paris.

In all Paris's villages, merchants are your real neighbors.
Your "Arab" convenience store, your druggist, baker and
hardware man become at least pro forma confidants. Fellow apartment-dwellers tend to be aloof, though moves are
afoot to favor conviviality. Once a year, mayors encourage
residents to put picnic tables out on the sidewalk and bring

food and wine – a practice raggedly followed. But a new website called *Peuplade* is taking off: it favors immediate-neighborhood get-togethers. Sneaky sub-agenda: online romance.

Yet of all the links that tie your village together, your *cantine* matters most. Feeding stomach and soul, it gives you an incomparable sense of well-being and belonging. Fickle as I am, I have four *cantines*, each for a different occasion. On a chilly day, I stroll to the *Brasserie Lutetia* for a fix of the most sinful, buttery *purée de pommes de terre* the devil ever imagined, with three pieces of tender chicken floating in a copper-pot of the stuff. Okay, I also go to ogle movie-stars: maybe Sophie Marceau or Juliette Binoche.

For a celebration, I walk seven minutes to the *Closerie des Lilas*, where Lenin and Trotsky played chess, Picasso imagined wild sketchings, and Hemingway hoisted more than his fair share. For a classy light lunch, I slip around the corner to *Bread and Roses* for a chat with my pal, owner Philippe Tailleur, over a gourmet tuna sandwich and a glass of velvety Bordeaux.

But my old-faithful *cantine* remains *Au Chevallier*, right across rue d'Assas from my ground-floor apartment. I drop in once a week when I sense my own cooking is poisoning me. With a three-course meal plus wine for twenty-seven dollars, I get friendship, sympathy and shared exultation.

But help too. Last year I cleverly locked myself out of my apartment at 10 p.m. I popped over to *Au Chevallier* to find Fred and four clients at the bar: a nearly toothless old man with a fund of appallingly crude jokes about then-presidential candidate Ségolène Royal; a young Mauritian; a mysterious Spanish lady; and a tough-looking handyman.

The handyman, it seems, was handy at break-ins, and just happened to have his tools. He tried to break my window, but amazingly couldn't crack the double glaze. We went back for Fred's moral and liquid encouragement. Fevered cogitations followed wild hypotheses, all aptly fueled. Finally, Fred asked: "Why not slip a piece of plastic between the door and the frame? Take a menu (plasticized) and see what happens." We did, and it worked – Fred and I hurling shoulders into the door in the spirit of Henry V's 1417 "once more unto the breach" assault on the walls of besieged Honfleur.

Gloating, we marched inside, faced my disdainful cat, then went back for a round (well, three) on me. Applause, laughter and self-congratulation. All six *habitués* agreed this was a grand victory – for international brotherhood, *Au Chevallier's* magic menu and, above all, our *cantine*.

Bread to live for

Around the corner from Fred's place is another place of conviviality, an unusual boulangerie-restaurant for daytime dawdling. And for dégustation – a word implying intensity and a little ceremony. The morning newspapers call for a second bowl of café au lait, or maybe a mind-sharpening (if not heart-stopping) double express. Bread and Roses camps at the corner of rue de Fleurus and rue Madame. Actresses Catherine Deneuve and Emmanuelle Béart have been spotted here, as well as Liliane Bettencourt, key shareholder of L'Oréal and richest woman in France. We're only fifty paces from the glorious Jardin du Luxembourg, arguably the world's oldest and most beautiful park.

We enter the little shop, whose English name dismays the language police charged with enforcing French-language sign-laws. The owner, Philippe Tailleur, steps out to greet us. He knows we are foreigners, vulnerable not just to bread and roses, but to bread, roses and poetry. After his "Bonjour, Madame, Monsieur," and a word of welcome, he confides:

"I am not in the service business, but the business of desire. If moist, chewy, sinfully tasty French bread is one of your fantasies, sit down and let me seduce you to a new vision of bread."

A lanky, mop-haired young genius allegedly 52, Tailleur breaks every French taboo of bread-making, business and culture. "Bread" to him is not those mythical bleached *baguettes* cradled by beret-wearing old men on ramshackle bikes. He doesn't even sell these long sticks – except in rare "health-food" versions, plain and multi-grain. He dismisses classic *baguettes* as either industrial cardboard or, when termed "traditional," phony relics.

His dozen or so breads are masterpieces of creativity and sensuality. Each uses only organically grown flours, some ground exclusively for Tailleur's cozy store. "Our bio (organic) bread is not just for health," he says, "it's mainly for taste."

Taste – and fanatical quality – are Tailleur's obsessions. Your taste-buds dance to his baker's music: dense multi-grains, tangy rye bread, yogurt-based Irish country bread, a huge, succulent loaf called (in English) "le brown bread," and a lush, grainy French *pain de campagne* that begs for a wild-boar pâté and a glass of cool Brouilly.

But the menu also lists more complex breads – one packed with figs, apricots and hazelnuts, another with chestnuts and walnuts, two Provençal-style twisted *fougasse* breads with black or green olives. Another flat, round, medieval-monk's bread uses rare Spelt wheat first eaten in 9,000 B.C.

Tailleur and his master Breton bread-maker Didier test their recipes like artist-scientists. "At each creation, we gather around the fresh bread, leaning over it, smelling it, tasting it, and asking ourselves: "'Is it good enough?'"

Tailleur preaches bread as the Dalai Lama preaches peace. To him, it's man's ancestral nourishment, the legendary staff of life. You should "never cut it, only break it with your fingers." His menu builds every dish – soups, fish, salads, *foie gras*, smoked salmon, deep quiches – *around* bread, not the opposite.

When Tailleur serves you at counter or table, he may whisper to you, as he did to me of his Marie-Antoinette *brioches* on my first visit: "This is a dream. It's for great moments of solitude on rainy days." Or, of his buckwheat-and-algae bread: "For Japanese intellectuals, this is pure Zen." Austerity with intensity.

Every food or drink is the best of its kind – a rare Spanish ham, Scottish salmon, English jams. Teas are from Taylors of Harrogate. Expresso is *illy's*. Fresh Gillardeau oysters and Billecart-Salmon champagne stand ever-ready for life's emergencies.

Once, Tailleur took me downstairs to his 120-square-meter "laboratory." He showed me gleaming machines for kneading and baking, and stainless-steel tables for pastry-making. His staff of ten includes three bread-makers. Two pastry-cooks make deep-blue blueberry muffins, maple-syrup-and-pecan delights, and murderous, dark chocolate-cakes. Partner-wife Carole devises salads and mile-high quiches.

Open since April 2004, *Bread and Roses* attracts artists, writers, movie-stars, cabinet ministers, and trendies who seek out only the best. Exquisitely tailored ladies, charmed by Tailleur's conspiratorial tips, surrender softly to chestnut-cream desserts. Tailleur's target clientele, welcomed by a fresh rose at each table, is unashamedly an élite of good taste.

The atmosphere of excellence extends to staff. Unlike many French retailers, they smile. And they seem happy to work as a team. That too is Tailleur's vision: "Money is not our target; it's a consequence. We are here to share a passion: to offer enchantment for the senses, and (echoes of Oscar Wilde) to make the superfluous essential."

Times are always tough for small businesses in France. All conspires to stifle initiative and play to class-warfare mentalities. A special tax police hounds entrepreneurs to pay crushing social charges on top of salaries. Unions fight apprenticeships. Intellectuals and politicians ridicule entry-level jobs. The now-scrapped 35-hour work-week, concocted by an economically illiterate Socialist minister, lowered productivity. Kafkaesque bureaucracy makes initiative heroic.

Still, Tailleur sees his store as the test-bed for a worldwide brand. Already Japanese are studying his formula. But they will have to find a way to reinvent Tailleur.

Tailleur rejects French chauvinism. He's a cosmopolitan with a weakness for things Anglo-Saxon. Both his menu-cover and front-door flaunt only English: "Welcome," "Push," "Pull." English-only "No Smoking" signs dismissed *Gauloises* and Marlboros even before the January 2008 restaurant smoking ban. Tailleur managed to convince the Ministry of Culture (which copied Quebec's French-predominant sign law) that *Bread and Roses* was really only, well, half-English, "Roses" being French…

What is Tailleur's ultimate goal? "To make the best bread in the universe!" Sliding an arm around Carole's slim waist, he smiles: "She keeps me young." She shoots back fondly: "And he makes me old."

Ah, the sweet business of desire.

Chocolate of the Gods

Across rue de Fleurus from Bread and Roses and up a bit toward Gertrude Stein's old apartment lies a grave provocation, the chocolaterie of Christian Constant. He and Tailleur are birds of a feather: Warriors for quality, they offer only the very best of everything. And everything, for master chocolatier Constant, a leading European defender of authentic, all-cocoa-butter recipes, is chocolate first, last and always. At the risk of convincing many women that great chocolate is better than great sex.

So, Madame, have you already wolfed down those Valentine chocolates that your top five admirers gave you? If not, listen to Christian Constant – France's pope of *la divine substance* – sublime, better-than-best chocolate. Scholar, wit and master *chocolatier*, this mischievous, bushy-eye-browed, mid-50s artist can help you blind-taste those swains into categories of quality (and, claims legend, love-making) from *Kit-Kat* to colossal.

The blind-tasting comes from Constant's family art of wine-making. He applies generations of grape savvy to taking chocolate back to the Aztec gods whence it came – for originally, as a drink, it was called "food of the gods" (botanically,

Theobroma cacao). In twenty years of travel to every cocoa-
producing country, cocoa laboratory and shrine, and in docu-
menting the amazing history of chocolate-making, Constant
has dramatically raised the level of chocolate knowledge and
appreciation. Before, people gulped down chocolate for the
tart taste and sugar-hit. Today's top connoisseurs, he says, can
discern not just the country coca beans come from, but the
vintage and percentage of cocoa butter and sugar.

Chocolate as aphrodisiac? Constant echoes neurobiological research showing that chocolate seduces your brain
into feeling sexual pleasure. Myth and anecdote – from
Casanova to Madame du Barry, Louis XV's mistress – lead
to expectations of ecstasy. Hence the delightful hint of
Valentine chocolate. But Constant believes the research
is basically sound, though in nature more Olympic than
Olympian. Winking, he confides at the tiny shop on rue
d'Assas that he keeps open 365 days a year: "Even if, chem-
ically, chocolate doesn't get you into bed, at least it fortifies
you for round two."

As with any alleged aphrodisiac, ingredients might
not really trigger neurobiological thrills. But texture and
shape can hint they do. Oysters, asparagus and *escargots*
slither suggestively down your gullet, and chocolate melts
at mouth temperature. Surely the illusion (this is love, after
all!) is what counts.

Countless illusions have followed chocolate from 16h-
century Europe onward. Immediately it became identified
with sin. It still is, though in a dietary, not theological,
sense. Bishops roared excommunication at parishioners
caught sneaking a bite of chocolate during Mass. Nuns
were forbidden this rapture. Noble ladies used it to 'flatter'
libidos between lovers. Polls today claim twenty percent of

all women prefer chocolate to sex – surely an incitement to flagging male lovers to eat *more* chocolate.

Sin-wise, the castle in Provençal Grignan points to a famous anecdote. A painting there of a fine lady served as warning to pregnant 17th-century women not to eat too much chocolate…lest, like her, they produce a black baby. The court tactfully forgot that the lady in question had a handsome African page-boy.

All of that is just fun for Constant. Friendly, grey-haired and fiftyish, he is a deeply serious artist and scholar – an Officer of the élite Order of Arts and Letters – and one-man crusade for quality and authenticity. In 2002, he led top European chocolate-makers to Brussels to fight a European Commission rule allowing *chocolatiers* to add vegetable supplements to their chocolate – instead of only pure cocoa butter. Constant, a hero to all Europe's chocolate lovers, won a half-victory: the "denaturers" could add non-cocoa junk to their chocolate, but would have to admit the crime on their labels.

Who, apart from Constant, makes the best chocolate in Europe? (My query about North American chocolate elicited a grimace). "The Belgians are honest," he says, "though like everything they do, theirs is a bit too rich." The Italians, surprisingly, are also in his good books, though chocolate consumption in Casanova's homeland is one of the lowest in Europe. "Germany and Holland make too-bitter chocolate." As for the Swiss: "I have to be careful what I say, for I have some stores there, but their chocolate is dreadful – full of fakery."

Constant stirs more than his chocolate. He animates many activities – samplings, lectures, associations – devoted to raising chocolate standards. His 23-year-old *Club des*

Croqueurs de Chocolat is limited to 150 members, all passionate Constant fans. One is Sonia Rykiel of fashion fame. She wrote the preface to one of his six, beautifully-written books on his passion.

His books teach, entertain, illuminate – a new one even lobbies to protect exploited cocoa workers. He tells you not just what makes great chocolate, but how to eat it: ideally, says Constant, with water, not to overwhelm the chocolate's subtleties. But a nice port, sherry, or even malt whisky can often enhance the taste. Champagne? "Well yes, for the romance of it, but it is not really the perfect companion for chocolate."

What is the perfect companion? Your most choco-late-literate lover, of course. Take him to chocolate's Vati-can where all sins are forgiven. And trust Madame Rykiel: "One should catalogue fine chocolates as masterpieces, as sculptures, as artists' canvases, and taste them slowly while drinking smoky Chinese tea at Christian Constant's in Paris, while listening to Mozart."

Le bon vin - no longer drunk on success

Port, sherry and malt whisky? All foreign beverages in a country whose liquid trademark is wine. But patriotic French imbibers see trouble in paradise, foxes in the chicken-coop, or rather "des loups dans la bergerie" (wolves in the sheep-fold). It was bad enough watching Italian and Spanish wine sneak into France against national prejudice, distributors' collusion and French wine-makers attacks on trucks bring-ing bottles over Alps or Pyrenees. Now France suffers the in-dignity of New World upstarts. Among those barging in: the U.S., Chile, Argentina, South Africa, and barbarian Ozzie-land and Kiwi-country – the Australasians having the gall to send flying-doctor vintage experts to teach the French "modern methods" of producing wine. Is there no shame? A stroll up to Montparnasse's rue Delambre and rue Bréa measures the disgrace.

Sixteenth-century satirist Rabelais called wine "the most civilized thing in the world." Nineteenth-century microbiologist Louis Pasteur termed it "the healthiest drink in existence." Twentieth-century novelist Colette savored its "licentious liberty." Twenty-first-century French, swallowing all this, just say: "Let's drink less wine, but better wine." The problem: France produces unsaleable oceans of the soothing stuff, and many people can't tell Petrus from plonk.

Synonymous with wine, and the world's largest producer (with Italy), France faces a wine crisis. Overproduction crushes many growers. Yearly domestic consumption, still the world's highest at 33 million hectoliters, has been dropping for almost thirty years. Per capita annual wine-drinking has fallen from 120 liters in 1980 to 55 liters in 2007. Half of French young people never drink wine. Trendy adults prefer whisky to Dubonnet.

Partly because of anti-alcohol campaigns, young people are turning to beer (barely considered alcohol) and sugary soft drinks – ironically triggering anti-obesity campaigns. Wine quality is uneven, now-corrected scandals in Bordeaux and Burgundy still faintly echoing. Price doesn't guarantee quality. Top Bordeaux reds are a speculator's playground: vintners love to hype current years as the greatest year ever. New Chinese clients (among others) buy this, along with the most absurdly priced wines.

Also hurting: Even knowledgeable customers lose their way in a Byzantine labeling system of *terroirs* (specific soils, placement and climate), regions, castles, and, of course, vintages. Acclaimed wine-masters also shape opinions.

Two foreign factors count. Over thirty years, U.S. wine guru Robert Parker's 100-point rating scale has achieved terrifying impact – not just on prices of wines he praises or dismisses, but on taste. Some major French wine-makers craft their wines to suit his personal taste. They slip oak chips into wine near the end of process.

Foreign competition also looms. French consumers, especially outside cosmopolitan Paris, are notoriously conservative – and patriotic. Drinkers here disbelieve a May 2006 repeat of a "shocking" 1976 blind tasting giving California wines the first five places against the best of Bordeaux. Why should we buy foreign wine, they argue, when France makes the best, most diverse wines? Yet visits to four quite different Paris wine emporia explain why some foreign wines are finding French shelf-space.

A sommelier at Paris's upscale *Grande Épicerie* thinks the complexity of French labeling intimidates. "Our clientele is sophisticated, and increasingly willing to try foreign wines. Foreigners' varietal-based labels are also less perplexing than many French ones."

A popular-chain *Nicolas* franchisee on boulevard Raspail doesn't think imports will ever get beyond their current five percent of the French market. But he warns that foreigners are invading. "Go and see the film *Mondovino*, which unmasks all the fakery and contrivances of globalized wine. Unfortunately, they often work."

The owner of small-producer store *La QuinCave* on cozy rue de Bréa scoffs at Parker – and at victims of his homogenized taste. "Making wine is incredibly complicated. These computerized, industrialized, one-taste-fits-all guys are simplistic and dangerous. But the import trend is up."

Finally, the boss of the *Comptoir des Andes* on rue Delambre explains why his Chilean-only wines succeed in France. "First, our wines are captivating. Their fruity taste explodes in the mouth." Next, "they are reliable: You can count on their quality, bottle after bottle – some French wines can be capricious." Labels are simple. "While building specific 'valley' identities like Maipo and Colchagua, and listing vintages, Chilean wines display grape varieties prominently. This helps new drinkers match foods and tastes."

Finally, price. "For ten dollars, you can get a good wine. For twenty-five, a superb one– confident but elegant." A few years back, TIME magazine claimed that a "good Chilean red is like Antonio Banderas in a suit by Giorgio Armani."

Quality, habit and national pride will always keep Frenchmen drinking mainly their own wines. The challenge is recovering worldwide market share – France was down from 23 percent in 2001 to 18 percent in 2006. Popular regional-wine exports dropped almost 16 percent in the first half of 2008. Spain, Australia, Chile, Argentina, the U.S. and South Africa have all taken markets from France, now only third-ranked exporter.

A French counter-attack has already drawn lessons from foreign competitors. For years, some growers have quietly consulted Australian experts on modern techniques. And with government help, they have ripped up lower-quality vines and distilled unsold production into pure alcohol.

More decisively, French exporters are discovering simplicity. With 470 AOC (guaranteed-origin) wines, 200 local *vins de pays*, France presents a dizzying choice abroad. Adopting foreigners' practice of highlighting grape varieties (Merlot, Chardonnay, etc.) is helping. Exporters are also inventing a few big mid-scale "brands:" Chais de France, Castel, and soon Chamarré (as in châteaux, Chanel and Champagne, wink marketers). Basic idea: combine label "readability" with quality and prestige at a decent price.

A sparkling solution. Plainly, somebody remembered poet Paul Claudel's words: "Gentlemen, in the little moment that remains to us between crisis and catastrophe, we may as well drink a glass of Champagne."

Champagne: small bubbles, big dreams

... And on that note, let's dip a tongue into a flute of the nectar of the gods. Now here we are clearly marrying (so to speak) love and ingestion, heart and tummy – or rather taste-buds. Taste meets illusion so intimately in champagne that one is never sure where one begins and the other starts. The occasion for drinking, and especially the drinking partner or partners, also shape the magic. If making love is the little death, a few, like a famous British lord, have thought of bubbles as their farewell libation for the big death. Surely a better drink than Socrates' hemlock to ease the way to the Next World ...

"My only regret is that I did not drink more champagne," groaned famed British economist John Maynard Keynes on his deathbed. In Reims, Champagne's capital, you share his regret. A dizzying 4,733 producers, 65 cooperatives and 284 mix-and-market houses offer the "heavenly stars" that Dom Pérignon perfected (but did not invent) in 1670. Tottering home after bubbly indulgences from the Champagne region's 250 kilometers of caves, you yearn like a rueful fisherman for the bottles that got away.

From the start, royals ("legitimate," or self-appointed like Napoleon), clerics, extravagant Englishmen and flighty ladies took to this heavenly nectar. Louis XIV and Dom Pérignon were both born the same day, and died the same day. The Sun-King's bubbly praise got the monk's well-blended, cleverly-corked new version of Champagne off to a giggly, if not roaring, start. Abandoned Queen Marie-Antoinette, awaiting Louis XIV's long-impotent grandson Louis XVI to rise to the occasion, found solace in the divine potion. By dubious legend, she designed bubble-killing Champagne glasses in the shape of her breasts – a pitch to her flagging hubby's imagination?

Seven British monarchs since 1884 have favored Bollinger Champagne – James Bond's tipple when not flirting with Moët et Chandon's *Dom Pérignon*. But pound-rich Brits today still like Pol Roger. Along with brandy, this fine blend helped Winston Churchill win the Second World War. His reward from Pol Roger: a case a week for life. For the afterlife: Winnie's name graces a special blend called *Pol Roger Winston Churchill*. (History disputes whether Churchill or Napoleon said: "I drink Champagne when I win, to celebrate...and I drink Champagne when I lose, to console myself.")

True to their wartime PM, who quaffed a bottle a day (plus brandy), Brits down gargantuan quantities of "champers:" roughly 37 million bottles a year. Serious boozers of anything except aftershave, they are by far France's thirstiest customers.

Another reason Europe's royals may like Champagne: For centuries, kings of France were crowned in the

Cathedral of Reims, "France's Westminster Abbey." It was there that Charles VII – aptly called "the well-served" – was crowned in 1429 in the presence of a famous groupie, Joan of Arc.

Clerics, adroitly ricocheting between heaven and hell, condemned this libido-stirring libation as the devil's drink. But the region got an early ecclesiastic boost: Pope Urban II (1088-1099), a local boy, hinted that offering him a quantity of Champagne wine (not yet even bubbly) might secure an audience. With a pope onside, marketers, adding bubbles, went crazy. Certainly Urban II did: he launched the First Crusade.

Today, many countries sell sparkling wines that surf on Champagne's reputation for celebratory prestige. Italy's *Spumante* and *Prosecco*, Spain's *Cava* and Germany's *Sekt* are the best known. Georgians and Americans, among others, have also exploited the "Champagne" name that France's diplomats and European Union trade negotiators fiercely protect. Even other French regions produce "Champagne-style" wine: *Crémant* from Burgundy, Alsace and the Loire is sometimes better than low-end Champagne. But the real McCoy, conferring top prices, comes only from the 32,341 hectares of the official Champagne region. Soon, by 2008 decree, the region will expand to meet exploding demand – "though without," authorities nervously insist, "diluting quality."

A visit to the chalk caves running beneath Reims's streets can chill you to 12 degrees C. (54 F.) as you watch workers giving millions of bottles a quarter-turn to help fermentation (mostly, machines do this now). Among big houses offering tours and tastings: Heidsieck, Ruinart, Pommery, Taittinger, Lanson, Roederer. But the real fun lies in discovering your own small *récoltant* among those 4,733 producers. Proud of their products yet trampled by the mass-market weight of the big houses, they will spend hours with you. You may form a lifelong attachment to a splendid brand nobody has heard of.

"It's hard work," confesses Josiane Daviaux-Quinet, who produces fine Champagnes with husband Philippe. "But it's a joy to craft exquisite tastes."

Much of modern Champagne mythology comes from the movies. Scores of them from *Casablanca* to *An Affair to Remember* use bubbles to tickle hearts. Perhaps the most charming film was *Gigi*, with a girlish Leslie Caron teasing older-man Louis Jourdan with these words:

> *The night they invented champagne*
> *It's plain as it can be*
> *They thought of you and me*
> *The night they invented champagne*
> *They absolutely knew*
> *That all we'd want to do*
> *Is fly to the sky on champagne.*

Madame Caron, now elegantly escaped from teenage delirium, runs her own enchanting inn, La Lucarne aux Chouettes, in tiny Villeneuve-sur-Yonne, 100-odd kilometers south of Paris in Burgundy. Her fine restaurant serves four top Champagnes: Bollinger, Pommery, Ruinart and Besserat de Bellefon.

"Sorry to disappoint you," she told me, "but I don't have a favorite because – to tell you the honest truth – I am like our new President, Nicolas Sarkozy, a non-drinker!"

Nevertheless, you can join her there to sip your own favorite. And, with a little luck, fly to the sky.

Bring a doggie bag

The street protesters dispersing, we sneak through the crowds to the colorful rue Delambre, just behind celebrated upscale restaurant Le Dôme on Boulevard du Montparnasse. Hunger gnaws, and we gawk not at mobs but at pretty girls.

We spot a frisky young woman with page-boy-cut black hair. She is – oh, about 28. Flouncing along, she steers her gorgeous companion into our cozy, famous-for-fish Bistro du Dôme. Rue Delambre was long a haunt of Simone de Beauvoir and Jean-Paul Sartre – sometimes together, often not. It's a small street of discreet hotels, bars and restaurants known to up-and-coming actors and fashion models. But it offers charming little surprises: a coals-to-Newcastle wine-shop selling only Chilean wine, a smokers-only eating club, a hole-in-the-wall Indian condiments shop, a superb cheese shop, a boutique wittily named Mi-fugue, Mi-raisin (playing off the "neither fish-nor-fowl" mi-figue, mi-raisin). It specializes – what a perfect idea! – in wine and classical music CDs.

The page-boy girl sits down facing me, beside her stunning blonde friend – a giant Afghan hound that starts slurping enthusiastically from a silver ice bucket.

Fido-Shah is the quintessence of elegance, lacking only Hamid Karzai's famous green cape. Throughout the meal, he sits up straight, as well-raised Afghans do, alternating bites of his raw meat with long-nosed pokes into the ice bucket. Not a soul stares. A few occasionally smile that the show is free.

French restaurateurs love dogs, and you often see pooches at or (usually) under the table. They add a homey, welcoming touch, and are probably less germ-laden than certain patrons.

Domestic animals, both dogs and cats, live well in France. Not just families with children, but many single or retired people increasingly find joy and comfort in a four-legged friend. (Let's leave parrots aside for now – Frenchmen don't like to be interrupted in full flight).

As elsewhere in rich countries, vast industries now supply French dog-lovers with "gourmet" food, and with fine accoutrements: collars, leashes and tartan winter cloaks announcing social, as well as breed, differentiations. Magazines and TV shows teach the art and science of dog care. Huge voluntary associations channel French commitment to canine happiness. Kennel clubs abound. Volunteer-run refuges find good homes for strays.

The biggest organization, with its own TV show, is called *Thirty Million Friends* – but it also cares for cats, zebras and pet boa constrictors. Publications like *Vos Chiens* deal exclusively with dogs, while many others cover only one race. Lots of discipline advice and news of health breakthroughs (e.g. identifying sources of pain), but also borderline stuff like pet horoscopes.

A popular novelty here is the dog-training system called "Agility" (the French use the trendy-sounding English word). What? Do humans need to teach dogs to be agile? If you watch it, as I have, you would say the dogs are teaching their masters, or that both are just having a rollicking good time.

Agility is a sport designed to bond dogs with their masters. Owner and dog race maniacally around an obstacle course, and try to go correctly over, under or through each obstacle faster than competitors. They cheer each other on, and jointly win ribbons. Pioneered in England in 1978, Agility has fans throughout France.

Until about 1950, the French tended to mock Britain's obsession with dogs – the real point of course being to mock Englishmen, whatever the pretext. Specifically, the French ridiculed mushy emoting, outrageous vet bills, dog fashions at Harrod's, and breeders' shows as regimented and Byzantine as the Royal Court. All of this fed amused contempt for *les Anglais*. No more. The French are now just as nutty about pooches as their hereditary enemies.

Another UK trend picking up speed in France is *zoothérapie*– or letting seniors have pets in old folks' homes. But the word sounds so much more scientific in French: one can furrow brows and espy philosophical underpinnings for common sense.

Apart from buying yourself some unconditional love, the best reason to get a dog in France, as elsewhere, is to get exercise. While walking your dog in Paris's grand parks, you enjoy a glorious, easy-on-eyes-and-legs workout. Also as elsewhere, you find an innocent ploy for striking up interesting conversations, including flirtatious ones.

Never mind those old stories about dogs defiling Paris sidewalks. Socialist mayor Bertrand Delanoë has noticeably cleaned things up: civic appeals failed, but huge fines didn't.

French politicians have not exploited the image-softening advantages of dog-owning nearly as foxily as Anglo-Saxon ones. For U.S. presidents, a dog – from FDR's Fala to Nixon's Checkers to Clinton's Buddy to the two Bushes' Spot and Barney – is a full-time campaign auxiliary. Even Canada's wartime Prime Minister Mackenzie King famously consulted his "little friend Pat" in this world and, by crystal ball, in the next.

Perhaps it's no accident that the French president who held power longest – fourteen years – was François Mitterrand. The most influential dog in de Gaulle's Fifth Republic was indeed Baltique, Mitterrand's black Labrador. Mitterrand, no doubt recalling Caligula's idea of naming consul his horse *Incitatus*, joked he might appoint Baltique to a prestigious body of economic and social advisers.

That didn't happen. Indeed Baltique was banned from a memorial service for the late president in the church at Jarnac, Mitterrand's home village. Baltique sat outside, restrained only by former budget minister Michel Charasse. Perhaps on grounds that Charasse had kept public finances on a tight leash.

Meeting the world at La Coupole

To end our romp through Paris eating, drinking and socializing, we meander to La Coupole, the most history-rich yet unpretentious great restaurant of Montparnasse. Here, apart from a long people-watching terrasse, is the largest bistro in Paris – 1,000 square meters, 33 painted pillars. Yet it manages to create a little island of intimacy at every table.

If a habitué, you might order the "historic" lamb curry served from a silver trolley by an Indian waiter in long white Punjabi servani, leggings and turban. The signature profiteroles au chocolat chaud follow by enchantment. If somebody told staff that today's your birthday, lights lower, and a procession of waiters marches to your table with a cake and sparklers, leading all 600 guests in singing "Joyeux anniversaire" (Happy Birthday).

*When you stop blushing, you can hoist your glass to an-
other procession: the hundreds of famous people who ate here
before you – or still do eat here.*

To eat at *La Coupole*, steps from Montparnasse's
ground zero, is to hug history: that of Europe's 20th-century
culture. A short drink away from *Le Dôme, La Rotonde,
Le Sélect* and the outrageously romantic, down-the-street
La Closerie des Lilas, it's one of the big five "*Monparno*"
restaurant-brasseries. But it stands alone, an always-come-
back first among equals. It's an understated, sleekly professional refuge where headwaiters marshal a brigade of
serveurs by lifting an eyebrow. Its gaudy *art deco* setting,
quirky traditions and gossipy tales tip hats to countless celebrated artistic, political, or otherwise eccentric clients.

Besides speaking of influence and luscious food, all
this hints at the raffish, madcap and libidinous. Great artists paid with sketches, boxing matches happened here,
women swam nude in a pool, literary and artistic quar-
rels resounded. Virtue sought vice, and found it here in a
"space of liberty" that made the world outside this room
seem stifling.

Until the early 2000s, *La Coupole* hosted basement
dancing (silky tangos a favorite), thus seduction, and it
still opens its big dance-floor for parties. But its reputation for wildness goes back to the 1920s and '30s. Then
artists passed around their groupies, notoriously the clever
Kiki de Montparnasse (who started as a nude model at 14),
and Ernest Hemingway hoisted anything that buzzed at
the bar.

Around the room crowd memories of legends, all customers. Among the artists: Pablo Picasso, Henri Matisse,

Amedeo Modigliani, Fernand Léger, Alberto Giacometti, Joan Miró, Paul Gauguin, Marc Chagall, Man Ray. Every Monday, to police dismay, would-be models swarmed a nearby street-corner "model market." Kiki was not the only famous model. Lenin, it seems, tried to become one – though certainly not nude – presumably for his expressive face. He failed. But he later became a model for a few others...

Writers? Of course Jean-Paul Sartre, Simone de Beauvoir, Jean Cocteau and Hemingway, but also *Maigret*-novelist Georges Simenon (who breakfasted in the bar), Henry Miller, Anaïs Nin, Eugène Ionesco, James Joyce, and a library-full of others.

Musicians? Dozens, including Sergei Prokofiev, Joséphine Baker (who always arrived wearing a live snake around her neck), Louis Armstrong, and George Gershwin, who heard here his first inklings of *An American in Paris.*

During the 1939-45 war, the *Wehrmacht* had one of its headquarters a few steps away from *La Coupole.* Henri Rol-Tanguy, head of the Communist Resistance, placed three German-speaking waitresses among the restaurant's servers. Meanwhile, General Charles de Gaulle's Resistance man, Jean Moulin, lunched with his wife here under German noses (he was tortured to death after his capture).

After the war, top politicians came back too. President Vincent Auriol liked to slide in discreetly. At Table 82 former President François Mitterrand ate one of his last meals. Left or right wing, politicians and intellectuals greet each other here on neutral ground.

All this notoriety, plus the dazzling décor of painted pillars and famous photo-portraits, draws Parisians and foreigners of every ilk: lovers, leaders, cultural creators, media stars, families (with small children on weekends), birthday-celebrants, and bug-eyed tourists from around the world. Says Assistant director Philippe Leroux, a 28-year *La Coupole* veteran: "We welcome people of every station and origin. Our 180-strong staff works three shifts from 7 a.m. to 1 a.m. and tries to make every visit unforgettable. To work here is to serve at the very summit of hospitality."

Mr. Leroux led a rare private tour of the gleaming kitchens, where a score of specialized cooks produce their marvels. Many dishes are multi-decade classics that regulars expect. "All of us, cooks and serving staff, know we are responsible to history and to quality. This is not a job for us; it's an honor."

It's an honor too, plainly, for *La Coupole*'s new owner, 49-year-old former-*Maxim's* cook, and famed restaurant-chain owner, Jean-Paul Bücher. Buying the famous institution from its founder, 89-year-old René Lafon, Bücher swears to respect the place's history, traditions and brasserie spirit. He has a sharp eye for service and price-quality ratio, and will probably extract even richer profits from his current 1.2 million yearly *La Coupole* clients. He is too shrewd a businessman to tinker with what works. And what works here is the pleasure of remembrance. The magic of touching a revered history and culture.

To preserve that feeling, Bücher doesn't want to submerge the magic in busloads of tourists with no concept of *La Coupole*'s past and meaning to Frenchmen. He wants it to stay the quintessence of Paris – first of all for Parisians who cherish the codes and well-known "secrets."

Symbols of fans' devotion: Lovers who kiss on the restaurant's benches are not termed couples, but *Coupoliens*. And when rumor named beloved singer-poet Georges

Brassens a candidate for another famous "Coupole"– the French Academy – a friend said: "He will never walk under *that* Coupole. He will only enter the unique, the true *Coupole*, the one on boulevard du Montparnasse."

∾

Chapter Two /

SCENES FROM AN EXHIBITION

Emerging from restaurant or *Métro*, you hit the streets of Paris. A spectacle of movement, agitation, often chaos. A kaleidoscope of colors, glimpses, gestures, flashbacks and fast-forwards. Show-time all the time, with men and women managing entrances and exits – each performer, blasé yet self-consciously, polishing "*mon look*." It's the Bard's all the world's a stage, in Technicolor. In film, fantasy or fact, it's Paris As You Like It.

Silent, empty streets beckon too. Daytime or lamp-lit nighttime, they soothe the mind and make you glad you're alive, here, and free. Offbeat *impasses, allées, passages, ruelles* and *rues* – even some *avenues* and *boulevards* – all may charm. And by the way (Trivial Pursuit time): did you notice how many English words for public thoroughfares derive from French? On a sunny afternoon, idling along an unknown street can delight a hundred ways. It may lead to a small restaurant, cozy bar or exotic shop, to a secret village, short-cut or intriguing alleyway, or even to a surprisingly famous square you'd lost sight of.

To feel and taste and smell the streets of Paris, read one of Georges Simenon's *Maigret* detective novels. This pipe-smoking, *bon-vivant* Inspector of *la Police Judiciaire*, a slightly better-dressed Lieutenant Columbo, reads these streets like a connoisseur of fine Calvados. The streets that lead you to a murder scene or a scruffy, hood-infested bistro brood memorably at night in a misty drizzle.

Speaking of rain, you should try to get caught in the Paris rain a few times. Cloudbursts blow over in a few squally minutes. A gentler downpour, in which you should get caught with a lover against a tree, will linger, holding you there – you, lover and rain all reluctant to leave.

A fold-up umbrella will save you many a time when the weather looks dicey. For living in Paris is like living in the middle of the English Channel: Weather can ricochet between threatening rain-clouds and blazing sun, and back, in five minutes. Under gloomy winter skies, you may curse Paris. Then, when the sun re-emerges to light your world, you forgive it everything: the noise, the pollution, the occasional rudeness.

To keep your spirits and sanity in this great capital, you need to spend a lot of time in parks. Your lungs will bless the micro-climates there. And your soul will bless the peace, perspective and joy Paris's many green spaces reserve.

But sitting around, even in beautiful parks, is not enough to cure ills of body and spirit. You need to walk and walk and walk. And ride a bike – Paris-as-Amsterdam's new signature, thanks to Mayor Bertrand Delanoë. For serenity and purest air, you should also high-tail it out of town as often as you can. The Paris region – called the Île-de-France – shimmers with beautiful countrysides, slower-paced towns, medieval villages, castles and fortresses. Try to rent a car outside the mad summer get-away dates, helpfully proclaimed by a thoughtful government. Better still, decamp by train.

Now let's visit some typical street scenes. For a change of pace and mood, we'll first enter the hurly-burly of people making points or fusses, and – really the same thing – having fun. Then, to recover, we'll explore a few restful parks before hopping on a bike for a look at a silent, lovely Paris almost nobody sees.

Street dramas and melodramas

*Not that we are obsessed with dogs and beautiful girls…
but when we walk down rue de Rennes to those citadels of
eggheads ("intellos") and star-struck toga-touchers in Saint-
Germain-des-Prés, we observe more of the same. Indeed plenty
more:*

Lanky legs, lush silhouette and tossing blonde hair her watch-me signals to sidewalk-café aficionados, the girl sashays past the Café des Deux Magots with an air of superb indifference. Oh yes, and with two bounding, pointy-nosed Russian wolfhounds on a leash. The crowd applauds. Flair with flaring nostrils.

This well-known story tells what everybody here knows: Paris streets are a grand stage of world and life.

A few scenes I recall:

- In a Brasserie near the National Assembly: We watch 50,000 students on their annual march for lower fees. The owner screams when a woman nearly impales his foot with her stiletto heel. He had accused her of stealing a postcard. The two of them rant for 10 minutes, while clients pick away at their *steak-frites*. The cops arrive in a black paddy-wagon. A *flic* languorously leaps off the back step, lifting a white-gloved hand à la Saddam Hussein as if to acknowledge an ovation. Blasé to a fault, he parts the pugilists, advising them to fight over bigger things – like the *Hollandaise* sauce?

- Parking paranoia: A French lady-friend of mine, ordered by a machine-gun-toting cop to move her car for a minister's limo, hurls her arms apart, Christ-like, and shouts "Go ahead and shoot me while you're at it! What are you waiting for, you coward?" Then both laugh.
- Three young guys in the *Métro*: they set up a theater curtain in a subway car, then entertain captive passengers with a Punch-and-Judy show on male-female seduction techniques. After five or six stops, they collect their money and move to the next car.
- Money in Montparnasse: Sirens blaring, five armored vans careen around corners. The middle one is a Brink's truck delivering mint-fresh euros. The four vans front and back keep side-doors open, with machine-guns pointing out. Is this Al Capone's Chicago? Can Hollywood do better?
- Outside the Pompidou modern-art center: A black guy tries with brilliant incompetence to make his wacky, one-man-band apparatus produce music. He drops a cymbal while reaching for a trumpet, loses his trombone-slide, entangles himself in wires, a crestfallen-but-game Charlie Chaplin. He has 200 people in stitches. He collects a ton of money. The nearby fire- and sword-swallowers don't stand a chance.
- My concièrge's 18-year-old daughter: From my ground-floor apartment I hear a crash and a scream, then running, shouting, and doors slamming. I dash out to find the girl in tears on the step and the concièrge's window broken. Her boy-friend was unamused at getting dumped. No less than five

cops come, each to assist the other. After an hour's debate on the doorstep, the poor girl points to her aggressor in the bar across the street. The cops nab him, scold him, then let him go. Never mind violence or stalking; this was *l'amour*. So what?

Daily mass demonstrations enrage immobilized drivers, but entertain strollers. The demo sub-culture deserves a separate look (see below). Yet smaller vignettes are quite enough to brighten your walking world.

Sidewalk artists chalk pastel masterpieces. Accordionists play all the old *I love Paris* tunes in the subway. A woodwind octet plays Vivaldi's Four Seasons in Place de la Sorbonne. At the bottom of la rue Mouffetard each Sunday, crowds dance and sing along to classic Paris songs: Édith Piaf, Maurice Chevalier, Yves Montand, Georges Brassens. You find such serendipity all over Europe; but here it wins eager reverence, and is everywhere now that spring is here. Bored at home or frazzled at work? Just take a walk and you will laugh, find delight, or cry.

Cry? Well, at least commiserate. For bent-over seniors and resourceful beggars strum your heart-strings. A few beggars, always young, kneel in the middle of the sidewalk with a sign saying: "I'm hungry" – just as you enter your favorite restaurant. Others hold open church or post-office doors for you, or offer you a street-people's newspaper. If you fail to give or buy, they loudly wish you a happy day.

Bare feet protruding from a face-covering *chador* work very well - even attached to a white European who can't spell Iran. Hard-hearted? Cynical? Alas, the phonies make you so, and you soon learn how to spot them. Gypsy moms with babies don't do as well now that police find some

Roma fathers at home are organizing teenage gangs to rob parking-meters.

There are two ground-level ladies I can't resist, though I did at first. A 35-year-year old woman (looking 55) has been knitting on the sidewalk outside my bank for five years. Before her: a diploma, and a sign bemoaning her layoff from a factory. She is plainly emotionally ill, and France's vaunted social security system and cult of "solidarity" can't seem to help her.

The other is an even younger, sadly disheveled woman who crouches at all hours in nearby doorways beside a bottle of cheap red wine. Giving her enough for a bottle earns you a beatific smile. And a chance to reflect that theater, on these charming streets, plays tragedy as much as comedy.

Demonstrative democracy

No TV story from France is complete without scenes of thousands of apparently furious protestors stopping traffic. The "street" is a very old weapon of angry Frenchmen, going back to the Middle Ages. But 'anger' doesn't convey the whole message. Hitting the pavement with your colleagues and sympathizers is a feel-good experience of deep resonance. It's a hormonal imperative, a reliving of teenage revolt, a seasonal celebration – in the end a party, often with beer, wine, barbecues, flirting and dancing.

Well-coiffed ladies with pearls marched with skinheads, Sunday-best farmers, small business people, workers and well-scrubbed youth –10,000-strong to acclaim far-right leader Jean-Marie Le Pen. About 400,000 scruffier counter-demonstrators, an alphabet soup of leftists, centrists, students, worried families and self-appointed intellectuals, denounced Le Pen as a fascist and Nazi.

That's how it used to be before mid-2007 when French voters virtually eliminated far-left and far-right parties. But demonstrations – known as *manifs* (for *manifestations*) – remain the routine way unhappy Frenchmen express themselves. What makes a *manif* in France, how do they work, and why do the French demonstrate so often?

Any cause is pretext for parading about in Paris, or indeed in any big French city. The most common excuse for a *manif* is wage demands, pensions or work conditions. These are routinely termed defending "acquired rights" and/or "public service" – especially when state-employed demonstrators are defending privileges private-sector workers lack.

Doctors, nurses, lawyers, farmers, laid-off workers, fishermen, teachers, students, name your trade – it's been in the street this past year or almost any year. The most shameless damn-the-public ones are striking transport workers: airline staff, air traffic controllers, baggage handlers, truck drivers, bus drivers, and railway staff of every kind. They are always ready to cripple citizens' basic needs to travel to work, visit relatives, or just eat. So strikes destroy people's holidays, cause elderly people to have heart attacks, and torment tired children? Too bad: workers' "rights" eclipse everybody else's. Only in 2008 did the government pass a law guaranteeing minimum train service.

Teachers are the champion *manif*-makers in terms of numbers, noise and predictability. Their massive education bureaucracy ("the Mammoth" or the "Red Army," termed it a former minister) shares a semi-official leftwing ideology and non-negotiable sense of entitlement. Invariably, it disguises its demands of more pay for less work behind slogans of serving children. This, while mobilizing children to march chanting union slogans backing teachers' demands.

Other *manifs* are social or cultural. Mothers demand more midwives (common in France); parents demand protection against schoolyard violence. Film-makers march to keep subsidies that make French cinema enviably creative.

The most scripted *manifs* are political ones. Party leaders march arm in arm with "compatible" union leaders and "outraged" intellectuals. Mobs of sympathizers trundle behind, mouthing authorized or prompted slogans. Such incantations stir collective frenzies, and make everybody feel righteous and triumphant.

Slogans are a vital part of *manif* culture. They should ideally sound aggrieved, angry, idealistic and witty – indeed, if possible, echo some reinforcing historical event. Marchers don't just make slogans, they chant them endlessly, with rat-a-tat rhythms that excite the blood and feed a sense of solidarity. Chants encapsulate a viewpoint, and hammer it home as threateningly as possible.

A *manif* needs costumes, bells, whistles, banners and cause-related props. Pig-farmers bring pigs to the Champs-Élysées, fishermen fish. Parading doctors carry stethoscopes, teachers dunce caps, plumbers pipes, and so on. Clowns, painted faces, stilts, whatever it takes to make a show: that's a *manif.* For high-falutin' causes, you need pretty girls on guys' shoulders waving French flags. Joan of Arc lives.

Such are the rituals, the liturgy of protest. Change is not usually the point – for most *manifs* defend those "acquired rights," a relic of Lenin's "irreversibility of socialist conquests." Besides, the *manif* is itself considered 'action.' It is mass, self-administered psychotherapy more often than not designed to *prevent* change. In France the left is far more reactionary than the right.

Unless you're aching to see grown-ups playing the fool, or you see *manifs* as an art-form, you will follow police warnings and change your bus or taxi route to avoid the nonsense. Off-limit routes often tell you which ideological flavor is on offer. Place de la Bastille and Place de la République for the left; rue de Rivoli and avenue de l'Opéra for the right. The Champs-Élysées for solemn national occasions, or for anybody with a pal in the Préfecture de Police.

Why this endless parade of parades?

- The French political system is so far out of touch with ordinary people that few think of approaching elected representatives. Politicians, "all corrupt and incompetent," won't listen unless a mob throws a tantrum;

- The French can't manage evolutionary change, only revolution – hence "the street." With a turbulent, myth-dominated history, they dismiss compromising gradualism. Entrenched élites hunker down and fight change until the kettle explodes;

- In so many ways, France is still an absolute monarchy. Memories of peasants with pitchforks and nobles' heads on pikes subliminally haunt today's 'kings,' and empower the street. Mobs incessantly remount barricades from 1789, 1830, 1848, 1871 and – the year they freaked out even de Gaulle – 1968;

- Back-scratching: Frenchmen accept today's traffic blockades because tomorrow they may want similarly to defend their own privileges: the street is automatically right;

- Union weakness: despite what foreigners think, barely eight percent of French workers belong to a union – a level far below that in most western countries. Propped up by secret donations from both government and bosses, France's union chiefs disguise their lack of real influence –reduced even more under President Nicolas Sarkozy – by organizing festive mob marches proclaiming their "anger." Fake fury, phony-façade 'Potemkin' protests.
- *Manifs* are fun. You get off work or out of school, inconvenience thousands, snag a few seconds on TV, maybe pick up a lover. Singing, chanting, bonfires – it's all a feel-good fête.

This may be the real secret of *manifs*. Notwithstanding the substance of a few demos, the French crave a party. Anytime, for any reason. As they say wryly about themselves: "In France, everything ends with a song."

Listening to summer's silence – the parks of Paris

Forget the frenzy. The tumult on pavement, asphalt and cobblestone may thrill, even amuse. Streets? They're just the paths leading you from park to park in Paris, or from quiet garden to enchanting little square. Nothing allows peace to seep into your personal Paris more deeply than do the glorious green spaces that an enlightened city government reserves for you. Find your favorites, and make them yours. Anytime is good, but try late June.

Raucous neighbors off on holidays. Rumbling cars and trucks subdued. A rare motorcyclist, without a muffler, proclaiming his manly inadequacies. Summertime, quiet time. Time to flee the tourist-rivers flowing down the Champs-Élysées. Time to hear yourself, your mind and soul. Time to seek peace in the 450 green spaces of Paris called parks, squares or gardens.

The great Paris parks thrill with spectacle and round-every-corner surprises: a statue, a pond, a bower, a tiny bridge, flower-beds, historic palaces. Their names: Montsouris, Monceau, Buttes-Chaumont, Invalides, Champs-de-Mars, Bagatelle, Belleville, Bercy and the astonishing Tuileries, Jardin des Plantes and Jardin du Luxembourg. All offer intimacy amid grandeur. They're places to watch people of all ages stealing a little happiness.

Amid such beauty, people cultivate private gardens of the mind. Each is different, but many offer what little kids really want: sailboats, slides, swings, merry-go-rounds, Punch-and-Judy shows. Inside the puppet theater, screaming kids explode your ear-drums. Outside, people hush their words.

The deep suburban forests – Boulogne and Vincennes – offer another silence. They suck you into their dark recesses, their high, overarching trees, their horse-trails, bike-paths, lakes and elegant restaurants: the Bois de Boulogne's *Pré Catelan* will do for your next wedding, Madame, or just a classy romantic rendezvous. If romance fades, ponder love's fragility in a famous cemetery: Bittersweet, Père Lachaise and Montparnasse echo Andrew Marvell's "The grave's a fine and private place / But none, I think, do there embrace."

Strolling alone or with friend, visit as many as you can of Paris's hundreds of small neighborhood parks. These pocket havens beg you to sit and read a book or newspaper, idly speculating on passersby or snuggling lovers on the next bench. Or maybe to daydream of life past, present and future.

Every district harbors several mini-parks – green oases amid the stores and six-storey apartment buildings. In the13th arrondissement, you can sit on a curled-back bench and hear only Cantonese. Beside Paris's *Grande Mosquée* (Great Mosque*)* is a tiny oblong park where you hear only Arabic and West African languages.

At Sèvres-Babylone's round little park, you will hear the choicest of plummy 7th-*arrondissement* French accents. Not 200 meters away is the charming little Parc Châteaubriand, hiding behind *La Grande Épicerie* and other chic food-and-drink emporia. At the bottom of the rue Mouffetard, an old Roman road, you can slip into a sliver of a park beside the ancient Église Saint-Médard. Just benches, a sandbox and a slide. On market days, you hear the hawking-cries of nearby farmers and fishwives. But that's OK. They're peddling sounds of life, not horns and exhaust fumes.

Almost every church has its little park. At Sainte-Clotilde, where César Franck wrote his revolutionary organ works and perfected his brilliant improvisational skills, the priest held an open-to-all Russian picnic in 2007. Attending: the Russian ambassador and a choir from Saint Petersburg. Normally, you hear there only birds and the sweet sound of silence.

Beside a more famous music church, Saint-Germain-des-Prés, you have two little parks – both *confidentiels* in the sense that people overlook them while admiring this

1400-year-old church at Ground Zero of France's intellectual life. A few stroll into the park along the busy Boulevard St-Germain. But almost nobody notices the even more
intimate little park on the church's other side, on rue de
l'Abbaye.

All of the above are seductive. Visit each on a whim,
often with a fresh newspaper or book. On art-market days,
stop at a well-hidden mini-park just off the animated Boulevard Edgar-Quinet. Another charmer is a small triangu-
lar park on the art-gallery side of the Institut de France, the
domed citadel of French culture that embraces France's linguistic Vatican, the Académie Française. There's an exquisite
small statue of a nude girl there, half-turned in a dance. Her
solitude makes this a magic, secret place. The Seine and the
Louvre lie a reluctant glance away.

My favorite of all little parks hides just across from
the Swedish Cultural Center in the richly textured Marais
district. An art-nouveau statue of another girl stands here,
arms stretched forward within a circle of almost always
empty benches. Around her stare Roman faces in broken
bas-reliefs. A weeping-willow hints again at Marvell: "Had
we but world enough, and time/ Your coyness, lady, would
be no crime."

I'm smitten with this girl. She's always there, always reaching out for a misty lover, always dancing
in this tiny corner of a *quartier* speckled with museums and galleries. I can read for hours in her company,
look up, and smile that neither she nor I has gotten any
older.

And what, precisely, is old? It's when, methinks, you
stop dreaming. Come to Paris, and briefly flee its glories
and grandeur. Go to a small park, and whisper a dream to

a dear friend. Stay young together in your very own *parc confidentiel*.

Heaven's Gate – the Jardin du Luxembourg

The lifelong "parc confidentiel" of untold Paris visitors is the incomparable Jardin du Luxembourg. See it before you die, and hope that earthly heaven turns out to be here for you too. Haven to every age from small child to senior, the "Luco" goes back to the Renaissance (with echoes of Caesar's Gaul), and shines as far ahead as the soul can imagine. It has soothed millions of your fellow human beings, and, in time, maybe it can help cure your ills of mind, heart and body as well.

If you can't get to Heaven this morning, come sit down on this sunny bench in the Jardin du Luxembourg. We'll watch autumn leaves float down against a cloudless sky, snack on some roasted chestnuts, then bless our fate: We're a galaxy away from the world's troubles. We're cuddling up to life as it should be.

Cuddling is what an epidemic of lovers are doing all around us on this nippy, dazzling day. Entangled in each other like doting octopi, sweethearts are seizing the day, the hour, the magic minute. And frankly, my dear, they don't give a damn about us.

Neither do the *tai chi* folks, *pétanque* players, *tae kwon-do* enthusiasts, oriental sword-twirlers, tennis jocks, wistful old ladies, kids on ponies, joggers, *képi*-capped guards, bistro waiters, chess-players, *pipi* ladies (50 *centîmes* for the loo, *s'il vous plaît*) or pigeons.

For the Luxembourg, almost since Roman times, has always been a public universe for private worlds. A place where 3,000 people can stroll, read a novel, a poem or *Le Monde*, sip a Kir, and savor solitude.

Or punctuate it, if eyes and interests meet, with a well-mannered word to a stranger that could lead to nothing or everything. Everything might be a coffee prelude to love in the afternoon. Or just a coffee and a memory.

A woman in the "fine flower of age" (that's any age a man finds charming) is likely to elicit an approach within minutes of settling onto a bench or chair here. If she leans even a little toward Catherine Deneuve (who lives down the street), say, fifteen minutes. Men? Even harmless pensioners can snag a smile and a chat.

The Jardin is a collection of many gardens, of secret places, each with its mysteries. At the center of a great French-style garden – all symmetry and subtlety – glows the exquisite *Palais du Luxembourg*, home of France's Senate. Built for Marie de Médicis (wife of King Henri IV) during 1615-27, its vast salons are ablaze with Rubens. Its three-storey façade gives 321 French senators a stunning view running up to the Paris Observatory a kilometer away.

Sprawl feet-up on two chairs facing the *Palais*: this will remind you of why you should have been, or married, a king. It reminded Hermann Goering of something too. In 1940, he installed here the western headquarters of the *Luftwaffe*. This is commemorated in bombing raids on your lunch of *poulet-chasseur* by the ubiquitous and, alas, incontinent, pigeons perching Hitchcock-like in trees above two outside *buvettes*.

Elsewhere, rioting English gardens play off classic French ones, with huge old oaks and splendid hide-and-seek bushes. Statues of poets – Rimbaud, Baudelaire, Lamartine, Verlaine – linger everywhere. So do statues of sculptors and painters. And of scientists who invented stuff you always thought some non-Frenchman discovered. Tragically, Chopin stands 200 meters from his mistress, George Sand. But maybe that's why their relationship has lasted so long.

The loveliest statues, surrounding the central basin, place twenty queens of France on pedestals. Ladies only, for the Jardin's mood is *la douceur*. My fantasy-love in this marble harem is Laure de Noves, a yearning of Petrarch's in 1327. Older women are in vogue, and she has aged beautifully.

In the wooded philosophers' walks toward Montparnasse, you can, I swear, hear the footfalls of Voltaire, Rousseau, Proust, Hugo, Hemingway. Just over there.

Tired of sitting? *Mais le jogging*! A lope around the Luxembourg takes you ten minutes. My own style of jogging I call enthusiastic shuffling. I can blitz the Jardin's inside perimeter in fifteen minutes, even stopping to wonder, again, at the achingly romantic *Fontaine de Médicis*.

Soul-food? The Jardin offers us four exhibitions this typical day: giant photos of volcanoes; modernist wood sculptures; a tour of French flora; and paintings by Raphaël. In the lineup for Raphaël, somebody carries a boom-box playing Mozart's clarinet concerto.

In the end, the Luxembourg's enchantment lies in the spell it casts on everyone entering its high gilt gates. A sudden hush, a tingly illusion tell you this is your personal paradise. Your secrets are safe here. Your heart is free to sing or cry here. Your mind, like your feet, can roam over capricious itineraries.

There are countless Luxembourgs, each defined by one person's memories. Almost always, these recall children or some long-lost love. Among the besotted, a complicity reigns: you keep your secret garden, and I'll keep mine. But together maybe we can walk a little, then sit a while longer on this sunny bench.

Now, have we eaten all those chestnuts?

Lady Godiva rides in from Amsterdam

Who are today's kings of the road? No longer can cars, trucks and buses arrogantly shunt aside those fragile string-and-paper contraptions called cyclists. Motorists are still good at killing them (as well as daredevil motorcyclists and scooter-riders) through accidents or the cancer-bearing fumes of their internal-combustion engines. But suddenly, as of July 2007, drivers have had to share Paris's roadways. Not really with pedestrians, whom Parisians-at-the-wheel still love to terrify and bully. But with another vehicle – that long-ridiculed two-wheel people-pedaled device called the bicycle. Quickly, of course, defensive road-hogs saw cyclists as a new threat to public order, indeed public morals. But the two-wheeled wonders are winning.

Bare bums on bikes? Cops torn between gawking and guiding, thousands of nude bike-riders swirled through over sixty cities on World Naked Bike Ride Day to pro-test dangerous, polluting motor-vehicles in cities. Fantasy and irony for the French: they claim they invented the car (Étienne Lenoir, 1862); and now, with Paris choking with micro-organisms only a cancer-researcher could love, many want to ban it.

Who started the biking-in-the-buff movement? Why, those sexy Spaniards – whose Mexican cousins offer toasts to "love, pesos and fat women on bicycles." Normally

French authorities welcome any excuse to party. From spring to fall, not a week slips by without some official fête: for music, the Internet, chocolate, cinema, gardening, journalism, comic books, and probably historic thumbtacks. Now bare bikers.

Surprisingly, Paris – where sex sells everything from coffee to scotch tape – saw cops banning the Lady Godiva-style protest. They arrested five cyclists (accidentally including a stunning blonde) for "sexual exhibition." In a city where sex clubs abound and national leaders prance through complex romantic entanglements, the arrests suggested a Paris version of the old Victorian rule: "Do as you wish, but keep your clothes on and don't frighten the horses." The horses today, presumably, would be distracted, accident-prone male drivers.

But nude cycling is just part of a much bigger story. Health, safety and the environment are galvanizing the French. Soon after his May 2007 election, President Nicolas Sarkozy made the environment a cosmic priority, along with tax and labor reform.

Until about 2002, Frenchmen greeted environmental dangers with at best indifference and fatalism, at worst denial and ridicule. France's green movement split into cliques, achieving nothing. The "romance" of cars also blinded people: pride in excellent French-made cars and a network of superhighways dismissed traffic fatalities (7,242 in 2002) as inevitable road-kill. Jacques Chirac as Paris mayor (1977-95) made cars street sovereigns, adding underground parking everywhere, and laughing at bicycles as quaint.

What's behind today's environmental reform? A murderously hot 2003 summer (15,000 neglected French elderly died), TV eco-star Nicolas Hulot, Hurricane Katrina, U.S. Cassandra Al Gore, and a devastating United Nations scientific consensus. Even the ineffectual but sexy G8 forum of major industrialized nations yearly urges faster action.

Although Paris's inner city hosts little industry, it drowns in cars, trucks and noisy, filth-spewing motorcycles and scooters. Buildings get so grimy that by law owners must have their façades sand-blasted every ten years – scaffolding causes eyesores lasting up to six weeks.

Adding up costs for health, sand-blasting, accidents and traffic-jams, critics claim motor vehicles bloat city budgets. They argue that bikes could bring cleaner air, easier parking and a gentler, quieter lifestyle.

By 2008, bikes were changing Paris. Socialist mayor Bertrand Delanoë extended bike paths to 376 km. and declared many streets bikes-only on Sundays. He encouraged members of bicycle club *Paris Rando Vélo* to explore the city in a river of self-policing hundreds. Police-protected roller outings also engaged over 15,000 enthusiasts.

In July 2007 he launched a program, pioneered to spectacular success in Lyon, to put 20,600 almost-free bicycles under Parisian bottoms. A deal with Cyclocity, a subsidiary of the gigantic billboard company JCDecaux, installed 1,450 high-tech bike stations throughout Paris where a person could take off on a *Vélo-lib'*, then leave it at any other station. Annual fee for daily short-run use: 29 euros (then about 39 dollars) – cost of a two-week Paris subway pass. Trips of under thirty minutes are still free.

JCDecaux invested $121 million in start-up costs, paying 285 full-time employees to run the computerized system. It reserves half of its billboard space for the city, and pays the city a yearly fee of $4.5 million. JCDecaux then gets to collect all revenue from the 1,628 city-owned billboards.

Dodging around Paris on a bike, I find the prospect of thousands more fellow-cyclists exhilarating. First, they help cut pollution: a year after Lyon signed with Cyclocity, its vehicle traffic dropped four points. Second, extra bikers even the odds a little against motorized Parisians who curse us cyclo-peasants as absurd intruders – even though we share some "bicycle" lanes with buses. Now at least we can smirk back.

Paris as Amsterdam? Not yet. But the bike vogue illustrates a new civic spirit. The government has banned smoking in restaurants, and is multiplying photo speed-traps, praising hard work, jogging and cycling. It's discouraging drinking, and is pushing law and order and traditional values.

Now they're arresting *cyclo-nudistes*. Where will it end? Could the future be – *mon Dieu!* – Paris as Singapore? As Ryadh?

No. it will "end" with bicycles becoming a so-called threat to something or somebody, just like the cars, trucks and buses. It has already started. Following several 2008 bike deaths where cyclists passed trucks on their right, raced down one-way streets the wrong way, or ignored red lights, the cops are fighting back against "dangerous" bike-riders. Their main weapons: fat fines and cooked-up media campaigns – all to the delight of taxi- and truck-drivers.

What can assuage motorists' fury at 'reckless' cycling? Nothing, but thank goodness France abolished the guillotine. Meanwhile, the streets of Paris are a bit safer, the air a mite more breathable, and traffic a shade more democratic. As long as you keep your pants on.

Owning Paris - early-morning nostalgia

Even on a bicycle, you should keep your wits about you. Or at least half of them. For it would be sad not to notice the seductions of pristine Paris as you pedal on. The best and safest time to appreciate monuments, interesting buildings and never-noticed shops or alleys – not to mention places of personal memory – is just before or around sunrise. Get out there on your bike between 5:30 and 7:00 a.m., and neither cars, nor cats, nor people will cross your path. Paris will be yours alone.

Cycling through the still-dark streets around 6:00 a.m. on a rough-and-ready Portuguese town bike, you're not thinking of beating Lance Armstrong. Or of cars or passersby. Pedaling at a good five-speed clip, and dodging through alleys and one-ways the wrong way, it's ten minutes from Montparnasse to the Louvre, and from start to finish you've got the City of Light (even without light) almost to yourself.

Why ride an early-morning bike in Paris when you could do something sensible like, say, sleep? Because dawn biking feeds body, mind and spirit. And because, of course, if you're nuts enough to ride a bike after 7:30 a.m., you risk a serious disagreement with a four-wheel rival. In Paris even women drivers drink testosterone, and pedestrians and bikes are mere Formula-1 track-blockers. A Green-friendly

City Hall offers a few special cyclists' lanes – after 7 a.m. usually shared with rambunctious buses.

The feel-good side of biking at daybreak draws on endorphins and one-upmanship. You're pumping hectoliters of oxygen into the old brain, and blasting out cobwebs. You also get an early-morning rush from *beating* the rush: that tingle of smugness you feel when you're up and at 'em, and others doze. You stop at a sun-lit terrace for a *café au lait* and buttered slice of fresh baguette, unfolding your morning newspaper. Friends snore? You sneer – though not too unkindly.

But oxygen-and-coffee cocktails are not the real thrill of Paris. History is. Evidence of kings and queens, their courtiers and lovers, of revolutions, writers, artists, musicians and scientists fill your eyes everywhere in France – and they are never more present than at dawn. Buildings and plaques memorialize them, well, to death. History-mania once led to spoof plaques announcing that "nothing happened here, ever."

On a bike ride from Left Bank to the Seine, the past comes at you from every corner. Two minutes from home, I whiz past the huge 18th-century Saint-Sulpice church. Its strange, asymmetric building harbored ferocious theological battles, and housed the Revolution's Temple of Victory.

Cavaillé-Coll's famous five-keyboard organ there draws the world's greatest organists – following composer Charles Widor (for 63 years "temporary organist") and master-improviser Marcel Dupré (38 years). Now the vicar moans that his church has become a mere way-station for tourist mobs – not pursuing Christ, but Dan Brown's *Da Vinci Code* fantasies.

A few other on-the-fly glimpses: the Place Saint-Germain-des-Prés, where literary and political cafés split clienteles with the square's ancient namesake church. Picasso's long-time home on rue des Grands-Augustins slips by as you turn the corner where, on May 14, 1610, a nine-year-old boy called Louis became Louis XIII. Emissaries told him there that his father, Henri IV, had just been assassinated.

Even the Louvre has bloody memories. It was from there that, on August 23-24, 1572, Charles IX ordered the St. Bartholomew's Day massacre of tens of thousands of Protestants. Charles's appalling sister, Marguerite de Valois, disgraced by lovers and booze, snagged a mansion you zip by on rue de Seine on the way to the gold-domed Institut, home of four state Academies.

The peak of this Easy Rider's joy comes when I wheel into the vast, empty courtyard of the glass Pyramide, the Louvre's spectacularly modern main entrance. The sun's first fingertip rays touch the ornate dark-grey chimneys, creeping down to the small round roof-alcoves, then to the tall, statue-laden arcades of the museum's grand inner façades. I careen six or seven times around the periphery, my private *vélodrome.*

By the time I leave, the massive courtyard is aglow. High up in the azure sky, white contrails betray the morning jets to North America, Africa and Asia. It's a surreal moment, past and future bracketing a luminous, solitary now.

Before heading home, I dash through Napoleon's Carrousel du Louvre, a mini-Arc de Triomphe leading one's gaze through the long Jardin des Tuileries, then up the Champs-Élysées to the real Arc de Triomphe about four kilometers away. A quick run up and down the high side-wall of the Jardin, then I scram home before cars and buses spoil the illusion.

As illusions go, remembering student landmarks and the friends you met there is more heart-warming than a millennium of kings and their often equally blood-thirsty women. Ah yes: This café was the Icelandic girl, that one the German girl. A third, just the old gang from that Sorbonne course where the French vowed they would "civilize" us foreign savages.

They didn't entirely succeed. But rolling back here fifty years later in the early-morning mist, and owning this great city for a few minutes each dawn, I decide that if life is but a dream, biking through Paris at daybreak is not a bad way to dream it.

But wait. There was one time when I did think of beating Lance Armstrong. Biking from the very top of an empty Champs-Élysées one morning before six a.m., I roared alone down the great avenue's cobblestones to the Place de la Concorde, coming close to shouting a war-whoop. For a good minute there, I was sure I saw Armstrong pumping hopelessly away…in my rear-view mirror.

෴

Chapter Three /

SEASONS OF CONTENT, AND OCCASIONAL DISCONTENT

In pre-literate societies sun and moon reckoned time, casting spells and pregnant shadows. Today scholars cite forty calendars still in use, including Chinese, Indian, Islamic and Jewish. A few Orthodox churches cling to the "Julian" calendar, cooked up by Julius Caesar after pillow-talk with Cleopatra. But most of the world plods along with 16th-century Pope Gregory's "Gregorian" calendar, which sprinkles the year with Christian memories that some revere, others ignore, and most gleefully exploit as work-free holidays – starting, but far from ending, with Christmas, Easter and All Saint's Day.

For the French, Gregorians to a fault, exploiting work-free holidays is a national sport. Workers claim eleven statutory days off, often juggled to make four-day weekends. If Christian feast-days can serve this fine secular cause, they reason, why not revere them?

French calendar-pacing is trickier than in many countries, starting with…starting the year. What are the universal rituals and joys of Paris seasons? How can you make sense of them, and serenely go with the flow? We pick just a few watersheds.

Back-to-everything time – early fall's "rentrée"

If any single word can make French men, women and children simultaneously cringe and rejoice, it's the word "rentrée." "La rentrée" makes September the most exciting, society-changing month of the year – especially since it can extend (who's counting?) to Halloween. With a little awe, ponder how it infiltrates every facet of French life.

Summer light wanes, a final *pastis* makes gullets tingle. The last bottle of chilled Alsatian white flatters picnic seafood to become a *cadavre*, dead on holidays' field of honor. A new year dawns. What, in late August? Yes. For in France, the "year" begins not on January 1, but September 1 – the ominous yet tingly-with-expectation eve of *la rentrée.*

La rentrée means 'returning' to whatever concerns you – school, work, culture, sports, politics, the economy, romance. Every country has its New-Year-in-September, but in long-holidays France, it's a time of almost unbearable anticipation.

Education being a state religion in France, the original 'return' was *la rentrée scolaire.* Serious business: school scripts children's lives for up to two decades with a rigor drilled into little heads from age three. Class ranking will later decide who gets into which élite school or faculty.

Every fall, teachers and high-school students ache to re-fight the annual battle against curriculum reform. After years of bringing down a classroom-full of ministers of education, kids and teachers can hardly wait to hit the pavement again while weather's good and street-protest partying is comfy.

Same goes for *la rentrée universitaire.* Bearded profs announce their course will be the same as last year. Witch-hunts against free-thinking faculty "rightists" will start up again: in 2008 a courageous Sorbonne rector got bounced for urging innovation and responsibility. The old Marxist students' union, UNEF, will urge the only activity it knows – a strike (actually a boycott with a chance to pick up a babe) – once again proving by pompous oratory that no shirt is too young to stuff.

The *rentrée culturelle* breaks down into literature (pre-eminent in book-crazy France), music of every kind, theater, movies, TV, dance, painting, sculpture, and limitless fashion trends. Every clan and coterie commands its *rentrée* and media insiders. Gossip abounds: the star news anchor, with a book to flog, reveals the non-secret that he fathered a fellow anchor's child. In September 2008, that same anchor – fired after 21 years from the top TV news program – exemplifies a creeping purge of media people Sarkozy dislikes.

The chattiest, most incestuous rentrée is the *rentrée littéraire.* Targeting the bonanza-producing fall literary prizes – the Goncourt, Renaudot, Médicis, Interallié and Fémina, publishers start hyping potential bestsellers in mid-summer. Driving the 2006 PR steamroller was the decade's bad-boy novelist-poet Michel Houellebecq with his *The Possibility of an Island.* Confronting the 632 other fall novels that year (few of which sold), he promised all the gimmicks of cash-grubbing *enfants terribles*: filthy words, cynicism, kinky sex, woman-hating and racism. But his syntax was exemplary! Critics saw a savior for the flagging French novel.

The 2008 *rentrée littéraire* dumped 676 novels on de-spairing booksellers. That year, women led the sex-mad pack. Catherine Millet recycled her impressive orgies. Christine Angot tarted up, so to speak, the *Kama Sutra* by detailing her upstairs-downstairs couplings with a Métis celebrity aptly called *Doc Gynéco*.

The big *film de la rentrée* 2006 showcased heart-throb Daniel Auteuil, plus boredom, hills, and a blind real estate promoter with Braille skills handy for wife-swapping.

September 2008 brought Houellebecq painfully to the screen, and painlessly a nothing-happens but esthetic stroll through Strasbourg called *La Ville de Sylvia.* It led, over the year, to a drumbeat of good, bad and indifferent French movies.

The big 2006 *rentrée sportive* featured the return to the national (*Les Bleus*) soccer team of Zinédine Zidane, captain of France's 1998 World Cup-winning team. Take the top ten NHL players and multiply their fame by ten, and you come close to "Zizou"'s celebrity. The huge sports daily *L'Équipe*, headlined a full-page color photo with: "The light returns." Rumor claims President Jacques Chirac, eager to lift national morale, personally urged Zizou to return.

Two years later, Zizou was kicking balls in memoir-land. And the season's soccer (*le foot*) melodrama at *rentrée* time was the endless travails of the coach of the Paris-Saint-Germain (PSG) team – the gang that couldn't kick straight.

The 2008 *rentrée politique* was a delight. Fratricide, that tribute of loyalists to rivals' talents, raged in both government and opposition. President Nicolas Sarkozy continued his year-long sniping at the man he most despised (replacing his predecessor Jacques Chirac): his prime minister, François Fillon. Sarkozy hated Fillon because he regularly beat his boss in the polls. On the left, the Socialist "elephants" renewed their ideological and personal rivalries (always the same thing) with beloved brothers and sisters.

Every government's potential Waterloo is *la rentrée économique.* In the fall of 2008, Sarkozy's economic reforms – another "rupture" with his love-hate mentor Chirac – turned out to be either damp squibs or so long-term in impact that Sarko would be collecting his pension before they bit. Assuming that, in the meantime, he didn't bankrupt the government's fast-depleting pension fund.

Unions and far-left allies – far more important symbolically than in membership – invariably promise what they do best: demonstrations (ah, *la rentrée sociale!*). Without growth, major labor reform, strict spending discipline and lower oil prices, nobody can much reduce France's still-high unemployment. For – shows each *rentrée budgétaire* – the state cannot invest in any of its grand plans, such as announced new nuclear-energy plants or Sarkozy's pet Union for the Mediterranean. As Fillon once blurted out: "The cupboard is bare, the state is bankrupt."

Can we ignore *la rentrée religieuse?* Not since Sarkozy told Muslims, Jews and Catholics that religion, far from being separate from society, was central – and that clergy were more effective than secular teachers at teaching morals and civics. Kicking it all off: Pope Benedict XVI's spectacular visit to Paris in mid-September 2008.

Amid such gloom, we are left with what really matters: *la rentrée romantique.* (One string-hyping lingerie firm calls this *la rentrée rose*, the "pink" *rentrée*). Summer romances cooling, the fall is wide open for new, more consequential liaisons. *Pastis* and *vin d'Alsace* make all of this perfectly clear.

Lights and delights of Christmas

Ever since Jesus kicked the money-changers out of the Temple, religious folk have struggled to reconcile faith and commerce. Not always comfortably: their own churches often save a little prayer for Mammon. For western societies with full traditions but empty pews, Christmas and Easter are times of ambiguity and flexible guilt. Paris does better than most great cities to declare a truce between Cross and crass – all while enjoying its trademark sensuality. Let's look back at a typical year.

Shimmering from the Champs-Élysées to the Eiffel Tower and the Latin Quarter's ancient, cobble-stoned streets, the City of Light is ablaze. Parisians, normally in a rush to go everywhere, anywhere, all at once, are on fast-forward for Christmas – or rather Christmases, each one pursuing its own lights.

First – shining the light of religious meaning: Christian churches and charities are alive with vigils, ceremonies, concerts, displays, colloquia, and welfare projects for the unfortunate. Twice-a-year Christians (counting Easter) are out in force.

Inside the huge Saint-Sulpice church, beneath vaulting arches in a sea of flickering candles, a twelve-by-four-meter Sicilian crèche displays a whole medieval village, with moving parts. Posters on the church's thick stone columns announce choir, organ and instrumental concerts: familiar classics, along with French organ-masters to show off the renowned five-clavier organ. Every evening until after New Year's, a sound-and-light Christmas Mystery show is playing, with Nativity images projected on gigantic screens.

Christmas Eve Midnight Mass here, and at the other great organ churches of Paris, Notre-Dame and Saint-Eustache, will be standing-room only. With thousands attending each service, many with burning candles, even atheists might wish a little to believe the Story.

Other great Paris concert churches – Saint-Louis-en-l'Isle, tiny Orthodox-rite Saint-Julien-le-Pauvre, Saint-Germain-des-Prés – offer multicultural as well as traditional European music. Two *Messiahs* are available, though a few grumpy Frenchmen object to standing during the "Hallelujah" chorus. One never knows if this is secularists' reluctance to stand up for Christ, or nationalists' refusal to stand up for England's King George II, who allegedly started the tradition.

St-Sulpice once oversaw a four-day *Village de la Fraternité* on its grand square. Some fifty wood-and-canvas stalls sold products made by, or helping, the mentally handicapped – jams, ceramics, word-work, and excellent beer and wine. Nuns and monks working with Down-Syndrome children were there, as were volunteers who visit the poor and elderly.

'Down' kids played wandering jugglers and clowns to amuse the crowds, and a small *a capella* group of them sang an impressive be-bop riff, topped off by some Swingle-Singers-style Bach. A Down boy played a beautiful trumpet solo, accompanied by the first-prize virtuoso pianist of the Paris Conservatory.

On rue Madame, the Protestant *Église Réformée de Paris-Luxembourg* offered more intimate Christmas concerts – a violinist, a singer. Its message boards focused on practical help for street-people, foreign students and immigrants. Having joined this church when I was 20 – mainly to meet girls, I admit – I knew it well. Its mix of austerity, familiarity, social commitment and back-to-the-Bible joy expressed a passionate Christianity, albeit usually in a minor key echoing ancient persecutions.

Next – this was France – were the lights in food-store windows. Temptations there could corrupt a saint any day of the year. But Christmas, the family food festival par excellence, triggered a month of elaborate scheming. Newspapers and magazines were hyping – as they always do – "authenticity" and "tradition."

Le Figaro newspaper promised a "neoclassical" Christmas, both at restaurant and at home. Yet "tradition," it intoned, was phasing out gigantic turkeys in favor of guinea hens and capons. Experts advised a single cheese – a Boursault or a Vacherin might do – instead of a gala assortment.

The rest, as always, remained gargantuan. It included such joys as *foie gras* "lifted" by bittersweet Sauterne, and/or champagne with oysters, smoked salmon, caviar and/or small *boudins blancs* (sausages of pork, bread, cream, eggs), then seafood bisque, followed by – with well-matched white and red wines – chestnut-stuffed fowl and roast potatoes, then a refreshing green salad, then cheese with a richer red wine. Finally, with more champagne: a huge, creamy mocha "Christmas log" as dessert.

Before reaching for the Pepto-Bismol, people had to leave room for cherries in brandy. After that, if they were serious, they could toss back a glass or two of 70-percent-proof Calvados apple brandy. Why? To "do the *trou normand*" – punch an imaginary hole in their tummies in order to start the meal all over again. A cigarette (though held far from that flammable Calvados) could add a naughty-but-nice, old-fashioned touch.

Other eaters whose eyes gleamed were the hundreds of thousands of unfortunate French residents too poor to buy much food. For them, and this is testimony to the great kindness of ordinary French people, help beckoned in a remarkable network of free food outlets called *les Restos du Coeur* (Restaurants of the Heart).

Another light – that familiar curse of the western world – was the light of lucre in the minds of merchants and, alas, the minds of thieves. Christmas and money, now Siamese twins, presented the real clash of civilizations.

Finally, the lights of Paris's grand city hall highlighted how well a few intelligent politicians served France's great village of villages. Inviting ice-skating below the beautifully lit City Hall façade was a symbol of a deep and wide commitment to ordinary Parisians. Authorities offered a fantastic array of free Christmas concerts, gospel-singing, crêches, parties and exhibitions. A favorite, for children in 19 districts, was a month of free merry-go-round rides.

For a French state aggressively secular, and increasingly multicultural, Christmas remains happily Christmas – with everybody feeling left in. The man behind much of this welcome-the-people extravaganza was well-liked Socialist mayor Bertrand Delanoë. When he became mayor in 2001, he drastically reduced his official living quarters to make an employees' daycare. He was also the man who expanded biking paths, restricted cars, and put summer beaches along the Seine.

During one of his all-night open-houses at the *Mairie*, Delanoë was stabbed by a crazy man and almost died. But back he bounced to throw open the City Hall and dozens of other venues. Now he seems a plausible candidate to become President of France in 2012 against right-wing President Nicolas Sarkozy.

Delanoë, who made the night-time Eiffel Tower explode year-round with light every hour on the hour, set

Paris aflame. In addition to major illuminations, he has lit up symbol-rich areas in five typical districts, and offered to back any others that want to brighten their streets.

In this City of Light, nobody asks the cost. They only ask: "Is it beautiful?" For pleasing the people with all this brightness – and for his beaches, concerts and merry-go-rounds – there is a word to fit this good mayor, the living spirit of his City of many Christmases: enlightened.

After you, Gaston - January wishes

Janus's month looks backward and forward. The backward part (in both senses of that word) comes with the exotic ritual of countless levees when ministers – and even some spear-carriers – present their "wishes" (i.e. brag) to captive audiences of journalists and lobbies. These catalogs of brilliance recap successes, real or fantasized, from previous months. They also hint at how these exploits position the Great Man or Woman for even greater things in coming months. Not really more instructive than tea-leaves or chicken entrails, such tip-offs can, however, set a mood. And they allow observers to see up-close how their leaders have survived holiday revels.

The forward-looking part comes in the semi-annual retail-store sales. Deep down, the State doesn't really believe that business people are qualified to set times for their own discount sales. Allegedly, to protect smaller merchants, prefects in each Département, including no. 75 (Paris), pick a few weeks in January, and later June-July, to let businesses do business.

First, put on your plumed hat and buckle shoes (or ball-gown), and prepare to bow to the fine folks Parisians ironically term "these princes who govern us."

Never mind April in Paris. For thrills, try January. Everybody's bursting onstage, faking entrances, strutting and declaiming. In most of the plays – from palace to stores to streets – history is barely a king or revolution away.

In France, this republic which loves its monarchs while despising them, January's most familiar stage-play is the *cérémonie des voeux*. A stylized expression of a leader's "wishes" (good and otherwise), this is a throwback to New Year's royal *levées*. In these, a monarch faced his courtiers, all standing, to deliver his views on past and coming years. Today, presidents, ministers, even mayors and backbench National Assembly members still deliver these set-piece messages.

An average minister may offer his or her "wishes" separately to colleagues, personal staff, clienteles and press. The president holds about a dozen "wishes" ceremonies – for government ministers, diplomatic corps, armed forces, state institutions, society's "dynamic forces" (business, unions, voluntary associations, religious groups), his home region, and the critically important press. If he doesn't greet somebody you're vaguely connected to, you're a nobody.

At the same time, the leader's main interlocutors get a chance to present their wishes to the top man or woman. The funniest ceremony? The intensely scrutinized public exchange of "wishes" between the president and his ministers , especially the prime minister – a person he sees almost every day. Each adjective, each omission, in their brief speeches signals favor or disgrace, friendship or enmity.

In a news-saturated world, you can mock these homilies as quaint. But they play two useful roles. First, they telegraph the speaker's opinions and goals. Second, the ritual conveys to attendees (optimistic by anticipation of later champagne) a sense of living within a well-ordered establishment. Frenchmen, always subliminally fearing their history of volcanic upsets and "street democracy," crave reassurances of order.

"Wishes" may also zap political adversaries. Listeners smile or scowl but stand patiently as this goes on, tugging forelocks to the kinglet before them and awaiting their next flute of champagne. And a chance, as connoisseurs of "wishes," to chuckle at each side's velvet sword-thrusts.

Another January stage-show precipitates mobs of buyers into semi-annual, government-authorized retail "sales." What? The government decides when stores drop prices? Well, how else could merchants possibly know what is good for them and their customers?

Each of the 96 central-government, departmental "prefects" in Metropolitan France (four others are overseas) decides exactly when, and under what conditions, sales will occur during the roughly six-week semi-annual blowout.

In January, Paris store-windows shout *Soldes!* (sales) with huge percentage signs, just as elsewhere. But storekeepers, on pain of fines, can't bring in new stock to flog if existing stock goes 'too' fast. Article L-310-3 of the Commerce Code says that "sales" can only serve to get rid of existing stock. A rat's-nest of other rules, defining prices and guarantees, keeps shopkeepers in line.

What's going on? Well, you might go back to Nicolas Fouquet, Louis XIV's financial superintendent. Fouquet, who freelanced on the side, managed the 17th-century king's money so cleverly that he built himself the world's grandest castle at Vaux-le-Vicomte near Paris. Proudly, he welcomed the Sun-King with an all-too-eloquent extravagance. On September 5, 1661, Louis took pretext of Fouquet's glory-theatening lifestyle to have famed musketeer d'Artagnan arrest him. Louis stole Fouquet's castle, used it as inspiration for Versailles, and poor Fouquet died in prison nineteen years later.

Lesson for today: Well, you just can't trust businessmen. Following Fouquet, his enemy Jean-Baptiste Colbert, for twenty-two years Louis' finance minister, tightened state control of taxes, but also of business: a three-time rule-violator selling cloth would be tied to a post with his cloth. Rules for today's *soldes* would have delighted Colbert.

But the most animated theater of all is the January strikes – each accompanied by raucous demonstrations, singing, slogans, marches and melodramatic echoes of the 1789 French Revolution. In 2008, President Sarkozy bragged that he had made strikes and demonstrations irrelevant. But with a little luck, you may still see January *manifs* of teachers, railway-workers, hospital workers, postal, gas and electrical workers, civil servants, or surgeons. And why not psychiatrists?

The shrinks, perhaps spotting a chance to chase ambulances, drool at ambient anger and pessimism – splendidly termed "sinistrosis." A consensus report of the 96 prefects, stating "French people no longer believe in anything," left room to believe in Freud. Better still, psychiatrists in mid-2008 reported a high percentage of patients suffering from "Sarkosis" – obsession with the here-there-and-everywhere hyperactivity of their "*Omniprésident.*"

Unfailingly, opposition politicians, to distract from post-holiday guilt of excess, claim every New Year's that France is "in crisis." As it has happily always been, and will forever be.

Voilà the January-in-Paris Show. But April, as the love-song goes, is just a "blossoming chestnut away."

End-of-season fun: bridges, fashion and music

After the gloom of winter, and icy-wet spring weather that makes a bad joke of "April in Paris," France's capital glides gleefully into summer. The most talked-about event takes place in Cannes at the mid-May International Film Festival. (The people and publicity there are of course pure Parisian). However, three home-town May, June or July customs offer Parisians escapism to shorten the race to warm, sunny weather.

First, the custom of extra-long weekends called *ponts* (bridges). Of France's eleven annual statutory holidays, two always fall in May (May 1 is Labor Day – as everywhere in the world except North America; and May 8 is Victory-in-Europe Day). But three moveable religious holidays – Ascension, Pentecost and Whit Monday) usually fall in May too. It's easy to tack together a four-day, even five-day, weekend when one of these holidays falls on a Thursday and another on the following Monday.

Paris in May is often a ghost-town. Families take kids out of school to a beach or summer home. Teachers goof off, alleging there are no youngsters to teach. Workers bail out for the cleaner air outside Paris. Young lovers camp inside the apartments their parents have abandoned. Shop-keepers (usually excepting Arabs and Chinese) shutter their stores, forcing stragglers to forage for food like Robinson Crusoe.

Unions fight tooth-and-nail to protect *ponts*, however implausible or repetitive they may be. Abusing the system a little, even a lot, is an "acquired right." But since everybody, even public authorities, exploits these happy coincidences, who's left to complain?

A second dance around the Maypole comes with the June-July, fall-winter, high-fashion showings. Presenting *haute-couture* is good fun for all, especially those who love mocking the unwearable absurdities that transform models into clowns. Of course, top designers – Christian Lacroix, Karl Lagerfeld, Jean-Paul Gaultier, Givenchy, Valentino and the trashy-dressed Brits who run Dior – do present some clothes your sister might conceivably wear. But they always toss onto the stage a few monstrosities just so the ordinary folks they despise can cluck at their madness.

In mid-2008, two great names got press for other reasons. Long-reclusive genius Yves Saint-Laurent died, plunging France into semi-official mourning. And bizarre, walking-high-collar-ad Lagerfeld posed for a public-service message in a government-promoted luminescent yellow-green highway jacket, saying: "It's yellow, it's ugly, and it doesn't go with anything. But it might save a life."

If fashion almost defines France, music makes it sing. Never mind that seventeen of the more than one hundred singers at the July 2008 *Francofolies* festival of French song sang in English; the spirit was international rock with a French accent. Since 1982, the first day of spring, June 21, has been declared *la Fête de la Musique*, a national music celebration. In a play on words that sounds both like "make music" and "music holiday," this summer-solstice festival sucks a whole nation of "cultural pagans" into an all-day, all-night music party. That day and night, anybody can express his or her musical joy in public – even, alas, with just drums under your window. Professionals and amateurs all come out, and no money is exchanged, just pleasure.

Every musical institution, from opera to music school to amateur group, joins with the oters in a vast volunteer network to echo and amplify the music in millions of pagan-for-a-day Gallic hearts.

On music night in Paris, you find crowds dancing on top of buses, brass bands marching, jazz animating street corners, a string quartet playing under graceful arcades, a lone singer on a curb. Every park becomes a place to see and hear enthusiastic players and singers. "Music everywhere, the concert nowhere." The slogan places music in the air in which people breathe, express themselves, and hear others. It's a festival whose actors are visible but whose 'product' is invisible. Yet, say neurobiologists, music transmits the deepest of our memories, the last thing Alzheimer patients forget.

By 4 or 5 a.m. the next day, the horns and drums and voices have stilled. Crowds have thinned on the main avenues. Mutual admiration and celebration have led to new friends, maybe more. Has the night launched a new career or two?

Never mind perfumes, wine and fast trains. The over one hundred countries that have copied this wild, crazy festival think *la Fête de la Musique* might be France's most beautiful export.

Aux armes, citoyens! – *Bastille Day*

"May our fields run red with [the enemy's] tainted blood."
When your national anthem ends with words like that, you really should mark your national holiday with a muscle-flexing, weapons-flashing military parade. In pomp, solemnity and sheer razzle-dazzle, Paris's annual July 14 spectacle on

the Champs-Élysées stirs hearts to sing "La Marseillaise" in street, living-room and shower. France outdoes everybody on earth with its parade. In nation-hugging tradition, it salutes all who protect the public, whether soldiers, sailors, airmen, police, fire-fighters, emergency medical staff, or Alpine and coastal life-savers. But after the marching and chest-thumping, it's back to those favorite French pastimes: parties and l'amour. Here's how it stirred patriotic hormones in 2008.

Choirs of firemen's children and French soldiers sang "*La Marseillaise*," greeting a slow procession of 65 air force planes flying in mid-morning over the Champs-Élysées. Then 145 United Nations peacekeepers from 25 nations, reinforced by units from 27 European Union nations, strode out to give the world's grandest annual parade an international cast. It was Bastille Day again, and no people, you mused, celebrated their national holiday with as much panache and fun as did the French.

Next came 4,268 French troops, led by *École Polytechnique* engineering graduates with swords and cocked hats. Soldiers marched, or rode the 241 horses or 312 armored vehicles, down the cheering, crowd-lined avenue. Each unit, proud to display its specialty and equipment, stepped smartly to the bands and drums pacing them. In all, 52 different units from land, sea and air forces paraded: plumed-hat St.Cyr officer-graduates, Alpine scouts, air-sea rescuers, medical teams, sappers, fire-fighters and gendarmes. Plus rousing bands, on foot or horse.

Last to go by: the ever-popular, white-*képi*'d Foreign Legion, with beards, axes and leather-aprons, marching at the leisurely, trademark step evoking their solemn mission: to die for France. Acclaimed by huge crowds, each unit saluted

President Nicolas Sarkozy and his main guest, United Nations Secretary-General Ban Ki-moon. This year's parade, welcoming that Blue Helmets' contingent, honored UN peacekeeping.

Sarkozy also hosted fifty-odd European Union and "Mediterranean" leaders, notably controversial Syrian President Bashar al-Assad. To mixed reviews, Sarkozy had launched the day before his pet EU-North Africa-Mideast project called Union for the Mediterranean. Aim: a sharpened focus on North-South relations he hopes will promote peace, including between Israel and Palestine. Highlighting the day of conciliation, just-liberated Franco-Colombian hostage, Ingrid Betancourt (a megastar in France), stood near Sarkozy too.

The parade's most powerful moment: when actor Kad Merad, identified as the classic ordinary guy, read in front of the foreign guests, including several frozen-faced, notorious dictators, the UN's Universal Declaration of Human Rights.

Then, a show-stopper: seven parachutists with red-white-and blue chutes, including a woman, precision-landed right in front of the official stand, unfurling UN, EU and French flags. The 90-minute parade ended with Sarkozy inspecting an honor guard, then standing stiff for another rousing "*Marseillaise.*" As the anthem faded, acrobatic jet-fighters flew high and fast over the Arc de Triomphe leaving red, white and blue contrails.

After the parade, the president held a garden-party for 8,000 at the Élysée Palace, where famous, infamous and deserving citizens jostled for bubbles and canapés. And for a photo with "Sarko" – or better still, with his dazzling wife Carla Bruni.

But the real fun of July 14 was at street-level. Most of France's 36,785 cities, towns and villages converted this nation and this day into an everybody-welcome village party. Bands good or bad, or just an accordion, inspired street dancers. Old and young, dutifully shrinking France's wine surplus, came to wiggle, contort and/or squeeze, all in laughing, carefree mood.

In big cities, the event of the night (often two nights) was the *Bal des Pompiers* – the "firemen's ball" held in most fire-stations. All the firemen were reputed handsome and virile, and all the girls (who lined up for hours) pretty and eager. Hey, wait a minute: 20,300 of France's 251,000 fire-fighters were women.

On *Fête nationale* nights, millions dance and flirt to celebrate the fall of King Louis XVI's Paris prison. People joke that in continental France the *quatorze juillet* (July 14) lasts three days, including hangovers. In Tahiti, part of semi-autonomous French Polynesia, two weeks.

These *bals populaires* aren't mere folklore. They draw the French together in easy, be-happy patriotism. They celebrate France with toasts and flags, but mainly with heart and body. For once, politics, ideology, religion, class, race and age don't matter. In giggly conga-lines, smoldering tangos, dizzying waltzes, and non-descript flailings, bodies have a habit of coupling – metaphorically or more. It's not just sky-high baby bonuses ($2,658 at first birth, plus a basic monthly $900-$1,693) that give France Europe's highest birthrate. Credit the *bals du quatorze juillet* too.

In Paris, a city of villages, squares large and small draw you in to fraternize. Nobody turns down a gracious offer for a twirl. Strangers are welcome because on

July 14 there *are* no strangers. A 40-minute Paris fire-works show easily draws 350,000 celebrants – many with champagne bottles – beneath the Eiffel Tower's exploding lights. In 2008, recalling France's European Union presidency, they flashed in the EU's blue and yellow.

The first Bastille Day parade, a year after the ancient fortress's fall, celebrated both the 1789 revolution and a restored king not yet condemned to death. Since then, the grand parade's forms and itineraries have changed many times. Today's Champs-Élysées extravaganzas date only from 1880. That year, the parade brought patriotic therapy after France's traumatizing loss to Prussia of both its 1870-71 war and most of Alsace-Lorraine. For four other awful years (1940-44), *Wehrmacht* Occupation troops marching down the avenue imposed searing humiliation.

July 14, 1945 saw a massive victory parade. Now, every year seems a victory. As each year's parade seems more dazzling than the last, as *tricolore* contrails and flag-unfurling parachutists land on a euro, we foreigners run a serious patriotic risk: Why can't we too be French? Just for a day?

Harmless summer obsessions

Summer frees, and often fulfils, the yearnings of each individual. Passions and interests just below the surface in winter burst out to remind us of who we really are, of what we care about, and of what we want from life. So it is with Parisians. But whether trapped in town or lolling about in faraway climes, they love to mix head and loins, with heart conceivably along for the ride.

Julius Caesar, Spinoza, Nietzsche: all summer magazine-cover heroes in philosophy-crazy France. But also Wynton Marsalis, Juliette Binoche, Zinédine Zidane and a zillion famous-for-a-season *pipole* (as in gossipy "people" magazines). High-brow and low-brow "stars" make up a sexy-egg-head show-biz State. Staples of France's summer rituals, such types are as predictable as the Seine, as unpredictable as a heat-wave-ending thunderstorm. They drive defining memories and rediscovered aspirations, as sixty million Frenchmen take a spontaneous bath of feeling good, of feeling bad, of feeling French.

But a fascination with history and ancient heroes betrays France's obsession with old exploits too. As lesson or hobby-fodder, hoary titans fill books, magazines, newspapers. Writers offer a titillating mix of facts, stories and ideas you wish you'd learned in high school. In just one summer 2006 week, daily *Le Monde* gave two pages to Hannibal crossing the Alps; the weekly *Nouvel Observateur*, sampling newly-opened archives, gave Stalin nine; and weekly *Le Point* ran a cover-story on Nietzsche. Popular histories met every taste: Cro-Magnon Man, Greek mythology, medieval religious wars, Aztecs, cathedral-building, the slave-trade, Balkan wars, royal mistresses.

The week of July 14, 2008, put Ulysses on the cover of *Nouvel Observateur*, Voltaire vs. Rousseau ("The War Without End") on *Le Point*'s cover, and Aristotle on prime space inside *Le Monde* – which, each week for months, had already been selling its own books on major philosophers.

History here is not all dates and damnation. *Le Monde* ran a series on famous gangsters of the past fifty years. Magazines fed us famous psychiatrists (Freud the "sulfurous" winner), and hyped those sure-fire paranoia-feeders, Free

Masons, Opus Dei and the CIA. Napoleon, of course, eclipses everybody, with de Gaulle immodestly creeping up.

Summer culture swamps every town and village of France. There are hundreds of summer festivals in France, each town choosing a specialty. A few: Avignon and Orange (high-class theater and opera), Marciac (jazz, with Marsalis a regular), Grignan (letter-writing), La Roque d'Anthéron (summit for professional pianists), and *thirty-five* festivals for comic books – here a serious cultural activity celebrating artists and styles. Paris, with both national and local authorities in the game, flaunts an Ali Baba's Cave of concerts, dancing, art and museums. Among the latest big draws: former President Jacques Chirac's *Musée du quai Branly*, a Louvre for native art worldwide; and the awe-inspiring *Cité de l'Architecture et du Patrimoine*.

Sports are a year-round drug (a dig at the pharmaceutically-challenged *Tour de France*?). By far the largest newspaper in France is *L'Équipe* (team). Summer games include any conceivable pretext for a race or competition. Cross-country motorcycle racing, para-sailing races, "Agility" dog races, probably snail races.

Beauty – with its modern twin, fitness – obsesses every beach-bound lovely and paunchy brute. But all this with that charming French mixture of innocence, earnestness and eroticism. As elsewhere, waistlines go up and down on clothes, in and out on bodies. Above all, they serve to feed a carnivorous fashion industry which, aping auto-makers' planned obsolescence, feeds neuroses of dowdiness – basically to disguise that the street, no longer *haute couture*, sets fashion.

Peruse the women's mags: the age-old dialectic between scrawny and full-bodied women pits expert against expert, with most men (and fatalistic) women plumping, so to speak, for Rubens. Happily, disguising time's ravages mobilizes L'Oréal and many competitors. Together, they sell enough cream to smooth out the Grand-Canyon-deep wrinkles of France-touring old rockers like Mick Jagger and Keith Richards.

Venus's other side, love? Puppy love, courtly love, romantic love, platonic love, true love, erotic love – summer serves 'em all up. *Nouvel Observateur*, swiping *Playboy*'s busts-and-brains ploy, once gave its cover to "Love – as seen by the great philosophers." In 2006, 70th anniversary of France's guaranteed annual paid vacations, family love was the big winner. (Maybe guilt played a part: remember when, three years before, those 15,000 old folks died in a heat wave when dumped at home by vacationing offspring?).

Sex for sexagenarians (and way up) now being celebrated, summer love's new conquests officially stir more hormones than before. In July 2008, daily *Le Parisien* ran a real-life, real-time series on how seductions were happening at every bar and beach. *Nouvel Obs*, famous for racy personal ads, again covered Paris *échangiste* (wife-swapping) clubs – an old summer specialty.

Journalists recycled perennial fantasies of hard-working *papas* cavorting with the maid in Paris while *maman* vegged out in the country with *les enfants*. In both licit and illicit adventures, meteorologists and shrinks assured that we could blame much of the groping and grappling on unusually hot weather.

What will we do when global warming gets really serious?

"Summer universities" – warming up for autumn quarrels

After a lazy summer, an agitation of neurons and adrenalin. Political parties and lobbies of all kinds hold informal policy clambakes called "universités d'été." In concept and action, these conferences or colloquia digest the past twelve months and kick off a new season. They try to define new policies, or update old ones. If their organization is in trouble, they set up a "beauty contest" of leadership rivals. They rev up the faithful for autumn's "new-year" battles. Above all, they make everybody feel – if not good, then confident they have something in common: far from a certainty.

In sandals, slacks and guarded grins, old friends and enemies (usually the same) share long tables of trustworthy grub and so-so wine. Panels, seminars and speeches barely muffle the sharpening of knives. At resort hotels all over France, it must be "summer university" time again – a time for shedding inhibitions, cranking up beach-fried brains, and girding loins for imminent combat, much of it usually fratricidal. At these weekend rituals of *universités d'été*, activists assess the rise and fall of the ambitious with the calibrated precision of Cold War Kremlinologists.

The *université d'été* is not a university as commonly understood: no courses, profs or marks. But it's a place where people with causes learn lots – who's up, who's down, and what's up in a given field. It's a yearly touch-base jamboree that allows organizations to take stock, and plot the year ahead. Informal and idea-rich, these end-of-summer events are the last sigh of holidays, and the first deep breath before players plunge into *la rentrée*, the frenzied September return to duty, work and struggle.

Take France's all-pervasive ideological civil war between left and right. On the left, a volatile cabal of groups still venerates Karl Marx, with various species of Trotskyites sometimes holding their own pow-wows. Many migrate to the grab-bag lefty group called Attac, whose summer shindig feeds late-August paranoia. It draws ideologues of every ilk opposed to "ultra-liberalism" and globalization – meaning the horrors of free enterprise, free trade and free thinking. Result: vicious rivalries and forced resignations drive militants to 'Attac' each other more than the evils of capitalism.

In August 2008 a Troskyite remnant, the Communist Revolutionary League, segued into a future Anti-capitalist Party at its summer university. To start in 2009, the new party is a vehicle for the personal ambition of nationally popular postman Olivier Besancenot.

Diametrically opposed to Attac and Besancenot is *Liberté Chérie*. It's a tiny movement trying to inject the subversive idea of freedom into French society – no cinch, when media, politics, schools and universities talk obsessively of enforced equality. Naturally, a privileged state bureaucracy makes some, Orwellianly, much more equal than others. *Liberté Chérie* gets zero media coverage and exerts near-zero influence on public life. Its *université*, when it holds one, looks like a band of early Christians cowering in the Roman Forum, waiting to be fed to the lions.

Infinitely more powerful is corporate lobby Medef, representing 750,000 firms. Medef attracts big business stars, plus drop-in visits from a few right-wing politicians daring to be seen with despised capitalists who shamelessly create jobs. Intellectually, it's way above the others, perversely dealing with real-world problems.

The most entertaining *universités d'été* are those sponsored by political parties. The Communist Party, bottom-feeding the pollsters' ocean floor, gave up its bedrock policies after Moscow declared them all wrong. It has become a nostalgia-ain't-what-it-used-to-be, pick-your-policy buffet party. Indeed, its leader is Marie-George Buffet. Her 2006 kick-off production (nicknamed after the party newspaper, *L'Humanité*) was the annual September *Fête de l'Huma*, a kind of boozed-up country fair. So harmless now are Communists that you find there everybody from dilettantes to ultra-left wackos. Buffet's 2008 exhortation was: "Change without losing ourselves" – a slogan voters had already rephrased as "You guys can't change, so get lost!"

The twenty scorpions in a bottle known as *les Verts*, the Green Party, have never missed an opportunity to miss an opportunity. A party that constantly devours its own tail, *les Verts* argue relentlessly about leaders – especially after just electing one.

The only political *universités* that matter belong to the governing UMP (neo-Gaullist) party and the Socialist Party. Only they can field candidates able to win major elections. The UMP is the personal plaything of the most brilliant, single-minded politician in France, Nicolas Sarkozy. Its September 2008 *université d'été* celebrated Sarkozy's mad-dash first year of reforms by mobilizing youth on beaches all over France; by showcasing Sarko's hirsute 22-year-old son Jean, already an elected official in dad's hometown of Neuilly; and by keeping fratricidal knives almost sheathed – all while nervously chattering about the party's cast-in-concrete unity.

The Socialists, as of autumn 2008, remained mired in a Royal mess. Ex-presidential candidate Ségolène Royal's fiercest enemies were still within her own party, not the UMP. Ordinary Socialists, like the public, loved her plain talk, pragmatism and close-to-the-people concerns of education, health and security. But the party's male notables, the "elephants" – at least five of whom also coveted the Socialists' leadership – were outraged at her continuing to top the polls. They still didn't dare attack her head-on, but in private they called her an "idiot," a "flake," a "lightweight." In recent years at the Socialists' *université*, all eyes have been grinning murder. Party secretary-general François Hollande could barely keep the spite from boiling over.

Complication: He too wanted to be the party's presidential candidate. But he trailed the leading lady hopelessly. Worse complication: Until his farewell party convention in November 2008, he had to act neutral toward all candidates, including Ségolène – with whom, by the way, he had fathered four children. Before François went AWOL with a blonde journalist during the 2007 presidential campaign, Ségolène had been his common-law "companion" – ever since, decades earlier, they had been classmates at a real *université*…

A case of bed-fellows making strange politics.

Chapter Four /

YOUR PLACE IN PARIS

"Where do you live?" When Parisians ask you that, they're really asking you "Who do you think you are?" Your identity in Paris starts with your sex and profession, flows from your personality and actions, sharpens with your style. But before you get far, you have to get close to somewhere: a home address. When somebody asks in what district (*arrondissement*) you live, your answer situates you financially, socially, culturally, often even politically. People play this game in every city. But Paris is so finely structured, with street-by-street histories going back centuries, that curiosity about your address is a sport for connoisseurs – preferably with a double doctorate in cartography and alchemy.

To simplify (or complicate) matters: Each of Paris's twenty *arrondissements* divides into four *quartiers* (some up to six*)*, roughly mirroring the compass. Like the *arrondissement* itself, the *quartier* is an electoral and administrative division. Even your national tax minders use it. It can place your little world unerringly – especially for culture, eating, shopping. When you get down to revealing your street, perhaps even your street number, any old Paris hand can pretty well nail your budget, tastes, politics and aspirations – and probably your schools, magazines and daily newspaper.

There are always surprises to defeat district detectives. Tiny enclaves, a revealing alley, a monument, a house, original architecture, a plaque all might shade suppositions. Shorthand: living in any of the first eight *arrondissements* gets you snob-appeal, with the 4th to 8th coming first. The 16e, like the 7th, gives you the instant class of old money, tradition and ministries-full of senior officials and state retirees. Unless you live in the 18th's pricey Butte Montmartre or show-biz compound avenue Junot, in the 17th, 18th, 19th and 20th you may need to learn Arabic and/or a couple of African languages. Or a few songs by Edith Piaf.

A few previously seedy streets in the 11th have been gentrifying. You can also spot islands of class and money bordering Paris's two magnificent forest-and-lake preserves: the western Bois de Boulogne (famous for horses, bikes, Brazilian transvestites and conjugal shenanigans) and the eastern Bois de Vincennes.

Politics cements geography. With twenty *arrondissements,* Paris's administration is compartmentalized into a score of near-city-states: Disneyland for Machiavelli. The city as a whole sports twenty-one city-halls – a palace for each *arrondissement,* then the grand *Mairie* for all Paris. Each local *mairie* is a mini-government, with mayor and deputy mayors, assembly, departments of economic development, social services and culture, often even a mini-foreign ministry. Why not? Well, how can anybody be proud unless represented by a smaller-scale Versailles and a local barracks of civil servants?

We have no room here to cover what needs a fat book or two. But vignettes of two favorite *arrondissements,* plus a memorable square and two famous streets, might suggest why Parisians develop mildly fanatical local patriotism.

You know all about Montmartre: Picasso, Toulouse-Lautrec, *Amélie,* the fly-by-night portrait artists in the Place du Tertre, and that white-domed Sacré Coeur Basilica with the touristy views and muddy-sounding organ. Let's take in those other five places, all with unique sights and tales.

History for everybody – the lovely, lively 6th

From Senate to Seine, the Sixth Arrondissement gains its prestige from memory, culture, romance and wealth. Almost every street carries plaques about great people or events. Left Bank intellectual and cultural life draws the famous and/ or talented here by the popular magazine-load: dotted with haunts of writers, painters, musicians and philosophers, "le sixième" breathes creativity. Anchored by the ancient, grandest-of-the-grand Luxembourg Garden, it reminds everybody of student days – of history, freedom, folly, ambition, and the sweet torments of love. Downside: sixième apartments sell or rent at sky-high costs per square meter.

Let's skip the laundry-list of the *6th-arrondissement's* Big-Name residents. Well okay, you could sneak in Catherine Deneuve – and maybe a score of other top actors, plus enough politicians to vote down a government. What really makes the Sixth work is strolling. Let's start along the Seine, walking from *l'École Nationale Supérieure des Beaux-Arts* to student-Mecca boulevard Saint-Michel. Continuing into the 5th arrondissement past Notre-Dame cathedral gives you the longest, most beautiful river views in Paris. For drinking in the city, meditating on life, or courting, this promenade is perfection.

As you start out from the *Beaux-Arts*, dodge into the magnificently renovated hotel where Oscar Wilde died: *L'Hôtel*, at 13 rue des Beaux-Arts. If impulsive and flush, you can rent for a bargain-basement $1,500 a night the room where Wilde died "fighting the wallpaper flowers." If you favor a leftish heart over cynicism and wit, you will find Peruvian poet Pablo Neruda's room here a lot cheaper.

Heading east, you quickly reach the gold-domed *Institut de France*, home of the French-language-police French Academy and three lesser academies. Each has a "perpetual secretary" – whose perpetuity usually lasts about four years. Ceremonial swords, costumes and droning speeches make the *Institut* a Vatican of French culture, with nobody accepted as pope. Almost next-door, you pass the *Monnaie* (Mint). Possibly worth a dash in to pick up a charming historic medal for a wedding or graduation.

At no. 51 quai des Grands-Augustins stands the historic *La Pérouse* restaurant. Founded in 1766, is has attracted statesmen, kings, czars, Dumas, Hugo, Flaubert, Maupassant and, in the old days, naughty old gents seducing teenage dancers or apprentice-milliners. Its small private rooms upholstered in crimson still boast huge mirrors – marked by the scratches women drew to test the diamond rings men gave them. For a major romance, *La Pérouse's* private rooms can lead to deep discussions – waiters knock before entering.

Turning toward the Odéon district, you run into scores of art galleries, expensive but often startlingly original. Long, narrow rue Visconti draws you in to linger in its alcove-like doorways, and to marvel at Balzac's old printing shop. Intimate *passages* on rue Dauphine invite you to tea-and-pastry shops – and speaking of tea, look for the astonishing blends and cakes at *Mariage Frères* at 13 rue des Grands-Augustins. Nearby at number 7: Picasso's longtime residence and studio. If you're lucky enough to sneak upstairs, you can study the light he painted by, and imagine the old macho grinning imperturbably as two women wrestled over him on the floor, as they once did.

Across the street on a small corner: the place where, in 1610, nine-year-old Louis became Louis XIII when courtiers told him of the assassination of his father Henri IV. At a feisty fifteen, little Louis bumped aside his hard-nosed regent-mother, Marie de Médicis, favored the arts, and went on to father Louis XIV, the Sun-King.

Move west to 56 rue Jacob. A plaque there notes that in this building, on Sept. 3, 1783, John Jay, Benjamin Franklin and John Adams signed with Briton David Hartley a little treaty recognizing the independence of the United States. None of this is as memorable as Ben Franklin's alleged retort to a lady who reproached him on a summer street with ignoring her. "But I was waiting for the nights to grow longer, Madame." Franklin had honed an already admired wit while U.S. representative in Paris. History doesn't record whether Hartley, George III's man, found him funny.

Time to drift up to ground-zero of philosophical and literary posturing, Saint-Germain-des-Prés. Name your writer or *intello*, they've all hung out here – starting, but not ending, with the iconic *Café des Deux Magots*, the *Café de Flore* and the *Brasserie Lipp*. Surprise: prices are not bad, and as you contemplate the 1,500-year-old church of Saint-Germain-des-Prés, you can easily convince yourself that you're in Paris.

Turn up long, shop-laden rue de Rennes for the Paris street adored by pollsters, because patronized by the "most average" consumers in Paris. Turn left toward the Place Saint-Sulpice and its church famous for five-keyboard organ and long tradition of famous improvisers. Sit at the terrace of the *Café de la Mairie* beside it, where movie-makers and occasional stars may hold court. As you sip your coffee or Kir, look up high on that building on your right: inside those tall glass windows lives *la Deneuve*.

Keep going to the glorious *Jardin du Luxembourg*, rhapsodized about earlier. Try to get a senator to write you a pass to visit the *Palais du Luxembourg* there with its Heaven-rivaling painted ceilings. If you have a small child in tow, put him or her on a pony out there in the garden, and say hello to pony-masters Mohammed and Karim.

Heading toward Montparnasse you go up the little shopping street of rue Vavin. Now it's almost wall-to-wall clothing stores for babies. But it still offers classy bargains for the elegant women trawling its small, fashionable stores. The cozy Square Vavin is worth an outside meal. Or take a short detour right to the intimate, private cultural center called *Le Lucernaire*: two live theaters, two cinemas, a restaurant, a bar, a second-hand bookstore all in one cobblestone alley.

Go a hundred meters further up rue Vavin and you hit the glitter of Montparnasse. Dozens of cinemas and, more vitally, historic bars and restaurants beckon. A few years back the *Lucernaire*'s founder, to get his government grant restored, went on a hunger strike. Somehow, he survived. Surely he didn't cheat?

Swamped in the Marais

Left Bank fun, Right Bank boring? Not at all. Cross a bridge near Notre-Dame and you will land in the most colorful, culturally enticing area of Paris: le Marais, the name recalling its ancient status as a swamp. High and low class, cultural opposites and a number of sexes mix, though rarely mingle. Live here, and let live here. For if you're lucky enough to find (and afford) an apartment in the Marais, you can meet all your needs, however strange, and see the whole world in Technicolor.

All the people Hitler hated live in the Marais: Jews, avant-garde artists, gays, free-thinkers, stylish rebels, the ragged end of the "caviar Left" (Gucci socialists?). Also lots of Chinese here. If you're a bit original, the Marais district of Paris's 3rd and 4th arrondissements calls you home.

It's high-energy, multicultural, riotously independent, unpredictable, blessedly tolerant of eccentricity. It's a place for people, as Barbara Streisand would say, who love people – especially people who don't crave assimilation into somebody else's mainstream.

Over the past twenty-five years, the Marais has become a trendy place to live. At least two stars of the forty-member French Academy live there, plus a chattering of other top cultural figures. To announce you live in the Marais is to invite this unspoken question: are you one of Hitler's hates, an unassuming genius, a bourgeois-bohemian (*bo-bo*), a socio-cultural voyeur, or just in favor of life?

It's the people – the wildly different, cheek-by-jowl communities – who shape the trendiness. Parallel ghettos of the mind get along just fine here. When black-hatted and -robed, bearded Hasidic Jews pass nose-ringed lesbians or bare-chested gays in the street, they don't lift an eyebrow. They just accept that the other guys belong here, and that's good enough. The word 'promiscuous' springs to mind – in both the English sense of frequenting many and the French sense of being up-close. Sometimes in each other's restaurants, but not in each other's pockets.

Everybody has his secret-public places here. Among mine: the Village Saint-Paul, a meandering walk through a string of linked courtyards with bookstores, antiques and intimate restaurants. I also like to visit mini-Israel around rue des Rosiers, or to drift into the superb museums: the Picasso, the Carnavalet (history of the City of Paris), the *Maison Européenne de la Photographie*, the National Archives, the exquisite 18th-century collections of the *Musée Cognacq-Jay*.

Dozens of other museums cover everything from Holocaust to locksmiths. The most startling building is the *Centre Pompidou*, specializing in modern and contemporary art. In the middle of a giant, tacky-but-fun square with jugglers, fire-eaters and buskers, the "Beaubourg" (as it's also known) contains ever-changing beauty, including painting, sculpture and film. But its outside surface is a modernist monstrosity: external pipes, air conditioning domes, stairways and garish colors. (For aggressive ugliness, its only rival is Barcelona's *Sagrada Familia* church – designed by the aptly named Antoni Gaudí and, I believe, Walt Disney on LSD. But I digress.)

For classically beautiful architecture, buy in your mind a magnificent *hôtel particulier*. Scattered throughout the Marais are dozens of these 16th- to 19th-century mansions. They are sumptuous, with carved façades and street-doors seven meters high.

For a quiet end to your day, slip into one of only three medieval residences in Paris – the *Hôtel de Sens*. Now also called the *Bibliothèque Forney*, it's devoted to decorative and fine arts. But its real charm lies in its look and feel as a castle. Queen Margot, tempestuous wife of Henri IV, lived there for a while, no doubt finding it restful after triggering a massacre of 30,000 Protestants in 1572.

After all this history and culture, let's get serious. Shopping is reason enough to wander around the Marais. Apart from a few arty boutiques, antiques, and in-your-face gay jockstrap stores (all flying huge rainbow-gay flags, some with semi-naked "doormen"), the Marais is trash heaven. Perhaps not coincidentally, leather is big: at least ten stores in a row sell dubious-origin handbags ("wholesale only here" to avoid sales tax). And there is enough costume jewelry to deck out caravans of gypsies.

Perhaps the best buy is a dance course at the *Centre de Danse du Marais*. Above a grubby-looking courtyard, this eclectic temple to Terpsichore can teach you anything from salsa to Thai, Balinese, belly-dancing, Irish jigs or a hip-swiveling *N'Dombolo*.

After waltzing around the Marais, you might prefer a stately minuet. But first, an elegant Square dance...

Place des Vosges – Paris's beating heart

If the Marais has a soul, and it does, it's here in this place of architectural perfection. A place to sigh and dream. A place to stop, sit down, and turn off the outside world. A place to think and wonder. And – as you see little children, lovers, families and old folks all finding harmony and joy – a place to be grateful you're alive.

Close your eyes. Four and a half centuries ago, knights jousted here. Now artists, musicians and dancers do, cheered on from above the enveloping arcades by ghosts of illustrious former residents. Built starting 1605 around the old jousting lists, it's a grand but intimate square 140 by 127 meters. Its three-storey stone-and-red-brick façades and slate-blue roofs whisper a thousand tales, their graceful symmetry making even blasé visitors gasp. It's quintessential Paris, the soul of French taste. It's the Place des Vosges.

Under King Henri IV, the randy Protestant *Vert-Galant* who switched from Rome to win France's crown, the square began as Place Royale. Assassinated in 1610, Henri missed its completion in 1612. After the 1789 Revolution, it became Place des Vosges, famously because that Alsatian *département* paid its taxes before others to the new people's regime.

Cultured or powerful people have always yearned to live overlooking the square. Today, it's still *chic* enough to turn friends green, even if you can only afford a garret. Among politicians preening here: Sully, Henri IV's finance wizard and strait-laced reformer (no petticoat-chaser, *this* Protestant); Cardinal Richelieu, Louis XIII's "grey-eminence" prime minister; Bossuet, Louis XIV's political cheerleader as well as court preacher – who, to test his sermons' clarity, rehearsed orations in front of his maid.

Among writers: 17th-century Madame de Sévigné, Paris's most virtuous (or discreet?) young widow, whose 1120 letters to her daughter defined elegant letter-writing; 19th-century poet Théophile Gautier, novelist Alphonse Daudet, and political philosopher Alexis de Tocqueville, author of ever-fresh *Democracy in America*; and 20th-century detective-novelist Georges Simenon. Oh yes, and a bearded fellow called Victor Hugo. You can visit his bedroom, touching the desk where he wrote standing up.

But the square isn't just a museum. It's a lively people place, a refuge where ordinary Parisians come to touch magic. Perhaps to fantasize that in some distant age they might have lived here as aristocrats? Five publics thrive here. Children play safely and noisily in the central park.

Lovers clutch and cling on benches or grass. Seniors envy lovers and kids, dream of happy times, and feed the pigeons. Tourists gawk, shop, drink and eat. And creative folk find grateful audiences beneath the arcades.

Apart from amateur easels, a dozen galleries offer a feast of medium-priced modern art. This includes painting, aquarelles, sketches, and sculptures so sensual you can't keep eyes – or hands – off them. For some reason, nudes and erotic art seem predominant here. But just smile, touch, and feel a little naughty.

On a typical weekend, you can catch uplifting free concerts. For a few optionally contributed *centimes* or euros, you can slip into an arcade to hear a cello-accompanied opera-singer; a classical guitarist; a jazz band; a string ensemble (Mozart and Vivaldi being surest crowd-pleasers); or a haunting counter-tenor (sort of male soprano), always at the high arch over side-street rue de Béarn. A gentle, ex-Paris Conservatory singer dressed in outlandish costume, he fled formal opera to sell his voice as a free man.

Under the arcades, you might also get lucky enough to watch some Flamenco dancers. Or a tango-dancing couple so sizzling they probably violate fire regulations. When people toss a few coins in their basket, they can pick up a pamphlet on – why not? – tango lessons.

By this time, you're hungry. Plenty of touristy-but-decent places beckon under the arches. Sidewalk cafés too, if you just want to drink, rest and people-watch. Only one top restaurant: *L'Ambroisie*. A three-star *Guide Michelin* establishment, it's where President Jacques Chirac took Bill Clinton to dinner. Cynics sneer that Clinton likely ordered a cheeseburger. Surely untrue – as Hillary said of Obama's alleged Islamic faith, "as far as I know."

There are other hazards here besides cholesterol. You might get sunburned, as I did once, lying face up on the summer grass. You might impulsively quit your job and start cadging *centimes* singing *karaoke* under the arcades. You might fall in love with somebody, or anybody, or everybody.

Just be glad you're not 400 years old and the cavalier immortalized in that equestrian statue commanding the central garden. He was the aforementioned Louis XIII, a king so little *vert-galant* that we know of only two romantic liaisons – some even say platonic, for heaven sakes. More credible rumors claim these were with *mignons,* handsome young male courtiers. Even if the good king spent too much time sailing, as the French put it, by both wind and motor, perhaps his devotion to the arts, and to developing New France in Canada, justify that statue.

In this square renowned for centuries of cheerful flirtations and conquests, maybe a difficult love-life was reason enough for the statue's downcast-in-stone allure. But Louis was probably brooding on his unfortunate ancestor, Henri II. Jousting here in 1559 against a Scot named Montgommeri, poor Henri got a lance through the eye and took eleven days to die an excruciating death. Doctors practiced on decapitated convicts to patch him up, but probably just killed him faster.

At least it was a Scot that killed him, not an Englishman. A lucky locale, after all, this Place des Vosges.

Ghosts of Rome on Paris hills – "la Mouffe"

Louis XIII and all those other 'historic' Place des Vosges folks? Mere newcomers to Paris compared with the gentlemen who, 2,000 years ago, marched up what is now the 5ᵗʰ arrondissement's storied rue Mouffetard. This is no place to come on a diet – it's a Roman banquet of cuisines, restaurants, bistros, snack bars and food markets. It's also a place for walking, gawking or, better still, partying day or night.

Tramping up the rough-hewn stone *via*, Caesar's legions climbed this hill to the heart of Paris, then a sprawling village called Lutetia. The Roman road, tracing a Stone-Age path, became today's magic rue Mouffetard. *"La Mouffe,"* as it's nicknamed, is the sassiest, liveliest people street in Paris. It's a feast for eyes and ears and tummy every day, dizzyingly so on weekends.

Six hundred-and-fifty meters long and six meters wide, Mouffetard is a cobblestone, downhill glide from just behind the *Panthéon,* national shrine where "a grateful homeland" salutes its "great men." Ah yes, and one 'honorary man', Nobel-Prize-winner Marie Sklodowska-Curie, pioneer of radioactivity.

Morning until late evening, *la Mouffe* teems with people. These often include classical or jazz musicians, a weird but lovable old lady shimmying to Dixieland, an ancient, bearded organ-grinder, avant-garde dancers and costumed actors. They command your attention while fruit-sellers squawk "unbelievable" bargains: *"Trois pour trois!"* or three boxes of raspberries for three euros. Well, that's at closing time when the berries are going to go bad next day.

Whether you mount or descend the long slope, curb-to-curb restaurants of every nationality guarantee you won't go hungry. So do food stalls and markets, large and small, some on locations reaching back five hundred years. Many specialize only in meat, fish, cheese, wine, fresh pasta, bread, coffee, or olive oil. Or regional French products, such as anything a goose or duck might waddle your way.

Side-streets also offer street-feasts or intimate dining, a wall or two needing a boost from outside beams. Narrow rue du Pot de Fer, where at no. 6 George Orwell wrote *Down and Out in London and Paris*, is restaurant nirvana. A few meters away is the delightful market in Place Monge. In this plucky little square you might see emerge from barracks – on horseback and resplendent in red-plumed silver helmets – the *Garde Républicaine*, the President's ceremonial 'legionnaires.'

Monge offers still more fresh produce, meat, fish and cheese, plus African, Middle Eastern and regional take-away dishes. Also, *petits vins* you can sample before buying. Chinese fruit-and-vegetable merchants, decisively undercutting French farmers' prices, draw long line-ups and sorely test clients' patriotism.

Back on *La Mouffe*, you drift past a blur of people and shops – affordable clothes, costume jewelry, souvenirs, hole-in-wall eateries, plus theaters, cinemas, a couple of narrow-aisled *Franprix* supermarkets. Impossible not to stop to enjoy lunch or a drink. Or to wander into one of the high-brow bookstores, a pirated-CD-DVD store, or the three-storey municipal library, where comfy chairs and sofas let you sample free books, magazines, videos and music.

Sprawling at the bottom of *La Mouffe* is a noisy, old-fashioned fruit-and-vegetable market. Farmers and wives 'melodramatize' their deals and joke with customers. Small wonders: open-air restaurants and cafés, an elegant five-jet fountain, a five-storey façade painted in exotic designs. Crowning all is a small, famous 12th-century church, Saint-

Médard. Here quarreled Catholics with Protestants and justification-by-faith 'Jansenist' reformers. Among worshippers: 17th-century philosopher-mathematician Blaise Pascal.

The church's agitated mystics so upset King Louis XV with sex-and-theology "convulsions" that in 1732 he banned miracles at Saint-Médard. Today the church's only agitations and miracles happen on its little park's swings and teeter-totters. From my second-floor apartment across the street I can watch tykes play there on a sunny day as church bells ring, and people chat, embrace, or inspect both fresh fruit and each other. On Sunday mornings, strangers dance to Christian Bassoul's accordion as amateurs, dressed 1950s-style, sing songs by Édith Piaf and Maurice Chevalier: a movie set from yesteryear, a cozy village-in-a-metropolis, a countryside Clochemerle-in-the-City-of-Light.

Ate too much good food? At the top of Mouffetard and over a bit, you can dive into a public swimming pool. At bottom, work out in a big public gym: cardio, African dances, *tai chi*, martial arts. Even a bowling-alley half-way up. You can rent a bike on a side-street – or, even cheaper, borrow an almost-free *Vélib'*, one of Mayor Bertrand Delanoë's 20,000 (ultimately 50,000?) bikes available all over town at 1,451 stations.

But you don't come here to exercise, though the walk up and down Mouffetard may burn a few calories. Two other pleasures get you back to the food and drink that define *La Mouffe*. Near its top is a geometrical contradiction – an intimate 'round square' called Place de la Contrescarpe.

Just steps from a struggling young Ernest Hemingway's one-room apartment at 74 rue du Cardinal Lemoine, la Contrescarpe, with its two main facing cafés, is a Mecca for people-watchers. And celebrations. Joining hundreds of jump-dancing soccer fans singing Village People's *YMCA*, I spent a night here after France beat Brazil 3-0 to win the 1998 World Football (soccer) Cup. Daytime, a *Kronenbourg* beer and fresh copy of your favorite newspaper are all you need to remember you're happy, lucky, and really in Paris.

At the foot of *La Mouffe* is a distant echo of Rome and its legions. It's a shop selling gourmet Italian food: daily-made fresh pasta, palate-teasing red or pesto sauces, spicy sausages and ingenious feast-dishes.

So what if Marco Polo only brought pasta from China a thousand years after Caesar? Today's Old-Roman descendants, the Italians, remembering how their forebears brought the Renaissance to France, just love to brag that Italy taught France to cook.

Wandering in the Elysian Fields – "les Champs"

Wherever you think you're going in this world, something tells you you've got there when you look all the way up – or down – "the world's most beautiful avenue." Grand yet strangely intimate, and dissecting the classy 8th arrondissement, it's the center of many universes, a place where history, beauty, and people great and modest come together: between 80 and 120 million visitors each year. Go there, alone or with a treasured friend, maybe at Christmas time. Make it your personal avenue, your private path to secret hopes, ambitions and loves. And let its magic flow over you.

No matter how many times you've crossed her path, there's a Paris lady who brazenly kidnaps your heart. Ever young, ever stylish, ever sure she's the center of the world, the *Champs-Élysées* knocks herself out to knock you out. Especially at holiday-time. A million festive lights hide in trees standing sentinel on her charms, igniting a river of flame two kilometers long and 70 meters wide. Tinselled windows showcase luxury of breathtaking taste and prices. Crowds stroll and swirl, multiracial Jezebels sashaying past shy guys strutting like Antonio Banderas. Some people actually shop here, but more come just to *be* here and to gawk. *Les Champs* is the Cleopatra of avenues, a look-at-me hormone-stirrer, a hair-tossing megastar, a gorgeous dame with a past of a thousand stories – possibly one featuring you.

Some of the great *Champs* tales recur. The stately Bastille Day parade down the avenue displays France's armies and civil defenders with a dignity that reassures and unites a nation. Another yearly event is the *Tour de France*. The race already won, massive crowds cheer as cyclists ride up and down the avenue to bask in glory. The winner drinks champagne while coasting to the victory stand.

Four hundred years ago, the avenue was fields and vegetable-gardens. Over the 17th-century, it grew from muddy mess to fashionable promenade. Baron-Prefect Georges-Eugène Haussmann finished the job during his huge 1853–1870 Paris renovations. For two centuries, the avenue has been a stage for grand events: marches (Victor Hugo's six-hour 1885 funeral procession drew over two million mourners), celebrations (1944 Liberation, France's 1998 World Cup soccer win), and that weird phenomenon of which France offers more kinds than varieties of cheese: demonstrations (De Gaulle's defenders in 1968, plus every species of discontented workers.). I remember inching slowly up the *Champs* as a student, with a huge crowd protesting the Soviets' 1956 crushing of the Hungarian uprising. We were young, outraged, and burning with solidarity for Budapest's victims, tossing our jackets on a pile to help the refugees.

Napoleon started his *Arc de Triomphe* in 1806 at the top of the *Champs*. Alas for him, he met his Waterloo in 1815, and King Louis-Philippe had to finish it in 1836. It's the avenue's crowning glory, a passionate metaphor for French grandeur. Hitler rubbed in France's 1940 defeat by having the *Wehrmacht* march under it and down the avenue, on foot and horse. The other end of the avenue bookends the *Champs* with its own heart-stopping greatness: the *Place de la Concorde*, where parades end with a flourish.

In 2007–08, the *Champs*' famous show-biz terrace-restaurant-hotel *Fouquet's* saw two dramas. On May 6, 2007, president-elect Nicolas Sarkozy celebrated his victory there. His ragtag group of friends, serious or flashy, waited over an hour for Sarko's pouty wife Cécilia to turn up. More happily, in mid-2008 a nearly-destitute 73-year-old lady called Lina Renault won a 47-year battle to prove she was the legal owner of *Fouquet's*. Selling it netted her a fortune.

Commerce now threatens the *Champs*' unique personality as national and cultural forum. Clothing stores, as elsewhere in Paris, are driving out cultural venues, killing bookstores, half the cinemas, even many decent restaurants. So are big-name stores like Virgin (music) and H & M, Zara, Gap and Célio (popular fashions). So are multinational firms eager to buy a world-famous address. Result: insane rents, running from a yearly $9,000 a square meter to $15,000 – on top of often multi-million-dollar signing fees. Class is giving way to *déclassé*. A major magazine in 2008 ran a cover entitled "*Les Champs-Élysées*: Chic or Cheap?"

Mayor Bertrand Delanoë has launched an emergency plan to stop the market from killing the avenue's image of quality, style, conviviality. Can he succeed? He'll be lucky to save a cinema or two – and to drive some tackier businesses literally underground. Beyond the flashier youth emporia, he'll leave stores to make you gape. Plus stores that are just fun: how about that Belgian beer museum?

The *Champs* still has lots to intrigue, day or night. True to character, it offers a touch of crass with its class. Racy night-clubs, and grandpa-thrilling girlie shows at the Lido. Movie-star hangouts like *Fouquet's*. A few night-time thugs from the *banlieues*. Pickpockets. Naughty fauna of the night: no longer Argentine *horizontales* prowling in white Mercedes, but *filles de l'Est*, stunning East European sirens. A little understatement remains: The exclusive gentlemen's club, *Travelers*, has no sign, just gilded gates.

But the only shady lady who seizes your heart, stomps on it, and flounces away with it, is still the great avenue herself. She's as old and as young as the Elysian Fields – a "heroes' resting-place" to the Greeks, a "paradise" to medieval Christians, an alley of dreams to you and me and everybody who, at a sudden breath-catching turn, crosses her path.

Practical, not poetic, the avenue's signature song puts it neatly: "Sun or rain, noon or midnight, there's everything you want on the Champs-Élysées."

PART II

PEOPLE FACING THEIR MUSIC

Chapter Five /

LES FEMMES

It's easy to peddle fantasies and fables about Parisian women. *Parisiennes* themselves invent them, and strive to prove them true in street, office and bedroom. Books and magazines fell forests titillating the credulous and insecure. Why do Paris women display 'legendary' sex-appeal? Because self-perpetuating Paris legends claim they do, and eager foreigners (include French provincial women) want to believe them. Just as they do tales of the mythical "French lover" (a fraudulent reputation, of course!).

A master peddler of *Parisienne* myths was 19th-century novelist Honoré de Balzac, a fat, smoking, coffee-swilling Class-A seducer. Presenting in April 2008 a routine section on where to meet the sexiest women in Paris, *Le Nouvel Observateur* weekly cited Balzac thus: "Does [the *Parisienne*] owe to angel or devil this undulating grace which plays beneath a swath of black silk, teasing its lace edges, spreading her balm in the air as what I would call the *Parisienne*'s breeze."

With such a fevered imagination, you can find any woman breezy. (Not a bad idea?) But couldn't you take your fever to Rome, Madrid, New York or blonde-paradise Moscow, and seek angels or devils there too? In fact, pick any small town where cheeseburgers don't meet Spandex.

Dress standards in Paris are indeed as high as the Eiffel Tower. Unwearable *haute couture* creates an intimidating mystique, and fashionable oases dot the city – pricey but usually exquisite clothing to drape princess or shop-girl. Reinforcing the standards: hawk-eyed women scrutinize how other women dress and behave. And men look, stare, ogle, leer, even audibly express admiration: an awed-but-eager whisper of "*ravissante!*" is manna to any mannequin, especially if she's an unofficial one, a slightly lumpy secretary or housewife strutting her stuff.

More to the point, how do *Parisiennes* behave? Parisian women of reasonable availability (a huge reservoir) of course respond to intelligent, tasteful and witty approaches by men. But don't women everywhere? French women are not especially loose, except in the sense of relaxed. Relations between the sexes in Paris are deliciously natural. No gender cops here: your biggest crime is *not* to compliment a lady. That's a sign of the gravest social misdemeanor – being *mal élevé* ("badly brought up"), or uncultured and lacking in social graces.

Paris is a city for women who want to remember what it's like to be a woman. Men, un-cowed by harassment paranoia, don't fear to flirt, flatter, hug, air-kiss and, in high society, hand-kiss (usually missing the hand). French women mostly enjoy this without running to a Human Rights Commission. Work-related harassment is another kettle of *bouillabaisse,* especially if tied to a "couch promotion." Then lawyers may (though rarely) enter the fray. If the harassment is mainly awkwardness or stupidity, and not job-threatening, many *Parisiennes* take a self-help approach: "What's wrong with those American women," I heard one female French manager say, "Don't they know how to slap a man's face?"

Les Françaises are just as guilty. No man is safe in a Paris supermarket vegetable section, never mind museums, bookstores and parks. For uptight foreigners, the first joy of Paris is just chilling out and rejoining, without stress, the ageless biological dance. Come here as political refugees... from political correctness. Once I observed to a newsstand lady that Sophia Loren, on a magazine cover, didn't look "too bad for her age." The kiosque lady feigned jealousy, retorting: "And what about me?"

Another time, in the Jardin du Luxembourg, I got carpet-bombed by a pigeon, from head to all points south. I went to the public facilities to clean up, and started wiping off my head and face in front of the horrified attendant – not the scowling "Madame Pipi" of legend, but Françoise, a cheery, round fifty-something. She started cleaning me off too, insisting that she wanted to help a "distinguished gentleman" (Who, me?). I tried to rebuff her, protesting that this was no job for a lady of her quality. But she persisted, all the way down. When I stopped her near a strategic place, she smiled and deadpanned: "But why do you want to deprive me?" Leaving a fat tip, I went upstairs to the *buvette* and returned with a blush-producing flute of champagne. Since then, Françoise and I have a bond only a Frenchwoman or a pigeon could appreciate.

In Paris as elsewhere, any man who claims he understands women is a liar, egomaniac or fool. Not or: all three. Given Latin expressiveness, generalizing about French women is especially hazardous. Are they sensual, passionate and romantic? Or flighty, brittle and neurotic? Wise, sensible and loving? Or cold, calculating and cynical? Mature, understanding and generous? Or childish, sulky and self-absorbed? Can the truth be: a bit of all of the above? Just like all human beings?

Does personality depend on context, times or lover? Any man stupid enough to give a clear opinion unmasks himself as an idiot. And the second he pretends he knows all about women, some very ordinary female – by design, perversity or accident – will certify his folly.

A man's surest defense is of course to plead ignorance. Not only does this parry accusations of arrogance. It guarantees that some woman will, out of pity or contempt, decide to take him in hand to explain it all. To *déniaiser* him, as that charming verb implies: to "make him a little less stupid."

Being a coward and a realist (essentially the same thing), I have no avowed opinion on women in general, or on French women in particular. That posture is not modesty. It's self-defense. As Andy Grove of Intel (maker of those little computer chips you love) once said: "Only the paranoid survive." And the best way to survive with women, methinks, is this: through cautious exploration, carrying a thick skin and a limitless willingness to listen.

How long should the exploration last? A lifetime, of course. Publicly, you search for the "perfect" woman – and chances are you may never find her. But to improve your odds, you can honestly claim that you need to study many women. Your journey may well be your destination. And if it proves to be only a journey, it's no tragedy. As British Airways's predecessor, BOAC, once proclaimed: "Getting there is half the fun!" If that sounds too frivolous, feed your friends this more noble explanation: Your risk of finding or not finding the perfect woman as akin to philosopher-mathematician Pascal's "gamble" on the existence of God.

If you die and find Him in Heaven, He'll reward your faith. If He's not there, it's cost you nothing. So believe, and enjoy the search.

My oblique path to "getting there" with French women BOAC-style (at least in print!) is to study a few remarkable, though not always exemplary, ones. In following pages, several such women illustrate roughly what quite a few French women may want. Obviously, they don't all want the same thing. Surprise! There is no typical woman, even French. These inspirational ladies are all over the map, emotionally, socially and professionally. But all demand, or demanded, two things: freedom and respect.

A good start on "understanding" women, as well as men? No *Vive la différence!* needed here, as the first two of our heroines show. Their examples prove again that everything in today's France began yesterday, maybe centuries ago. So let's choke down a bit more history. This may set the stage for some women in our times, as we move from women's courage to boldness to flamboyance to simple confidence. Beyond that, we collide with sexuality – in its never-stale, infinite variety of expression and impact.

Olympe de Gouges – famously unknown revolutionary

How have Western women won long-delayed rights? For Anglo-Saxons, Susan B. Anthony and Emily Pankhurst may spring to mind. But you can make a decent case that Marie Gouze (later Olympe de Gouges: 1748-1793) started it all. Never heard of her? That's because her many enemies went to outrageous lengths to bury her memory, and because the English-speaking world tends to be parochial. De Gouges rocked so many boats in her time – despotism, slavery, censorship, patriarchy, and revolutionary corruption – that the "boys" had to stop her. Tragically, as you will see. Her eclipse matched a two-century intimidation of feminists. But in recent years, France has begun to salute her seminal contributions: see shake-the-cage reformers Gisèle Halimi, Élisabeth Badinter and Ségolène Royal. Today's French women cannot find a more vivid and thrilling model than their 18th-century sister Olympe.

Her death and systematic effacement from public discussion crippled women's rights in France for ten generations. Who was Olympe de Gouges, and what battles did she fight?

Born thirty years before the French Revolution to a butcher's family in remote Montauban, she married young, had a baby, and quickly became a widow. Matrimony couldn't have been enchanting, for she promptly declared marriage "the grave of confidence and love." During her life, she had enough lovers to show at least tactical forgiveness to the male sex. And she was smart enough to escape financial pressures by moving in with a well-off Paris senior civil servant. She had adventures enough, but her liaisons were minor-league compared with the aristocracy's frantic bed-hopping.

As a Paris lady of leisure, she took to writing plays, then political tracts. The court-dominated *Comédie Française* ridiculed her plays as amateurish. Its real reason for attacking her: her first play condemned mistreatment of blacks in French colonies. This upset the court for its portrayal of despotism; but even more, it enraged slave-owning aristocrats.

She campaigned against slavery on and off the stage, writing another pro-freedom play and a devastating book. She faced not only boycotts and insults, but death threats. She refused to shut up. The Abbé Grégoire, a leading anti-slavery proponent, named her in a "List of Courageous Men [*sic*] Pleading the Cause of Unfortunate Blacks."

She went on to plead for decent treatment of poor mothers and children, and indeed of beggars. These writings laid the philosophical foundations for important elements of France's modern social safety-net. With revolution and renewal in the air, de Gouges worked with La Fayette, Condorcet, Malesherbes and many other public figures to promote a constitutional monarchy. They failed – the radicals wanted a king-free Republic.

A republican herself by 1792, she begged Maleherbes to let her help defend King Louis XVI's life before the out-for-blood Convention. She was allowed to attend a ceremony commemorating the Revolution, but Malesherbes and others dismissed contemptuously her plea to address the Convention. Women could not speak in public. Her response: "Women have the right to mount the (guillotine) scaffold. They have the right to mount the podium."

A year before, she had written to Queen Marie-Antoinette to seek backing for her campaign for women's rights. Crystallizing her views in the most provocative manner possible, de Gouges published her own version of the revolutionaries' Declaration of the Rights of Man and the Citizen: a "Declaration of the Rights of Woman and the Citizen." In it, she turned the men's self-important words into a sharp-eyed, ironic manifesto for male-female equality.

This alone earned her the enmity of the grandstanding revolutionaries, an increasingly nasty lot bent on spilling blood. A rare critic, she opposed the death penalty. She continued to bombard their extremist "*Jacobin*" leaders, and the public, with her ideas on how to build a better society where citizens could live under laws for all.

She smelled a blood-thirsty dictatorship coming, and was right. She could easily have escaped her prison-cell, but wouldn't run away. To the end, she stepped up to the podium. And on November 3, 1793, recognizing her parallel right, the revolutionaries let her mount the scaffold.

After two centuries of silence, Paris has recently begun to recognize de Gouges for her brave ideas. A street and a square now carry her name. Universities have found room in courses for her. And former 2007 presidential candidate Ségolène Royal has proposed carrying her cinders to the resting-place of France's heroes, the *Panthéon*. Noting how history still plods, Olympe would enjoy the irony: Its chiseled-in-stone legend proclaims "A Nation's Gratitude to Its Great Men."

George Sand – pen, cigar and scandale

Born under Napoleon I, she died after Napoleon III. This brilliant minor noblewoman lived through the greatest events of France's 19th century. Taking a man's name to seize personal and literary freedoms, she turned intellectual France on its ear. She faced, even courted, scandal, living as freely as a man. This, at a time when mothers told unmarried daughters to "be quiet and be beautiful," and women of riper years learned to be good or be discreet. Though born in the country, Sand was no mousy, dreamy Madame Bovary. She did become a close

*friend of the author of that famous novel, Gustave Flaubert –
who, by the way, had already pre-empted the title by confessing
that "Madame Bovary is me." Sand's playground of mind and
body was Paris. And that's where her soul-sisters still thrive,
even as feminists worldwide celebrate her as a pioneer.*

Victor Hugo revered her, Chopin loved her, France's
"good society" despised her. She was a dozen wild, controversial women under one man's name: George Sand. Born
two hundred years ago as Amantine-Aurore Lucile Dupin,
she blazed her way through French intellectual and cultural
life for 72 years, and passionate fans and foes dispute her
standing to this day: in 2004, highbrow daily *Le Monde*
handed them almost a whole weekend magazine.

Sand drew her own caricature. Men's clothes, cigars,
relentless social climbing and networking. Her personal
life was her public life, and she delighted in shocking her
upper-bourgeoisie relatives by flaunting a scandalous lifestyle. She paraded lovers of at least two sexes. She defied,
then left, her husband in a no-divorce France to live alone
in Paris. Even when she went off to Venice with a young
poet-lover, Alfred de Musset, she betrayed him with an Italian doctor, leaving the poor lad limp with perplexity.

She wrote ceaselessly – some eighty novels, each usually in a few weeks, twenty plays, and uncounted short
stories and articles. She also wrote at least nineteen thousand letters to people great and small. In both fiction
and letters, she never planned themes or structure; she
just took her pen and let creative passion ("logorrhoea,"
sniped enemies) sweep her along. Most now call her tor-
rential novels mediocre – all gush, no shape – but a new
generation of readers, perhaps dismayed at the aridity

of today's French novels, are finding them engaging again.

The George Sand pen-name came about for the same reason that her contemporary, England's Mary Ann Evans, wrote as George Eliot: women writers, in the 19th century, were not taken seriously. (Even Eliot wrote a piece called "Silly novels by lady novelists" – an echo of W.S. Gilbert's *Mikado* slap at "that singular anomaly, the lady novelist").

Sand laughed last. Her novels sold widely. Happily, her grandmother left her a splendid little castle in Nohant. Throughout Sand's stormy life, this was her haven, her security and her freedom – confirming again the dictum that there are very few situations in life where the possession of large sums of money cannot be of some assistance.

In ideas and enthusiasms, Sand lived without restraint. Although her early novels tapped into the romantic vogue, her lust for justice and equality later drove her to back socialist, even revolutionary, ideas. On both counts, she was a soul-sister to Hugo. Both were hell-raisers, both fearless, eloquent, and determined to live as they wanted.

She didn't harp on feminist theory. She preferred to apply it. And that's why you find her on all the better gender-studies programs everywhere. She didn't peddle Freud-like hypotheses about cigars; she smoked cigars. Stomping with stogie into editors' offices, she demanded to be treated like a man. "I ask the support of no one," she proclaimed, "to kill someone for me, gather a bouquet, correct a proof, or go with me to the theater."

Her network of friends, especially celebrated friends, probably inspired the Rolodex. A dinner-party at Nohant might include any of Chopin, de Musset, Flaubert, Lizst, Balzac, Turgenev, Heine, Delacroix, plus a princeling or two. History doesn't dwell much on her lady friends, though Sand called actress Marie Dorval her one true love. The queen-bee syndrome may have been at work: she junked years of letters from a good friend, the Countess d'Agoult, telling her they were worthless.

Sand was a piece of work, but a masterpiece of work to many. She would not shut up, whether as writer or conversationalist. Driven, industrious, obsessed with expressing herself, she used others as her fuel and foil. Was she, as a child early abandoned, achingly insecure? She was, strangely, modest about her reputation. "They will forget me in fifty years," she said.

Well, they haven't. And all points to her seizing minds a lot longer. She was just too original, too gutsy, just too don't-give-a-damn independent, at a time when women crocheted, nodded at husband's whims, and bowed covered heads to the priest. Even if her writing becomes passé, her example will always stir free-thinking women. And maybe make freer-thinkers of a few men.

Today's sudden rage for Sand has unearthed an unsuspected side of the acerbic public figure. As she grew older, she lived more and more in her village, forsaking the prancing and preening of Paris. What a dazzled public now finds, in witnesses' letters, is a profoundly kind and simple woman. Outside her circus of celebrity, the peasants she walked with to gather flowers or inspect the crops adored her. She tended to their children and their illnesses, and shared their joys, just as a good neighbor.

One female biographer calls Sand "a reasonable feminist," given the limited possibilities of her time. But it was her unreason, not her reasonableness, that made this woman a better man than most.

Françoise Sagan – Bonjour tristesse, et au revoir

No crusader, this one. She was instead proof that, as Cyndi Lauper sang, "Girls just wanna have fun." But what a girl, and what fun! Her first public fun was shocking the world with a cynical teenager's view of love and lovers. Waif-like, totally self-absorbed and irresponsible with money and cars, she was insanely generous with friends. Almost as prolific as George Sand, Sagan wrote as she drove her sports cars – wildly, thoughtlessly, and without regard for consequences. Posterity so far only remembers the scandalous novel she wrote as a precocious school-girl: "Hello Sadness" remained her fate. In her agitated, full-speed-ahead life, she had plenty of friends high and low, but few real ones at the end.

Fast cars, fast pen, fast life and death. Writer Françoise Sagan, leprechaun of a taboo-breaking postwar generation, rocketed to wealth and world fame in 1954 at age 19. Her novel, *Bonjour Tristesse,* termed "a masterpiece of cynicism and cruelty," led admiring Catholic writer François Mauriac to call her a "charming little monster."

The monster could write like an angel. When she died in 2004 at 69, destroyed by poverty, illness, debts, tax arrears and lawsuits, she left all France in tears.

Front pages and magazine covers pictured her wide-eyed innocence throughout the decades. Paris mayor Bertrand Delanoë told a million street-revelers that his all-night *Nuit Blanche* festival belonged to her. National politicians rushed to grieve – and to seize a piece of history.

Sagan (a name borrowed from Proust to spare her rich family embarrassment) wrote her totem-novel sitting in a café in the summer of 1954. On May 7, France had suffered a spirit-shattering defeat at Vietnam's Dien Bien Phu. Elites and all authority drew contempt.

A year before, Brigitte Bardot had burst on the scene, defying parents, fashion and society. Bikinis swayed on beaches. Jean-Paul Sartre and his accomplice Simone de Beauvoir smoked cigarettes and cynicism at Saint-Germain-des-Prés. The world-weary times sought a focus for rebellion. *Bonjour Tristesse*'s 17-year-old heroine supplied it. She chronicled her dashing father's womanizing, and, with premature sophistication and careless brutality, plotted heart-breaking manipulations. The book gripped readers by its clear-eyed scheming, then found scandal in the author's age. A girl who made love without being in love? Only boys did that.

Her image shocked even more because she was a "girl of good family." She was "well-raised" (the ultimate French compliment) and spoke beautiful, slightly old-fashioned French. This only spiced up her extravagances: expensive sports cars, lovers of both sexes, constant night-clubbing, hobnobbingwithsometimesdubiousfriends(manyfamous), treating her life as trivial. Among many who never read her, she passed for just another airhead – famous for being famous.

Fame too soon and bad advice were her downfall. Her father, learning she had earned a fortune for her first novel, didn't tell her to save. He told her to blow it all quickly before it corrupted her. She did, impulsively. She gave it away (including cars) to friends, leaving a box of free cash on her mantel for visitors. She even sent money to unhappy women for nose jobs.

Later get-rich schemes involved her in shadowy oil deals in Kazakhstan and dealings with wealthy Corsican speculator and racing-car driver "Dédé-la-Sardine." Influence-seekers abused her innocence to get to top people. She was close to at least two French presidents (Georges Pompidou, François Mitterrand), and could probably call, and meet, anyone she wanted in France.

Fame drove her to alcohol: whisky gave her courage to face journalists. Her escapism pushed her to drive her Jaguar XK 140 barefoot at crazy speeds. A near-fatal accident got her hooked on drugs, including cocaine. Never able to keep track of accounts, she faced years of agony in the bankruptcy courts, fighting off the dreaded *fisc* (the tax department).

Even in her late-life miseries, she could be hilarious. "Make people laugh. Laugh at yourself... Whether sweet or sardonic, laughing is the dazzling, irresistible proof of our freedom." This from a girl kicked out of convent-school for claiming that "God is a big rabbit." Incorrigible teenagers, she and singer-lover Juliette Gréco made jokes an endless badminton game.

Decade after decade, and at breakneck speed, Sagan churned out novels, plays, screen-plays and articles. Quality roller-coastered, but she always kept her signature style. At its best, it was fluid, shimmering, inevitable. At her every stumble, critics dipped pens in acid. They couldn't forgive her for so much talent, and for writing so much, so quickly, so almost carelessly.

Like many ever-young creators whose troubles eclipsed their creations, Sagan may gain new fans devouring media praise on anniversaries of her death. For artists, early death (even at 69!) can be a smart career move. Sagan has left enough masterpieces – three or four novels, a movie or two – that she will keep a place.

But for French and foreign admirers of her halcyon days, her death closes the mythic time of Montparnasse. Near his end, she would take a blind Jean-Paul Sartre there to *La Rotonde* to cut his meat, both of them giggling as they escaped Sartre's "dragon-lady," de Beauvoir.

As with Mitterrand, the tender complicities of old man-young woman warmed those next-to-final years. Destitute the last few, she camped in her old Normandy house, lent back to her by a kind owner. She sat forlorn and a little befuddled in her wheelchair, her loneliness deepened by a chattering TV set.

She had only wanted to "write very good books." She couldn't understand where all the money had gone, and why the *fisc* was still so vindictive.

Three Simones show how – Signoret, de Beauvoir, Veil

No one woman can sum up the dizzying progress of women in society over the past forty years. Birth control, abortion, workplace promotion, breakthroughs in politics, sports, even the military. French women's gains, while far from complete, are everywhere evident today. In this revolution, every woman – even those who prefer more traditional roles – has countless new choices. And each woman brings her own values, talents, experiences, ideas and sensitivities to redefining dignity.

Let's look at three different women of recent times and see how each, in her own way, won respect and new freedoms for women. All that seems to link them is a common first name. But they have two other things in common: courage, and insistence on stating and living their own standards.

Three ladies called Simone. Between torrid actress Simone Signoret and icy philosopher Simone de Beauvoir shines a warm but steely other Simone: politician, later top judge, Simone Veil. All three Simones have helped French women advance.

Signoret, in her sparkling memoir *Nostalgia Isn't What It Used To Be*, told how her career soared on raw talent – and how, by shrugging, she commanded lover Yves Montand to crawl back from Marilyn Monroe. De Beauvoir showed women how to split the difference, man-wise: hard-nosed feminist soul-mate to Jean-Paul Sartre, while girlish mistress to her "precious, beloved Chicago man," novelist Nelson Algren. In her male-dismantling *The Second Sex,* she gave all women a bible to thump. And a mantra: "You're not born a woman, you become one."

But it's Madame Veil – an 81-year-old Auschwitz survivor – who most speaks to French women. For 35 years, she has flung herself into the least woman-friendly of all professions in this macho country: politics. Rising to be Minister of Health, then of Social Affairs, then President of the European Parliament, and then member of the Constitutional Court, she has long been the most respected woman in France. The one who led women into politics.

She followed a thorny, sometimes deadly, path. In 1791, as we saw, Olympe de Gouges lost her head to Robespierre. In 1994, killers linked to corrupt male politicians assassinated pushy female MP Yann Piat. Big names surfaced, but police enquiries got nowhere.

In France, politics has always been a patriarchal affair. Even today – in spite of a law saying parties must offer half of all candidacies to women – only 18 percent of France's 2008 National Assembly members are women. (They sit low on party lists, and, in single-member ridings, get to "die" against big names). Percentages of women in parliament elsewhere: Sweden (47), Finland (41), Denmark (38), "macho" Spain (36), Germany, including Chancellor Angela Merkel (32), Canada (21), USA (17). French regional and local politics, though electing more women, deny them executive power: only seven percent of mayors of towns with at least 3,500 inhabitants are women.

Political culture is the flip-side of French daily life. Relations between men and women, we have noted, remain more relaxed than in politically correct North America. That tired slogan about the good old days when "men were men, women were women, and everybody knew the difference" makes more or less innocent flirting almost a national duty in France. But there's a price for charm: in government and business, women get praise, rarely power.

France's obsession with its own history entrenches the idea that men should do the dirty work of politics. Women, as men's muses, always inspired, encouraged, advised, supported, consoled. Oversimplifying: Women in post-Renaissance courts became, even more than in troubadour times, the alcove civilizers of men. Female literary salons from 17th to 20th centuries shaped taste and ideas. They even cleaned up language and jokes. Gradually, salons became more political. Napoleon's female nemeses – Madame Récamier and Madame de Staël – lost salons, and won exile.

Lagging behind Anglo-Saxon and Nordic countries, France gave women the right to vote only in 1944. For another forty years, it stuck female politicians mainly in symbolic or 'family' ghettos. Then, over a raging decade,

woman seized control of procreation – thus the practical
opportunity to enter politics. Legalization of birth control
in 1967 led to Health Minister Simone Veil's all-changing
1975 law allowing abortion. Backed by a 1971 "Manifesto
of 343 Sluts" (including Catherine Deneuve) who admitted illegal abortions, Veil became the heroine of women's
access to political power.

This prospect infuriated old-line male politicos of all
colors. Female parliamentarians suffered unspeakably obscene catcalls about their bodily shapes and functions.
In full National Assembly and Senate, audible mutter-
ings about "whores" and "dykes" were common – with
much worse on the hustings. One remarkable member of parliament, feminist Gisèle Halimi, quit in 1984.
Prime Minister Edith Cresson (1991-92) faced misogy-
nist martyrdom. In 1995, "reformer" Prime Minister
Alain Juppé (later scandal-laundered in Quebec, now the
excellent mayor of Bordeaux) named twelve female ministers. These *Jupettes* (mini-skirts) outwore their tokenism:
He fired eight of them six months later.

In 1999, women politicians of all parties joined to
launch the *Chiennes de Garde* – literally "bitch-watchdogs."
They publicized every sexist insult, and managed to cow the
yahoos into…not silence, but discretion. Senator and ex-
Culture Minister Catherine Tasca told me: "Men are more
careful now. But condescension is rampant. The other day
a male senator ended an attack on a female colleague's ideas
with the putdown: 'Nevertheless, madame, I still find you
charming'."

In recent years, the "elephants" (male bigwigs) of
major parties have grown apoplectic. Barely getting used
to a female minister of defence, Michèle Alliot-Marie, they

seethed at two other smart women who stepped into the limelight. Françoise de Panafieu ran for mayor of Paris. And Ségolène Royal, a bright (and, I hesitantly report, beautiful) 52-year-old, was a Socialist candidate for the 2007 presidential election.

Neither won. But others – thanks to Sarkozy – have captured key posts: Finance, Economy and Foreign Trade, Justice, Interior, Higher Education and Research, Human Rights, Ecology, Labor Relations, Health and Sports, Housing and Urban Affairs, Culture and Communiocations, Family and Solidarity.

The old boys can't mock these jobs as tokenism. The responsibilities they carry lie at the very heart of modern government. The women exercising them of course succeeded on their own merits and efforts. But thanks to the three Simones, and some other gutsy women, they had inspiration, examples and, in the end, a chance.

Ségo, Cécilia, Carlita – cherchez la femme fatale

After Sarkozy won the May 2007 presidential election, three other women seized public attention, and not always in edifying ways. Not one looks like having the historical impact of the above ladies. But give them time.

With thirteen female ministers, Sarkozy's first cabinet certainly delivered the gender-equality goods. His Spanish pal, Prime Minister José Luis Zapatero, went further: in 2008, he named a majority-female cabinet, including a very pregnant minister of defense. Among Sarkozy's most visible appointments were two women of North African parentage and a young Senegalese. Before his marriage to current wife Carla ("Carlita") Bruni, Sarkozy used to take some of the more exotic young ones along on his foreign trips, often commenting publicly on their "beauty." No male ministers have yet won the accolade of being handsome. But maybe they can swing that when France again gets a female prime minister.

For sheer day-to-day presidential obsession, none of Sarkos's female ministers have shaken his cage as much as the following ladies – one fighting him publicly, the other two doing their best to contain him at home.

Impressed that almost half of French President Nicolas Sarkozy's cabinet is female? France's three most interesting political women are elsewhere. One, Ségolène Royal, played Joan of Arc in 2007, then Alice in Wonderland, and finally – claims the title of a tell-all book she published – *La Femme fatale.* The second, Cécilia Ciganer-Albéniz, played an exotic second wife who humiliated her then-Interior Minister husband (Sarkozy) by running off to the Exterior (New York) with her lover – an "events organizer" who, this time, clearly outdid himself.

The third lady, a rich, smart, man-eating model-singer called Carla ("Carlita" to her besotted "Nico") snagged Sarko on the rebound from Cécilia. As they say in the serials: to be continued.

The first lady – and the only political woman in her own right – is defeated Socialist presidential candidate Ségolène Royal, ex-companion of ex-Socialist Party boss François Hollande. Her campaign promised salvation, then went all fuzzy, ending in recrimination.

The Royal-Hollande couple entered Socialist Party politics together in a Bill-and-Hillary-Clinton pact, coordinating careers but pursuing them separately. Hollande, who passed for a jokey, indecisive apparatchik, whipped his party on with a wet noodle. Royal, until her run at the presidency, passed for a lightweight: minister of the environment before that became serious stuff, then of elementary schools, then of family and childhood.

Her sudden sweep of the party's presidential primary left poor Hollande – who wanted the presidency himself – looking even more the hen-pecked loser. *La Femme fatale*, a devastating look at the couple's romantic tensions and political rivalries, was prelude to a June 2007 post-electoral party bloodbath.

Even late in 2008, the issue remained: Can the Socialist Party finally pry itself loose from lingering Marxist fantasies of class war, and join Europe's Tony-Blair-style social-democratic mainstream? Eight years before, Royal's defeated prime ministerial boss Lionel Jospin dared to risk this slogan: "Yes to the market economy; no to a market society."

For leftist theologians, this contradicted Marx's theory that economic systems define societies. But Jospin – long a Troskyite mole within the Socialist Party (a deceit considered a mere youthful indiscretion in France) – opened the door a crack to reality. In 2007, to Jospin's anger as a would-be come-back kid, Royal went further. She deadpanned that Blair had decent ideas on youth employment and investment in public services. The furies of French Socialist hell descended on her.

Smeared as a "Blairite" by her Marx-nostalgic colleagues, she backed off and never mentioned Tony again. Two clans leapt on her "lapse:" her party's archeo-Marxists; and leadership rivals also seduced by Blair, but lacking her guts even to hint at Blair's merit.

The party's cobwebby ultra-left-wing acclaimed former Prime Minister Laurent Fabius, a rich man no more a socialist than your cat. Secret *blairistes* latched onto former finance minister Dominique Strauss-Kahn. And for a year – with French voters sending all lefties to a much warmer place – only "DSK" remained standing against Ségo. Both want to "renew" their party. But each as king or queen of the Socialist castle.

Meanwhile, in mid-2008, Martine Aubry – a real Socialist queen as daughter of Mr. Europe, Jacques Delors – came out of the woodwork to challenge Ségolène. The War of the Queen Bees. Fantasist of the 35-hour week and parachuted mayor of northern city Lille, Madame "Aubry is the perfect anti-Royal candidate," chortled diehard lefties.

Forget the alcove gossip about spouses and lovers. The big story here was that a woman, with steel for a backbone and grappling with modern dreams, was having a serious go at dragging a major, macho, reactionary French party into the 21st century. Fluffy tales of "French power women," highlighting Ségo's bikinis and Cécilia's runaway lovers, delight us all. But on May 6, 2007, seventeen million French voters, many holding Marxist noses, backed historic change with Ségo. In Hillary-math, 'seventeen million cracks in the glass ceiling.' That was virtually one in two French voters in a race Sarkozy won by only 53 percent to her 47 percent.

That ain't society news. It's startling political news, and Marx was spinning in his grave in London's Highgate Cemetery. Ségo, now *there's* a femme fatale, as Sarkozy well knows. Long after her defeat (which she called a victory), she was still tracking him night and day, denouncing his every step with the acid tongue of a spouse who knew his worst secrets.

Psychologically, Royal is to Cécilia as Margaret Thatcher is to Paris Hilton. Cécilia's role in politics, had she stuck around, was to focus on four roles: giving Sarko the family anchor his hyperkinetic personality needed; influencing personnel decisions; drawing him further into his bad habit of getting powerful media cronies to censor negative coverage of himself and Cécilia; and wearing Prada.

In the end, the Cécilia story remained palace gossip. For years, the press analyzed her every glance, every absence and every Sarko caress. Was this or that a harbinger of some new, mad Cécilia dash for freedom? The volatile, Spanish-mothered Cécilia was indeed quite a pan of paella. But she clearly had a fragile temperament. Her political impact proved only indirect, anecdotal and picturesque.

Paul Simon (of Garfunkel fame) brilliantly prophesied our French-Spanish Cécilia's roller-coaster effect on Sarko in his famous 1970 song of her name in the aptly-named album *A Bridge Over Troubled Water*:

"*Cecilia, you're breaking my heart / You're shaking my confidence daily...*" ending with "*Jubilation! / She loves me again...*"

Alas, she didn't. And after helping him get elected president by playing political wifey during the 2007 campaign, she took barely four months before taking up again with French-American lover Richard Attias. Her marriage to Sarko ended formally in November 2007.

Within days, a rich pal fixed up Sarko with another wild Latin. She was singer-model Carla Bruni, ex-lover of several glitterati stars, and a woman who titillated (or horrified) matrons by professing that monogamy "bored" her.

Clearly, being presidential spouse doesn't bore her. Since their February 2008 marriage, Sarko has let her record and sell her whispery, super-amplified love songs — the most notorious song comparing her lover (Sarko? Another?) to Colombian cocaine and Afghan pot. But she's an intelligent, cultured woman who tries to lift his horizons beyond sports, politics, trash-TV and burnt-out rock stars. A wife who tells him to calm down and not swear at everybody in sight. Startling progress.

After not even a year on the job, the president's "Carlita" gets credit for civilizing (a bit) her new love. And for winning the respect and admiration of most French people. She may claim, as only a rich heiress can, to be "left-wing." She can delight in consorting with Gucci Marxists – even scruffy writers for left-loving daily *Libération*. But, as "*le bon peuple*" expects, she slips easily into the palaces of the Republic. If the people of monarchy-nostalgic France can't see a dignified king on the throne, now at least they can admire a woman who acts like a queen.

Some hiss that maybe she shouldn't have posed on the roof of the Élysée Palace in a slinky black evening-gown for that summer 2008 *Vanity Fair* cover-profile. And the jury is still out on how she can reconcile her pop-music career with arranging the state-banquet silverware.

Cynics claim she too will decamp someday. How nasty, how ghoulish, how drenched in anticipatory *Schadenfreude*! But betting is she'll stick out at least one presidential term, even two if Sarko wins one. Let's not be cynical. Many signs suggest this is true love. Besides, isn't the roof of the Élysée Palace a perfectly logical place for a fashion-shoot?

Iron elf in a Maserati – Laurence Parisot

If women are cracking glass ceilings in politics, what about that even more macho activity, business? Generally, women, even from top business schools, are still making their marks in middle management. The old-boy network reigns with no complexes in France: moves to put women on boards and promote them to CEO status are hit-and-miss, if not folkloric.

One spectacular exception is Anne Lauvergeon, CEO of the huge French nuclear conglomerate Areva. Her top-notch studies and patronage of President François Mitterrand won her a raft of powerful jobs in science and industry. She is now the most powerful woman in France and – according to Forbes magazine – a woman directing the world's largest workforce.

A woman with broader and more vocal, if less direct, influence in French business is Laurence Parisot, boss of the Medef employers' organization. As such, she speaks for big business and ends up in all the political and social battles that implies. Her originality is to have succeeded not as Lauvergeon did – via the state apparatus – but through managing the family furniture business, then spreading her wings on her own in other economic activities. Her unapologetic defense of free enterprise, her attacks on France's sacrosanct Code du Travail (Labor Code), and her blunt, commonsense language make her France's most society-changing trailblazer for women. Her father gave her the perfect gift for a woman in a hurry: a red Maserati.

Laurence Parisot may be the toughest woman in France. With teasing blue eyes and enough freckles for an Irish milk-maid, the 49-year-old president of France's employers' group (*Medef*) is the "boss of bosses" of French industry. In 2005, her first year on the job, she forced allies and adversaries alike to ponder how an enterprise-friendly society might solve many of France's intractable economic and social problems. The worst:

unemployment, sluggish growth, government deficits, suburban violence.

She has pushed this agenda ever since. To appreciate Parisot's revolution, remember that France's élites – politicians, civil servants, teachers, intellectuals, journalists – live mostly in a mythical consensus of state-revering, mushy leftism unconstrained by reality. Class warfare allegedly pits workers and their intellectual vanguard against an oppressive "rich" minority. The word "*libéral*" (here meaning a believer in markets) is, with rare exceptions, an insult. It conveys greed, selfishness, and harsh, anti-social Anglo-Saxon brutality. Almost invariably is carries the prefix "ultra," as though by nature it's extreme.

Medef, representing over 750,000 firms, was re-founded in 1998 by Ernest-Antoine Seillière (usually mocked as the baron he is). It fights a lonely battle to defend markets, thus the entrepreneurs who alone create jobs. "It is time," said Seillière, "to put the entrepreneur at the heart of French society." Parisot echoes this and vows to make the French "love markets."

To do so, she has shaken up the French business patriarchy in two ways. First, she replaced old male *Medef* warhorses by five brilliant mid-career female executives with impeccable credentials. Two women (from zero) sit on her executive committee; eight out of ten directors are women. They run *Medef*'s key sectors of oil, banking, taxation and finance. Tagged her "girl team," these women bring youth, competence and media savvy – vital to changing the anti-capitalist public culture.

Parisot's priority? Removing state shackles from small and medium businesses – the ones that create three quarters of all new jobs. Although adversaries often caricature all business people (even taxi-divers and newspaper vendors) as fat, cigar-smoking titans, seventy percent of Parisot's member-firms have less than fifty employees, thirty-five percent less than ten employees. To defend them, she speaks out with shocking bluntness. In 2006, she attacked the "statist logic" of Prime Minister Dominique de Villepin's proudly announced economic road-map, ridiculing its "cost and irrelevance."

Later she denounced President Jacques Chirac's job security ideas as absurd. She slammed the "mess" of state aid and the "Kafkaesque complications" of entrepreneur-punishing taxes. She attacked the job-protecting (actually job-killing) Labor Code Chirac defended. She mocked the "incomprehensible paradoxes" and "contradictory injunctions" of Labor Minister Jean-Louis Borloo, provoking apoplexy within this supposedly business-friendly, right-wing government.

Eyes a-twinkle, Parisot assured she was not looking for fights (subtext: as men do), but would fight whenever necessary. Unafraid to put cats among pigeons, she invited to *Medef* meetings all manner of speakers hostile to *Medef* – the jaw-dropper being Yankee-baiting, nationalizing, Venezuelan President Hugo Chavez. Others included Euro-MP "Red Dany" Daniel Cohn-Bendit and rough-talking soccer defender Lilian Thurman. The guest-speaker list of her *Medef* "summer university" is always a *Who's Who* of top business leaders.

The 2006 meeting's agenda was (a pretty good Parisot job description) "reconciling the irreconcilable." The title itself a provocation in polarized, all-or-nothing France, the colloquium kicked off with Chirac's *bête noire,* European Commission President José Manuel Barroso. It chased herds of sacred cows to slaughter: "reconcilable democracy," with

Jewish leader Théo Klein teaching negotiation from Israeli-Palestinian experience; "confronting socio-economic models," with World Trade Organization boss Pascal Lamy; and the "world geopolitical context," with terrorism guru Gilles Kepel.

Later Parisot blasted the government for proposing class-action suits against French business. In a powerfully argued brief, Parisot tore the idea to shreds. Another initiative showed off her background as a creative communicator. To sell her ideas for youth training, she set up a partnership with *Skyrock*, a radio station purveying music by such scruffy rappers as NTM (their name taking filial piety to unprintable excess).

Parisot is a media star, but not a show-off. She shares PR duties with other colleagues, though nobody grabs the headlines as cleverly as she does. Citing Montaigne on being a woman, she wraps logic in charm to pitch ideas offensive to this socialist-minded nation: the minimum wage is too high, pensions cost too much, bosses should fire incompetents, the state must live within its means. Such stuff is banal in most free-market societies. In France, it's anathema, an assault on the cherished "French social model."

In France's manly business world, Parisot is *not* one of the boys. She's a steel-magnolia leader who lobs hand-grenades scented with Chanel No. 5. The "boys" now respect, even admire her. And, no doubt, secretly envy her that little toy her papa left her, the red Maserati.

Gigi – still dreaming of romance

Some of us never grow up. And some of us never should. That's the case with Leslie Caron, a beautiful French woman who will never grow old – first because that's her nature, and second because she's immortalized in celluloid as a bubbly, naïve 17-year-old. Indeed, when we met her earlier, the topic was bubbles – champagne. Ballerina and modern dancer, Oscar-nominated Hollywood actress, lover of many famous, infamous or even discreet men, she still works at this season of her wisdom. First, as an actress always game for her next role. Then – being a romantic yet sensible French woman – as an inn-keeper in the gentle Burgundian countryside.

Facing the slow-flowing Yonne, just above the rolling vineyards of Burgundy's greatest wines, Leslie Caron's *La Lucarne aux Chouettes* (Owl's Nest) inn redefines idyllic. Intimate, embracing, her hostelry-restaurant has become one of France's must-visit romantic getaways. Robert De Niro thought so; so did Kristin Scott Thomas (*The English Patient*). Fans expect, and find, the exquisite, understated taste of the great actress-dancer-singer Caron in every nook and cranny.

You have seen Leslie Caron in scores of movies. But if you're lucky enough to be over 55, and remember her as the 17-year-old *ingénue* Gigi in the 1958 film of that name, you'll forever see her as a rambunctious, pixie-like child-woman. In some ways, she still is – as I found out dining with her one night at Paris's vine-covered *Closerie des Lilas*.

A pixie? Well, even at a bit over 17, she still sparkles. Rambunctious? Still active in TV and films, she has opinions on everything under the sun. She also runs her enchanting inn – and she's no absentee landlord. When not traveling abroad, she supervises the place from either Paris or her suite at the inn itself.

On a day-to-day basis, "Leslie" (as she insists even new acquaintances call her), entrusts the inn to her onsite manager Dominique. Everywhere at once, and (without hovering) eager to please, Dominique conducts the young staff like a string quartet. And she ensures that the inn's superb Japanese cook, her husband Daïsuke Inagaki, has all he needs to torment your taste-buds with light, innovative dishes. Once you've tasted his baked-onsite breakfast breads, you'll never sleep in.

Each of the inn's four rooms is spacious but different. Madame Caron personally decorated them all – as she did the whole inn, right down to napkins and silverware. Old movie-posters show "Leslie" in many of her movies, a treat for movie buffs. When you leave, another sweet surprise: the rates are extremely reasonable. This is no tourist trap – once you come, you'll be back.

I had already interviewed Leslie Caron by e-mail about champagne (see Chapter One above): she had celebrated it in a long-ago movie-song. This time a friend and I met her for dinner at the *Closerie*. She brought another guest: her little Shi-tzu "Tchi-Tchi" (not "Chi-Chi," she cautions). He listened sagely as she told wonderful tales of Old and New Hollywood. "My first big break came as a 'hoofer' in *An American in Paris*" (1951)." Based on music by George Gershwin, it featured classic songs: "'SWonderful," "Our Love is Here to Stay," and "I Got Rhythm."

A few months before filming, legendary dancer Gene Kelly picked 17-year-old Leslie out of a ballet to partner with him in the movie. You can catch her in this on *YouTube*. She's also there limbering up with impossible suppleness. "I was warming up in a corner," she says, "and Gene handed me a book to hold. It made the warming-up sequence worth watching entirely on its own. He was inspired, and such fun"

Ready for anything challenging, Caron has made 54 movies. Twice she was nominated for Best-Actress Academy Awards: in 1953 as star of *Lili*, and in1963 as leading-lady in *The L-Shaped Room*. Not bad for a self-described "hoofer."

Leslie Caron talked of her many "adorable" leading men: Louis Jourdan, Fred Astaire, Cary Grant, Mel Ferrer, and "rather grouchy" compatriot Maurice Chevalier. In recent years, she's done everything from comedy to drama to subtle fiction to TV series (*Law and Order, Falcon Crest*). Recent co-stars include Jerry Lewis (*Funny Bones, 1995*), Juliette Binoche (*Chocolat,* 2000) and Judi Dench (*The Last of the Blonde Bombshells,* 2000*)*. In 2007, she won a Primetime Emmy Award for *Law and Order*.

Such a record – running from ballet to movies to TV – is astonishing. Madame Caron is happy to talk about the past, and hearing her stories is like watching a movie-archive unfold onscreen. She talks so casually and colorfully about the actors and directors she has known (on and off screen) that you wonder why somebody hasn't signed her up to host a TV series called *The Story of Hollywood with Leslie Caron*. She could dazzle in that role, even without highlighting her highly picturesque private life. "I did know quite a few interesting men."

She's writing her memoirs just now, and had to leave the *Closerie* a bit early: "I need to get off to a good start each morning to get it done." But her mind and energy are turned as much to the future as the past. She has strong

views about where France is going: "Thank God for Sarkozy. He will finally fix the economy." And she intends to
keep acting: "Why stop? Is there a legal cut-off date?"

But you sense that her special joy these days is that cozy
little inn on the Yonne. "It's my secret sin. It's a refuge to
contemplate past…and future."

෧

Chapter Six /

LES FONCTIONNAIRES

One quarter of all French employees work for the state. Their salaries and pensions (including arm's-length agencies) make up 55 percent of the state budget. Three quarters of all French youth aged 15-24 want to be civil servants – envied, privileged *fonctionnaires.* The other quarter may not be that ambitious, though a million or so of the most resourceful and talented under-35s find opportunity abroad.

Facing over 20 percent unemployment – due in great part to that job-discouraging Labor Code – more youth are trying their luck at starting a small business. Unfortunately, surviving France's business-hostile bureaucracy demands fanatical dedication. For France's huge army of civil servants love the world as they see it: a republican monarchy in which every clerk with a rubber-stamp can leisurely lord it over selfish 'dissidents' trying to make their own way.

How did this happen? Most credit (or blame) goes to 17th-century finance minister Jean-Baptiste Colbert's belief in state intervention in the economy. This mindset led to selecting firms as "national champions" – a habit even 'free-enterprise' Nicolas Sarkozy favors. It fostered a national religion distrusting individual initiative, and presenting the state as the country's salvation. France's education system – especially its "Red Army" or "Mammoth" bureaucracy – has rooted this idea in generations of young French.

Public services often comfort and protect citizens. And France offers some wonderful services: healthcare, nursery schools, cultural and community centers, super-modern trains, even a couple of good TV channels. The term "public service," however, tends also to mean that the public exists to serve public-service union leaders. Mention the phrase *service public* and everybody salutes. When unionists shut down the Jardin des Plantes for a pay dispute, depriving thousands of pleasure there, they hung this sign on the gates, with no sense of irony at all: "Closed to defend public service."

Astonishingly, in spite of paralyzing strikes, barely *eight* percent of France's workforce belongs to unions, and these splinter into several ideological clans. Thanks to endless marches, strikes, blockades and occupations, France's leftist élites have succeeded in portraying France around the world as a mob-rule joke. Rightist leaders, indulging in daggers-drawn rivalries, legislative flip-flops and deafness to public opinion, have also helped make France look like Disneyland with *foie gras*.

Young people here, as in other European nations, are terrified of living less well than their parents. At least until recent slow-economy years, they and their parents have tended to think that the state owed them a living – immediately and forever. A life without risk. And, as civil servants, a life with richer pensions than unlucky, 'ordinary' citizens.

Like children denied expected favors, French youth routinely throw tantrums, and earn praise for "social vigilance." France is the only country where students smash property and commit street crime with impunity – then sing the Communist *Internationale* to defend bourgeois privilege. But they are just following the example of their elders, including most teachers.

Besides the bloated, reactionary education ministry, France's other immobilizing institution is the *École Nationale d'Administration* (ENA). Finishing-school for the political and administrative élite (again Siamese twins), ENA sends out graduates with an impeccable spirit of public service. But they come with we-know-best smugness and only a skimpy knowledge of real-world, free-market economics. They go straight to top state jobs, a minority choosing the private sector. Yet few of them, methinks, could run a profitable corner fruit-store.

But let's not smear everybody wielding a rubber-stamp. In spite of a genius for devising job-creation programs that create mainly more civil service jobs, *les fonctionnaires* do a few good things easily deserving two cheers. Alas, their repeated strikes and juicy privileges make a third cheer a dubious option.

Fed up with strikers, and sure he has crippled them through charm and toughness, Sarkozy hopes to trim civil-service ranks by attrition. He is cutting 30,726 *fonctionnaires* in 2009. But others ferociously resist. Can he really beat the unions? Can Hercules defeat Hydra?

Playing post office – le facteur

No civil servant enjoys as much trust as the man or woman delivering your mail. Your facteur brings messages and packages right to your door – and, if you meet up, does so with a friendly word. No wonder mail-deliverers

have become the most popular symbols of a helpful state –
surprisingly often even ending up as movie heroes.

Tramping, cycling or driving six days a week over
70,000 itineraries in navy-blue uniforms with tell-tale yellow stripes, 100,000 posties evoke a France of slower, gentler times. Of times before e-mail, instant-messaging and
pagers, of dreaming village spires, of letters touching hearts
with joy, sadness or (hello taxman!) dismay. As much a part
of traditional village life as the mayor, teacher or priest, *le
facteur* is a familiar, reassuring figure. He talks to everybody
on his rounds, and everybody talks to him.

He – now as often she – is not just a person delivering
letters and packages. He represents *La République*. Message:
public services are central to French life, and *La Poste* –
a profit-making public enterprise owned by the State –
serves all Frenchmen equally. And intimately: he conveys
everybody's secrets (love, money, good and bad news), but
keeps them in sealed envelopes. Complicity, hope, dread,
joy, all delivered discreetly.

Books and movies romanticize the postie's role. Crime-
writer Georges Simenon loved to parachute a postman into
his famous Inspector Maigret tales, from *Maigret voit rouge*
(Maigret Sees Red, 1963) to *L'Inspecteur cadavre* (Inspector Corpse, 1968). Dozens of Simenon's books and spun-
off movies used letters to hint at mystery, menace or sus-
pense.

Films of '40s-to-'60s stars like tough-guy Jean Gabin
and clownish Louis de Funès (*Le Tatoué* or Man With a
Tatoo, 1968) wove postmen into celluloid dramas or
comedies. France's classic postman flicks first came from
postwar humorist Jacques Tati, creator of the acclaimed

film wacko Monsieur Hulot. His 1947 *L'École des facteurs* (Postmen's School) and 1948 *Jours de Fête* (Statutory Holidays) are comic hallucinations praising the dreams, adroitness and pluck of hapless countryside mailmen.

Deadpan Buster-Keaton-style disasters littered Tati's first film. The second showed a richer, more lovable character who, during rounds, would stop at the village café for a "small glass of white" – or even put down his mailbag to help bring in a crop threatened by rain.

Fast-forward to 1990 and another postal comedy: *Promotion canapé* (Promotion by Sofa). In full French-farce tradition, this one surfed on the mass arrival of women in the French postal system. Pre-politically correct, this crude, cynical satire portrayed vertical advancement proceeding horizontally.

The year 2008 saw fictitious posties star in the biggest French hit movie of all time. *Bienvenue chez les Ch'tis* drew 20.2 million viewers to 793 screens over 19 weeks. A sweet, wacky comedy, it thrilled everybody but a few sourpuss critics.

France, of course, is not the only country to romanticize posties. Italy's touching *Il Postino* (The Postman, 1995) showed a simple, idealistic postman fantasizing about his idol, Chilean Communist poet Pablo Neruda. Hollywood gave us *The Postman* (1997) with Kevin Costner.

But the French may have developed the richest, most influential postal mythology. Tied to the religion of public service, France's postal people are revered. As we saw, 76 percent of French youth yearn to join the set-for-life civil service, and their first choice is *La Poste*. Job satisfaction? Gossiping counter-clerks may irritate clients in a slow-moving

post-office line. But the mail-bag hauler earns only gratitude as the all-weather servant of French tradition.

Take the Christmas calendar that every postie offers
free (well, in sly expectation of a tangible *merci*). Oblivi-
ous to political correctness, every day on it lists a saint's
day. Church and state split in 1905, yet this harmless little
anachronism makes everybody an honorary Catholic. Neither Muslims, Protestants, Jews nor even atheists seem to
mind.

Certainly not Olivier Besancenot, France's most famous
postman. Atheist and Che Guevara fan, he has twice run
for President of France for the Revolutionary Communist
League, one of several Trotskyite sects. At 27 in the 2002
election, he won 1.3 million votes. Four years later, he got
almost 1.5 million votes, 4.08 % of all votes cast. Still carrying his mail-bag on regular rounds, he parades his far-
left views to delighted TV studios, street demonstrations
and platforms. The New Anti-capitalist Party he is gearing
up to launch in early 2009 is scaring the proletarian pants
off his increasingly marginalized "brothers and sisters" of
the official Communist Party.

Back to the post office. If all employees argued politics there, blood would flow, or at least deafness would
ensue. Anyway, there may well be no Trotskyite way to
lick a stamp. Providentially for workers' solidarity, a government plan to start privatizing postal services in 2009
will rally all posties to a common "save-the-*service-public*"
cause.

Besancenot's ideas are antediluvian, but *La Poste* strug-
gles to innovate. When I was a Paris student in 1954, to be
heard you had to yell into the post office's pre-war phones.
But with help from Canada's Northern Telecom, France

leap-frogged forward. Paris was already ahead with its subway-routed network of pneumatic tubes (a mid-1800s Scottish invention). This system let you have a love-letter delivered in a 12 cm. *pneu* anywhere in Paris within three hours – carried from the destination post office by a bike-riding *facteur*. In a dicey romantic situation, a potential love-saver, if not life-saver.

La Poste continues modernizing. In 2007, it announced a total makeover of letter-carriers' lives: new high-tech electric bikes and scooters, GPS telephones, even new dark-blue uniforms with those nifty yellow stripes.

As the TV-launch cameras rolled past the bikes to a young female modeling the elegant uniform, the announcer suavely intoned: "In the postal war against competitors, *il faut séduire*." Now in French, *séduire* may mean merely to please, not necessarily seduce. But this is France, and *La Poste* clearly wants to deliver pleasure.

Call the flics – but which ones?

Paris is crawling with cops but, as the saying goes, when you need one you can never find one. Because uniformed officers fine even cyclists now, and their traffic auxiliaries ticket parked cars, they are not excessively loved. But the neighborhood cop does represent protection, however ineffective, against criminals. So people don't insult them to their faces anymore – partly because this is now an infraction carrying a nasty fine. In any event, the 26,000-odd Paris cops (18,643 in uniform) are just a small part of France's police repertoire. Ponder the many varieties of French police – all of which, in the end, are responsible to somebody in Paris.

A sunlit bistro on the boulevard Saint-Germain. A student demonstration rock-and-rolls endlessly by. A woman by the cash register screams, a man howls as she stomps her stiletto-heel on his foot: he claims she stole a postcard. A fight ensues, with insults impugning the sexual charms of both. Soon a police van glides up, and a dashing young *flic* casually drops off the back with white-gloved hand in the air to settle the fuss.

A fine memory for thinking about France's legions of men and women in blue. For no democratic country seems to have so many cops, kinds of cops, and obsessions with cops, as the land of Inspector Maigret (or Inspector Clouseau, as you wish). In elections, police are front and center. For a crucial issue – tied to hot-button immigration and national identity – is always *la sécurité*, law and order.

France's first real police began with Louis XIV in 1667. Before, public order was often private disorder. Brigands roamed free, vigils and law officers were corrupt and/or incompetent, jurisdictions a rat's nest, citizens' arrests common. Louis XIV assigned his police a multitude of tasks: catching criminals, but also upholding edicts, fighting fires, regulating business, cleaning streets, censoring, and watching potential enemies. His police played politics as much as they fought crime.

Under Bonaparte, serving the political master became all. Napoleon's much-feared police boss Joseph Fouché – a clerical dropout, then raging atheist – made his name by helping push Louis XVI and scores of others to the guillotine, and by crushing royalist peasants. His ruthlessness, scheming and sprawling network of spies made him irresistible to Napoleon – even through multiple fights and betrayals.

Throughout the 19th century, police got increasingly professional, and spread all over France. Their political missions expanded. In 1855, Paris created les *Renseignements Généraux* – the shadowy *RG* – a domestic espionage and "analysis" service reporting to every interior minister. (President Nicolas Sarkozy held that job twice, and still keeps intimate tabs on police and intelligence activities).

In the last half of the 1800s, the Industrial Revolution led to both more crime and social-political tensions. Victor Hugo's vengeful Inspector Javert in *Les Misérables* sharpened the police's hated image. As the century ended, communists and anarchists became prime police targets. This continued until some shamefully collaborationist French police in 1940–44 eagerly helped Nazis round up Jews, even Jewish children.

Since 1945, the French police have become as modern and professional as the best anywhere else. Not counting the 17,000 members of the mainly rural *Police Municipale*, consider France's two main police bodies:

* *Police Nationale*: Its 150,000 members play many roles: counter-espionage and counter-terrorism; border policing; uniformed patrol and response; traffic duties, and criminal investigations (Maigret-Clouseau). Its *Compagnies Républicaines de Sécurité* (CRS) are the much-feared bash-first, ask-questions-later riot cops you see by the busload around "sensitive" streets. No sense of humor at all.

* *Gendarmerie Nationale*: France's 104,275 gendarmes (slang: *pandores*) work with investigating judges in criminal cases. They also act as sea and air police. But to the average Frenchman, they act as small town, village or countryside police, catching highway speeders or drunks, rescuing citizens in disasters, and handling airport

and train-station security. More thrillingly, they supply the 3,300 members of the élite *Garde Républicaine*. Apart from protecting president and prime minister, the *Garde* parades in gleaming, plumed silver helmets on splendid horses. Eyeing them on the Champs-Élysées, you'd swear France was a monarchy.

More than ever, police roles are a political football. Friendly beat cops or nasty beat-'em-up cops? Citizens' protectors or politicians' spies and bully-boys? As French public opinion moves to the right, you find even traditionally anti-cop left-wingers admitting that too many ghetto kids are running wild. Socialist presidential candidate Ségolène Royal demanded a "just order" and military supervision for delinquents. Every riot of ghetto youth – in the steaming *banlieues* or at Paris's huge *Gare du Nord* – only makes police look more welcome.

When Mr. Law-and-Order himself, Nicolas Sarkozy, became France's president in May 2007, he promptly placed protégés at the top of key police and spy services. And in mid-2008, knocking heads together, he fused the old RG domestic snoops with their hated rivals, the counter-espionage *Direction de la surveillance du territoire* (DST), to create a single, internal over-4,000-strong super-spy outfit called the *Direction centrale du renseignement intérieur* (DCRI).

Sarkozy's adversaries caricature him as psychologically unstable (his conjugal soap opera helping), a crypto-fascist, a fanatic who would secretly love to deport all immigrants, then fling everybody else into the slammer. This is convenient for Sarkozy. For it shows that he frightens law-breakers, and it isolates his anything-goes, soft-on-crime rivals.

But Sarkozy also scares many ordinary folk. The trick for him is always to show he's not just on the side of the law, but sides with the law-abiding. He did so in September 2008 by questioning an already approved, scandalously intrusive filing system called *Edvige*. "Enriching" RG snooping, *Edvige* planned to open computerized files not only on tens of thousands of elected, union and religious leaders, but even suspicious 13-year-olds, noting views, health and sexual preferences.

Whether significant changes ensue is another story. Once snoop-files get set up, they tend to stay – and get used. But in rapping the knuckles of Interior Minister Michèle Alliot-Marie over *Edvige*, Sarkozy danced elegantly on his public-confidence tightrope. All he needs now is to buy some white gloves and practice casually hopping off the back of a paddy-wagon.

France Télécom hangs up

An empire-within-a-country, France Télécom long held a monopoly on telephony. This grew out of an old Post Office known as the P.T.T. (Postes, Téléphones, Télégraphes). Now "FT" – also called "Orange" to facilitate competition in several other countries – has rivals, and is chastely known as "the historic operator." Even though facing competitors, FT-Orange keeps its imperial hauteur, and plenty of the fonctionnaire mentality. Also, as we see below, a rare talent for screwing up.

The French, we know, adore talking. Heck, they invented wit, flirting and literary salons, *non*? But the telephone overwhelms them. Within 100 meters of each other and my apartment, two addresses sum up this disconnection between titillation and technology.

At 27 rue de Fleurus is Gertrude Stein's famous apartment, hangout of *literati* (and even writers, such as Hemingway) of the '30s, '40s and '50s. And in the courtyard of the Institut Catholique at 21 rue d'Assas, you can see where Édouard Branly in 1891 invented the "wireless telegraph" – precursor of today's cell phones.

All of which surges to mind when I digest my nearly eleven years with France Télécom, still state-dominated but now independent. To be fair: FT has been grappling, like everybody, with an alphabet-soup of technologies Branly never imagined: ISDN, ADSL, FTTH, FTTB, AONs, PONs, EFM, IEEE 802.3ah – the constant one being HELL. Besides, who cares about acronyms when you just want to order Indian food or dally *à distance* with a lover?

But FT has a record of doing what's fun for engineers, and to HELL with customers. The worst betrayal of clients, especially youth, was FT's long, late-'90s rearguard battle to derail the Internet. The public reason: to protect $1.2 billion in revenues from FT's handy-in-its-time Minitel – a closed, bill-collecting cash-cow for FT. Apart from train schedules and students' rankings, half of this revenue (marginal in FT's budget) came from sex ads. FT – and the state – living off the avails?

The real reason for protecting Minitel via sky-high Internet dial-up rates was FT engineers' pride – plus a deep suspicion of the U.S. FT' s president once denounced a visiting Canadian telecom regulator as "an agent of the Pentagon" for talking up the Internet – "We all know the Internet came from the American Defense Department."

But I digress. The nastiest story is what FT routinely does to its clients. First, if you are an *Internaute* (Internet-user), you will deal with three companies, all really the same: France Télécom, Orange and Wanadoo. The old FT shell-game: you call one, and they send you to two others. Same game between sales and "service" – endless phone-tag, with nobody aware or responsible.

Another trick: FT re-assigns cancelled phone numbers after only six months. First, FT gave me a number previously assigned to the *Pitié-Salpêtrière h*ospital where Princess Diana died. For two years, I fielded medical calls – proudly without losing a single patient. Next FT gave me the after-sales service number of *Darty*, a massive consumer-appliances chain. I got to offer invaluable advice on fixing refrigerators.

Next up (on my fax line) was a restaurant chain called *Chez Clément*. I always recommended the chicken, pork and beef rotisserie, rounded off with the all-you-can-eat, chocolate-and-cream *profiteroles*. My least happy wrong number (one digit off) was the *Cétélem* consumer-credit bank: seven out of ten of my incoming calls for four years made me financial adviser to profligate households – a bartender serving drunks. I got my counsel down to two seconds: "Dial 41, not 42."

Spotting a new low-cost FT "triple-play" offer of telephone, Internet and TV, I leapt at the bargain. Alas, the "*LiveBox*" high-speed modem tying it all together quickly became a DeadBox. I had to visit the sales office twelve [*sic*] times to straighten out trivial details. FT technicians were mostly subcontractors with little clue as to how this new stuff worked. All four gave up, confessing FT's chaos and/or incompetence. But they were all aces at billing: almost $300 in all for pointless onsite visits, plus hours on the "help" line at 51 cents a minute.

FT kept me in line, if not online. They cut off my secure Internet (for e-mail, banking and free Internet *Skype* calls) for six weeks. They killed my land-line phone for three weeks. FT's advice: "Look in the phonebook for a technician. We don't know of anybody to help you."

Aching for technology that worked, I fell for a snazzy new cell phone from Orange (FT), thinking they couldn't mess *that* up. It worked, but with 48 hours of stand-by battery-time, not the advertised 250 hours. Nearly all the cell messages I get were from Orange... trying to sell me more lame-duck-*à-l'Orange*.

Thank God, I told FT *not* to put a referral recording on my old *Cétélem* number, for that would continue sending borrowers to my new number. Uh-oh, they forgot: unwanted credit-seeking calls pursued me. But FT said they would gladly fix it if I would send them a fax. Pity again: they had destroyed my fax line. But I found one at my new (permanent?) triple-play home: the cyber-café beside Gertrude Stein's apartment.

One FT guy, hearing my odyssey, offered consolation: "Well, all this has made you a well-informed client." Indeed. "Besides, the other phone companies are awful too." Then – perhaps coining FT's next brilliant marketing slogan? – he bragged, "but we're the least awful."

Le fisc – loving the tax (wo)man

Tax-collectors, like cops, dentists and hit-men, learn not to take things too personally. And in France, one is happy to report, the fiscal folks generally seem a reasonable lot. You can call them up, ask for advice, plead with dignity, or grovel with wit. And often get the benefit of the doubt.

France may have lost the Franco-Prussian War of 1870-71, but it never adopted the literal-minded rigidity that, through Bismarckian maneuvers or immigration, Prussians inflicted on other countries (Guten Tag, Deutschland! Good Morning, America!). As with all French civil servants, the tax people have a gigantic rule-book, but many are delighted to help you find a loophole. Or just to chat with a client who's not fuming-mad at them. Strategic helplessness also works, especially if you're dealing with a person of the opposite sex.

It's easy to deal with the French tax system, familiarly called *le fisc.* And if you live in France for six months plus a day in any calendar year, you *will* deal with them, for that makes you a 'tax resident.' Your home country likely has a treaty preventing double taxation – though if you're American, you may find that Washington's Prussians pursue you still. In any case, no panic. To develop a happy (or less terrifying) relationship with *le fisc,* you just need to follow some simple advice.

First, take for granted that the tax people believe everybody cheats, and that they have seen much greater crooks than you. They discount every statement at least a shade, and assume that a little larceny shines in the purest of hearts. It's a matter of how much greed is acceptable. They do not admire secret foreign bank accounts.

Sympathy for cheaters starts in-house, for senior tax officials enjoy a number of succulent breaks and bonuses that common mortals can't access. (Same goes in many state administrations, including semi-autonomous Electricité de

France and Gaz de France, where even junior employees get cheaper kilowatt-hours and gas equivalents).

Classic advice of French tax advisers (even bankers): "To live happy, live hidden." That is, don't suddenly leap out from the crowd with tricky revenue streams, a Taj Mahal residence, stables with prize-winning nags, and a garage full of Bentleys. Tax department sleuths mine the newspapers and magazines for ostentatious consumption not already 'legitimized' by Old Money or a bling-bling, tax-deductible lifestyle clearly needed to tart up your show-biz image.

Your accountant will tell you the same. He or she may even tell you, as an expat, not to buy property in France: "giving hostages to the *fisc*." Staying liquid is a wise and accepted way of being a trouble-free expat. And tax officials will be amazed at how honest you are if you unblinkingly reveal offshore revenues they have neither time nor inkling nor even means to track down. You can collect "reputational" brownie points – handy in later situations where your taxman has discretion.

Second point: Get used to complexity. When you see paycheck deductions of thirty items and a Chinese water-torture of different kinds of tax claims the *Administration fiscale* can throw at you, you may blanch. But strive to stay Zen. The system is deliberately complicated. That's partly because the French never like a simple solution when a complicated one will do. And partly because labyrinthine procedures allow *fonctionnaires* to keep the upper hand. Let me count the ways they Mau-Mau you:

- Split jurisdictions: Until 2008, the income tax department was *two* tax departments – one to assess your tax, the other to collect it. Separate

ministers, mandarins, methods and unions –
and neither side liked to talk with the other. A few
years back, unions drove out a minister who tried to
join the alienated twins. Now Sarkozy has rammed
through a fusion, and it looks like sticking. But
count on continuing historic 'cultural' conflicts:
the assessment people tend to be understanding and
open to dialogue; the collectors like to barricade
themselves behind plastic screens, to scowl and to
threaten penalties. The old shell-game may go on –
even though the state will try to buy off union leaders with (only for them!) more paid time off, fancy
offices and new computers, as it did in 2008 while
fusing its two unemployment agencies.

- Multiple taxes: France doesn't like income taxes as a
single, fair, direct way of taxing people. Millions of
French don't even pay income tax. But they get hit
with several others: the "habitation" tax (a tax on
breathing), property tax, the public-service-TV tax,
several social security taxes, general solidarity tax,
and wealth tax if they own (not earn) too much –
meaning a total estate of over 770,000 euros.

- Small business: Don't start one. As often mentioned
here, owners face a snowstorm of taxes, each more
ingenious than the other, that can cripple you even
before you start generating revenues. The brutal,
autistic tax-collecting URSSAF you will face took
lessons on pillaging, and indifference to suffering,
from Genghis Khan.

Third rule: prepare to deal. Your assessor is probably a fair-minded person. He or she is well-trained to be
friendly and helpful. As long as you don't invent egregious

fibs, you will get a sympathetic ear. Especially if you're famous (Catherine Deneuve once got called in to explain a cash-filled envelope). Or filthy rich (France's Elvis Presley, Johnny Hallyday, seems to get prompt understanding even while toying with French, Monégasque (Monaco), Swiss and Belgian nationalities). Bernard Tapie, both famous and rich, walked away from a complex case with possibly 40 million euros because of rumored sympathy from a well-placed tax official named Sarkozy. He is undoubtedly innocent of any wrong-doing.

If you're just an ordinary drudge, show unfawning respect for your interlocutor. Tell a plausible version of the truth. Don't volunteer unasked- for information. And don't become too "interesting." Above all, ask for advice.

Humor, irony and modesty can help. So, where natural, can a touch of flirting. I know a man who, with helpless charm, persuaded a tax-lady to fill out his return. Quite coincidentally, she found he had no tax to pay.

Taming the Red Army – a work in progress

"One politician and a million employees." "A massive, clumsy dinosaur." "A mammoth with a flea [for minister]." "A machine for producing strikes." "A guillotine for ministers." For decades, that's been the image of France's Ministry of Education. A hundred thousand whistling, drum-beating, laughing unionists fill the Paris streets, demanding that the latest hapless minister resign…because he wanted to do something. Anything. Now, starting with a clever, tough new minister backed by President Sarkozy, change is in the air.

Until brilliant scholar and wit Xavier Darcos became its minister in 2007, France's ministry of education was an insane asylum run by the inmates. Roughly a million employees followed a cadre of left-wing ideologues opposed to any and all reforms.

Split into slightly different historic flavors, French education unions gained a reputation for regularly shutting down schools in order to 'protect" pupils. It would be excessive to compare this thinking to that of U.S. generals in Vietnam: destroying villages "in order to save them." But the unions' mentality was and still is not entirely dissimilar. For French education (see later) has suffered disastrously from outdated pedagogy and obsession with wages and tenure.

Incessant strikes have gravely damaged education. With transport workers, teachers have been the most mindless and selfish of all public employees. Their idea of dialogue has been "our way, or the street." The "street" has often included brain-washed elementary and secondary school students carrying banners with slogans defending teachers' "acquired rights" – trumpeted of course as protecting children. Scared-of-their-shadows governments long caved in every time.

Why did Darcos, named by Sarkozy in 2007, make a strong start on taming his rebellious troops? Because he was the first minister of education a) to stand up firmly and intelligently to his anti-reform unions; and b) to get unconditional backing from his president and prime minister. All his predecessors rushed to make "concessions" to bureaucrats and teachers, forgetting pupils. And when protesting "educators" filled the streets, every minister ended up being betrayed by a nervous president or prime minister.

Whether curriculum reform, standards, textbooks, teaching methods or pupils' facilities, almost anything new a minister proposed used to get shot down by employees and their unions. Infiltrating parent-teacher groups until they became teacher-teacher groups, staff would gut anything and everything remotely affecting their rights and/or privileges.

The results are clear: standards (measured internationally) have fallen. Students attack teachers physically in high schools. Drop-out rates soar. Far too many youth get shoveled into university, then fail in first year. And, as the Shanghai Jiao Tong world university rankings show, France continues to fall behind in higher education: the top French university, Paris VI, stands an embarrassing 39th.

Darcos is slimming down the Mammoth a little by cutting some 13,000 jobs in 2009. But that's not enough to free up serious money for better teaching and learning. At the higher-education level (separate from Darcos) it's also hard to see major French progress: the 2009 state budget adds 1.8 billion euros to research, but cuts 900 research jobs.

What's new in education is not just Darcos. It's Sarkozy. Though he spins off more ideas before breakfast than predecessors could in a year, he believes in the essentials: basic skills, good values, hard work, discipline, respect for elders, including teachers. To ram through his changes, like Darcos he displays craftiness, courage, perseverance, determination.

All this makes the taming of the "impossible" *kamikaze* ministry a bellwether for a whole country's success. The Sarko-Darcos recipe: Seduce, then attack. Scarcely cricket, but the unions always beat the cricket-players. The game now is hardball – with a steely smile and a scholarly witticism.

྇

Chapter Seven

BUT HOW IS YOUR LIVER?

There's more to Frenchmen's health than the "French paradox" – that semi-Mediterranean diet causing fewer heart attacks. But that's a good start. Any country that encourages you to drink red wine with your red meat – and that still gets no.1 rating for healthcare from the World Health Organization – knows something about living well. And living long: France's average life expectancy at birth, mixing men and women, is almost 81 (in UK almost 79 and U.S. 78).

French, and many European, doctors take a whole-person look at patients. Morale, psychology and culture count along with blood pressure and hemoglobin counts. Latin physicians in particular believe happiness is part of health. And happiness includes not punishing yourself too much with drastic diets – invariably yo-yo diets. Eat a little of everything, emphasizing the "little." And drink a bit every day, not fearing to have a glass or two extra on holidays.

"Your North American doctors are Puritans," a Paris cardiologist once told me. "You need to live, to have a few indulgences, to make life worthwhile. He sent me for tests one Christmas Day, and nurses offered me a glass of their own champagne. Following days they gave me a choice of red or white wine with meals. This told me right away I was healthy.

French healthcare is quite as good as the WHO says. Waiting-lists are reasonable, often rare. And home-visits are a low-cost marvel. Healthcare is cheap, and often free. But often bureaucratic: Instead of funding the national health service out of income taxes, the state injects layers of players and papers to spoil your satisfaction. Nothing seems likely to change this taste for elaborate bureaucracy – part of France's DNA.

But there's more to healthy people than doctors and nurses. There's clean air, natural food and a sound environment. And there's exercise: an inspiring example of cardiovascular health, though not all can play at it, is that rogues' game of rugby. Let's take that whole-person look at all these topics – noting that hygiene outside hospitals remains another kind of "French paradox."

Bending principles, curing ills

Health-care debates in nearly all countries turn on the relative merits of public versus private service, payment and administration. In a given country at a given time, you usually have to vote for whatever "public" and "private" seem to mean. Ideology clouds the worldwide dialogue, and terminology generates dictionaries of dogma. In France, debate on healthcare is as vigorous, indeed as fractious, as anywhere. But surprisingly, the French display more pragmatism than do many Anglo-Saxons.

Big news in 2007 for healthcare: Doctors now get $44.15 for home visits instead of $42.70. Unless you're old enough to remember doctors with long black bags visiting sick kids at home, you'll think you've died and gone to hospital heaven. Alas, the above raise for doctors happened only in France – and, of course, in euros.

Despite widespread growling and a few prickly problems, most French patients and health-care professionals admire their health system. Many loved Michael Moore's 2007 satirical movie *Sicko:* it praised French, as well as British and Canadian, healthcare while panning U.S. scandals. By almost every standard – longevity, healthy children, top facilities and equipment, quick, wide access to fine care (including operations and cancer treatment) – France is a good place to get sick. Or avoid getting sick.

France achieves this while spending only a little more per capita on healthcare than western countries' average: 9.5 percent of gross domestic product (GDP) instead of 8.3 percent. (Private-run U.S. healthcare costs 16 percent of GDP, heading for 20 percent in 2016 – and leaves 47 million people uncovered. Canada's system covers all residents for 9.7 percent of GDP). France's spending gives it rather more doctors per capital than most countries: 3.3 per thousand residents vs. a western average of 2.9 per thousand (though well below Italy's 4.4 per thousand). However, France has 15,000 midwives, an almost unknown species in many countries. These serve as well-trained professionals between doctors and nurses.

You can get fast, high-quality service in France, while in Anglo-Saxon countries you may wait months for critical operations. The French state begins by protecting patients' rights, including a right to speedy service – even ownership of your own files, such as X-rays. It also carefully plans hospitals, locations of specialized facilities (transplants, neurosurgery, emergency wards) and allocation of key equipment (MRI, CAT, PET scans).

But the main answer (apart from sustained, not yo-yo, financing) seems to be that the French – routinely mocked as doctrinaire socialists – have long allowed private medicine to work side-by-side with the state health-care system. But fully integrated with it. *Service* is universal, but *delivery* of service can be state or private. Private service-providers are free, under state supervision, to deliver innovative approaches.

Example: a service called SOS Médecins, a cadre of young doctors who whiz around in small cars to meet home emergencies. Once I called them at 5 p.m. for a sprained ankle that I had to stand on that evening. A young doctor came within twenty minutes, patched me up, and left with a check for thirty-five dollars – his full, state-reimbursable fee.

Working with SOS Médecins is SAMU – a public-private emergency triage-and-treatment service in Paris and 350 other localities. Dialing 15 gets you immediate expert advice and, in crises, a hospital alert plus specialized on-site medical staff in under ten minutes. SAMU ambulances often carry a doctor to start on-the-spot care. (Note: "scoop-and-run" UK ambulance staff blamed SAMU's "stay-and-treat" approach for delaying arguably life-saving hospital treatment for Princess Diana). Private ambulance services, with partly reimbursable fees, exist everywhere.

Publicly-supported private hospitals handle half of all surgical operations and 60 percent of cancer treatments – in both cases cutting wait times drastically. These 2,139 for-profit or not-for-profit facilities add over 170,000 beds to the 316,000 beds offered by 1,032 public hospitals and clinics. They inject into the system an accordion-like flexibility. Their competitiveness keeps costs down.

Privately-delivered services are funded by the state healthcare system, known as *la Sécurité Sociale* or *la Sécu*.

Normally, you pay a small fee – *la Sécu* reimbursing 75 percent. But if a doctor decides you need help, he can waive this and get you 100 percent reimbursement – automatic for big expenses like operations.

As usual in France, bureaucracy and history create a system of unbelievable complexity. Depending on your job (worker, farmer, self-employed), you may get *Sécu* reimbursement from one of three funds or *caisses*. These are financed and run jointly by employers' and employees' groups, with top-ups from income taxes. No invisible single-payer here, as in the UK and Canada.

As everywhere, budgets balloon; but the state is attacking costs on several fronts: controlling doctors' fees and, where possible, imposing generic drugs over brand-name prescription drugs. Serious anti-drinking and anti-smoking campaigns also reduce illness.

To cover the 25 percent of costs not routinely reimbursed, nearly all Frenchmen take out extra private health insurance, called a *mutuelle*. France now offers free extra coverage to poor people – but limited by a means test.

Why can't France borrow a simpler health-payment system from single-payer (i.e. government-paying) nations? Its current *Sécu* funding runs massive deficits partly because of its complexity. Paperless, income-tax-based funding for no-fees, all-covered care could save France countless administrative dollars each year.

Frenchmen, as we've seen, are used to making separate "transparent" tax payments for home, TV license, income, "social charges" (health and much else), plus "solidarity" and "fortune" taxes. To fund free healthcare via income-tax alone, citizens would choke at higher marginal tax rates – even though they wouldn't pay separate payroll charges or have to buy extra *mutuelle* policies. Switching to all-income-tax funding would demand a huge, multi-year PR campaign. And the will to face down entrenched public bureaucracies and private insurers. Another big one – the biggest? – for Sarkozy.

But countries with publicly-run, free universal healthcare could learn from France too. Their left-of-centre politicians tend to believe that *anything* "private" would turn free-for-everybody healthcare into a Yankee-style, rich-man's jungle leaving millions of people uncovered. France's example of coordinated public-private services proves that ain't necessarily so.

Skeptical? Picture shorter lines –- and maybe that old-time doctor hauling a stethoscope out of a black bag to reassure a frightened, home-bound child.

Pasteur would be shocked...

As in many branches of science, the French have long explored the frontiers of medicine. They continue today, with top doctors engaging simultaneously in research, teaching and clinical practice. Their work translates into generally fine, innovative care. But one stunning lapse stands out: the nation-wide blind-spot about basic hygiene in public places – restaurants and – shockingly and persistently – in schools.

As names of Paris streets and hospitals remind you at every turn, France is also an *inspiring* place to get sick. A few pioneers of medical disciplines: 16th-century Ambroise Paré (surgery), Louis Pasteur (microbiology), Marie and Pierre Curie (radioactivity, vital for X-rays), Paul Pierre Broca (brain-speech research), Claude Bernard (physiology), Luc Montagnier (HIV). René Laennec invented the stethoscope, a key diagnostic tool.

If your problem's in the head, 12,000 French psychiatrists yearn to plunk you on a couch. Their terminology (the world's most common after Greek) can fit whatever ails you. It might even help you analyze the sudden 2008 marriage of President Nicolas Sarkozy to Carla Bruni, spitting image of his just-divorced wife Cécilia: *folie à deux* (shared madness), *la belle indifférence* (feigned by Cécilia), *logorrhée* (ceaselessly chattering Sarko).

The shrinks may also tell you the French are hypochondriacs. They pop more pills than anybody on earth. They delight in discussing their illnesses and operations: a *crise de foie* (inflamed liver) wins you universal sympathy. Blood-test labs and exotic pharmacies await you on every corner. Weekly newsmagazines publish exhaustive report-cards on the "best" or "worst" hospitals and clinics. Try to resist looking up your own.

By that scorecard, French medical and hospital care is indeed first class. As an occasional consumer, I can confirm that doctors and nurses are top-notch, and their equipment up-to-the-minute. Not to mention their wine-cellars...

Now Sarkozy is attacking Alzheimer's disease. Dealing with both treatment and research, he's tacking on a tiny "dementia tax" to each medical visit and prescription-drug purchase. This will increase France's total four-year Alzheimer budget to almost $2.36 billion to fight an incurable illness afflicting 860,000 French citizens. In twenty years, rising longevity will double the number of victims, gravely straining health budgets (as elsewhere in the West). But Sarkozy's strong, focused effort should make a difference.

France is already a pioneer in cancer and AIDS treatment and research, as well as heart-rhythm problems (Prof.
Haïssaguerre, Bordeaux). It will prove a leader in Alzheimer's too. Trials underway, instead of 'warehousing' patients,
are successfully postponing inevitable dementia by several
years – a huge savings in both money and human happiness.

Sadly, there is one public-health area where France is
not just behind, but a disgrace. It echoes and magnifies
the appalling hygiene in rest-rooms of many French restaurants and even on first-class TGV trains.

A 2008 national study based on 30,000 children in 900
schools all over France confirmed that almost *half* of all primary school children have stomach-aches. Why? Because
they can't bring themselves to use their schools' revolting
toilets. One in five children suffers urinary infections, and
15 percent suffer acute or chronic constipation – thus poisoning their bodies.

A similar report came out in 2006. But school inspectors, teachers and mayors (the latter responsible for primary schools) buried it. Local authorities, fearing expense
and embarrassment, consider dirty toilets for children a
taboo topic. Yet the 2008 study, conducted by Internet
since local authorities refused to help, depicted a national
horror-show: lack of sinks, soap, towels, toilet-paper and
toilet-brushes, broken toilet-seats.

Girls and boys often share toilets, where open-at-bot-
tom doors, already embarrassing, may not even lock. That's
only one reason children avoid them. The main turn-offs
are the stench (73 percent), filth (57 percent) and fear
(14 percent) – barely 30 percent of toilets are supervised.
Accidents and bullying cast shadows.

With doctors shouting about this, where are the parents? Some parents' groups commissioned studies, but their associations are often dominated by teacher-parents who resist change. Result: says this year's report, the problem infects education from nursery school to university. Bladder and urinary-tract problems especially harm teenage girls. The report adds: "This is a major health problem demanding attention. It causes children deep unhappiness, sometimes academic failure."

Will the 2008 report provoke a revolution? Not likely. Cost and public humiliation will almost certainly block effective action again. History and culture also discourage a clean-up. Toilets at Versailles under Louis XIV were glorified chamber-pots, and not always used: When you have stairways, and servants to mop them up each morning, why bother? It's not like that today. But visiting most (except upscale) restaurants still illustrates old priorities: Make the food and décor wonderful, but don't spend too much on clean, properly-equipped washrooms.

Enjoy your breakfast. And remember the man who made your milk safe. He argued for better sanitation (as well as red wine!) and never let ridicule or taboos stop him from saving lives. Hating both germs and hypocrisy, Louis Pasteur would have found a way to protect the kids.

Breathing green – Nicolas Hulot

The most vital medicine in every country is clean air – carrying the oxygen that keeps every cell of your body alive. France was slow to care about ecology. But, as in many of its late-arrival reforms, it's now joining world leaders. Imitating the dynamics of most good causes, politics and personal

*rivalries slow change. France's Man-in-a-Hurry, its universally
admired prophet of greenness and a healthy environment, is
smart enough to stay out of politics. He has a wildly popular
TV show: Why seek a government job?*

Wild black hair flopping over deep-lined forehead,
Nicolas Hulot, like Shakespeare's Cassius, hath a lean and
hungry look. His leanness belies hyperactivity, his hunger
eagerness to save the world. "Al Gore as Indiana Jones,"
53-year-old Hulot is France's Mr. Environment. His best-
selling books, apocalyptic warnings, and especially his hit
TV show *Ushuaïa* (Tierra del Fuego's southernmost city)
generate stratospheric popularity.

Haunted by global disaster, and long half-threatening
a run (later abandoned) at France's presidency, Hulot was
courted by every major candidate in France's 2007 presidential election. All signed his "*Pacte écologique*," a ten-goal, five-
proposal manifesto putting environmental virtue at the heart
of public policy. Hulot insisted that a new president could
implement his program immediately with no technical or
legal obstacles.

Endorsed by over half a million citizens, what did Hulot's Pact demand? Its ten "goals" were motherhood: renew
energy; reduce consumption; produce in new ways; stop
endless city growth; favor rail and river transport; assess the
real value of nature's benefits; protect biodiversity; favor
preventive medicine; use the environment to stir innovation; take international initiatives.

The Pact's policy "proposals" aimed to lock politicians
into making the environment central to state activity. The
list: a deputy prime minister in charge of sustainable development; a carbon tax to reduce pollution by four times;

a generally organic food market; public consultation on plans for sustainable development; public education on the need for such development.

The Pact ignored several issues demanding debate, especially automobile pollution in cities. Although Hulot argued that his carbon tax went to the core of this, its effect would be too long-term to make an early difference. It didn't confront the powerful French automobile lobby (whose 2008 sales are again flagging). And it didn't encourage public transport, hybrid or hydrogen-fueled cars, or indeed Dutch-style city cycling. Meanwhile, the cost of scrubbing down the façade of every building in Paris every ten years exploded. Traffic and parking squeezed out pedestrians. And lung problems infected children and elderly at horrendous cost in health and money.

Hulot also sidestepped nuclear-generated electricity. Atomic reactors – of a proven-safe French design – supply almost 80 percent of France's electricity. Yet large-scale disposal of nuclear waste, a longer-term problem than anything Hulot mentioned, remains a postponed priority.

Repetitive and preachy as it was, the Pact at least focused public attention – in a dramatic, understandable way – on a strong, pro-environmental direction. Hulot did what Arkansas farmers advised to get a donkey to move: Hit it over the nose with a two-by-four. The donkey here was government, and Hulot didn't believe in subtlety. He was right. For in late 2008, backed by a president swearing to make radical breaks on many fronts, his crusade has set all France aflame with environmental zeal.

A one-man *National Geographic*, Hulot eclipses the official Green Party – whose greenness glows mainly in the personal jealousies gnawing at its half-dozen leadership rivals. Other ecologists have fallen into the French vice of obsessing over doctrinal nuances and tactics, invariably to serve personal ambitions. Hulot lunges for democracy's jugular. He draws on the unequalled credibility he's gained through his globe-girdling TV adventures illustrating environmental disaster.

How exactly does his magic work? By a multi-year, multi-media assault on public opinion, anchored by his compelling TV documentaries. Imagine watching this passionate, eloquent daredevil floating out on an ice-floe to "interview" a dying polar bear. Or crouching beside farmers in Chad starving beside a dried-up lake. Or climbing ancient Nepalese glaciers melting to inundate dozens of inhabited valleys. Or nodding at the anguish of Bangladeshis telling him that, by 2050, rises in sea-level will drive fourteen million of them from their lands.

In showing the scandal of man's depredations, Hulot speaks of impending catastrophe. But also of hope. In this, and in bringing the masses along on his expeditions, Hulot belongs to a well-established French tradition of environmental educators. Among them: the Comte de Buffon (credited by Darwin as a precursor of Evolution), Louis-Antoine de Bougainville (South Pacific explorer whose namesake flower delights), Maurice Herzog (conqueror of Annapurna), Antoine de Saint-Exupéry (pioneering aviator-author), and especially the unforgettable undersea explorer Jacques-Yves Cousteau with his *Calypso* diving-ship.

No wonder you see Hulot on magazine covers every other week. He's a seductive personality – likeable, honest, expressive, and above all terrifyingly well-informed. In 2007 the influential weekly *Nouvel Observateur* even handed him its entire pre-Christmas issue to shape as guest editor-in-chef.

In his lead editorial, Hulot spoke of the "massive tragedies awaiting us." He denounced "our worst enemy, fatalism." But unlike many Cassandras, he offered hope of "another possible world." A world "where being is not sacrificed to having." With his floppy hair and scruffy turtleneck, Hulot doesn't need public office. He has public power, the power to move France.

Rugbymania excites France's women

Exercise isn't fun. But watching hairy giants pumping muscled thighs as they dash around, scramble forward while tossing a ball backwards, pile on each other in muddy shorts, and grunt animal noises, looks like fun to many French women. No doubt because it evokes more agreeable forms of heavy-breathing? "Whatever it takes" to get fit? A fine slogan for inducing the slothful to take up running, jogging, or enthusiastic shuffling. In the 2008 Olympics, France again proved that whatever it took to win its 40 medals, many took it. Plainly, today's French youth don't hate exercise as much as did their grandparents – whose main exercise was bending elbows.

Sébastien Chabal – nicknamed "the Caveman" – is a Central-Casting monster, a black-bearded, rat's-nest-haired, 1.92 meter-tall, 114-kilo hulk who runs like a rabbit and collides with opponents like a loose cannon on HMS *Bounty*. When he explodes across the rugby-field, broken bones, blood and despair all follow, and they are not his. Sex-symbol of France's team at Paris's 2007 World Cup Rugby finals, he delighted millions of "chabalistes" fans with his size, speed and unpredict-able behavior – like stomping on opponents and tackling referees.

La rugby-folie has captured Frenchmen. The game will continue selling big flat TV screens for years. But as well as thrilling couch potatoes, it has become a metaphor for exercise and health.

Football, soccer, rugby. All trace their ancestry from early 19th-century games at the aristocratic English school in Rugby. (Naturally, the French claim it all started in me-dieval France, even in Roman France). Eventually, three different games emerged.

North American football – with pre-programmed, cheeseburger-fed robots patting bums and bursting out of huddles for only a few seconds at a time – looks like the Prussian Army on maneuvers. Soccer ("football" in Euro-lingo), runs cardiovascular marathons, sometimes kill-ing young players to produce scores of 1-0 in a game like hockey.

The third game, the "game played in heaven," is rugby. Legend claims it started on a soggy field at Rugby in 1832 when a schoolboy named William Webb Ellis, exasperated by a too-slow soccer game, grabbed the ball and ran with it – instantly inventing "rugby." Tackling, scrumming, and serial, on-the-run, backward passes flowed impulsively. Chaotic action and much-higher scores made rugby a game for both "butcher-boys and gentlemen."

History doubts that Wellington really claimed the 1815 battle of Waterloo was won on the playing-fields of Eton. But rugby's toughness, resourcefulness, initiative and team-spirit likely helped scattered armies of soldier-bureaucrats to hold and expand the British Empire after the 1830s.

Rugby was the game of hard men – and for women who marveled at them.

Four out of ten French stadium fans are women. Women from grannies to teenagers praise rugby's values: courage, comradeship, courtesy. Players respect adversaries and referees. Hooligans stick to soccer.

French women look misty-eyed describing players' hard, well-defined bodies. Uniforms help. American football-players, note female fans, wear goofy, below-the-knee pants and wimpy pads. Soccer guys wear nondescript mid-thigh shorts. But *les rugbymen* wear really short shorts, revealing those powerful thighs.

Making leaner soccer men look effete, hunky rugby stars fill magazine spreads. A nude rugbymen's calendar ("Stadium Gods") outsold a famous Paris naked firemen's calendar. Chabal, of course, is the ultimate wild-man fantasy, say women. His "gentle, twinkling" eyes torment Beauties to his Beast.

Funnily, few French except hard-core aficionados know quite how rugby is played. National TV networks, magazines and newspapers offer seminars explaining 'rucks and mauls', 'locks', 'no. 8s', 'scrums', 'drop kicks' and 'converted tries.' During tournaments, even Paris billboards play with rugby jargon to enhance the festive mood.

As in many things French, juicier "sidebar" tales sometimes overshadow what's happening onstage. Apart from customary players' gossip, media interest focused in 2007 on two men in the wings who later became PR allies: now-former French rugby coach Bernard Laporte and – can you tell any French story today without him? – "Omnipresident" Nicolas Sarkozy.

Tall, bald, squinty-eyed Laporte was not just a coach. He became France's Secretary of State for Youth and Sports. This, because he had a chance summer drink with a Sarkozy bodyguard who wangled him a lunch with then-candidate "Sarko." Laporte's sports fame and sixteen personal sponsorship contracts made him doubly attractive to Sarko, who loves hanging out with celebrities and successful "businessmen."

Another Laporte magnet: France's national soccer team infuriated Sarko by disinviting him from the 2006 soccer World Cup in Berlin. So he latched onto Laporte and his rugby squad to prove sportsmen still loved him.

France's winning the 1998 soccer World Cup allegedly won polls for former President Jacques Chirac. Superstition? Not if you believe the 577 inhabitants of Larrivière-Saint-Savin in southwest France.

Commemorating an accident that killed three local rugby boys, they restored an abandoned chapel and renamed it Notre-Dame-du-Rugby. A stained-glass window shows the Virgin Mary holding a small boy gripping a rugby ball, with players jumping below them.

If you watch the wild hugging and inspired improvisations of a real game, you can easily believe that rugby is indeed the game played in heaven. But it's a stretch to imagine hairy, scary Sébastien Chabal as the model for Larrivière-Saint-Savin's stained-glass baby Jesus. He couldn't even have made a convincing choirboy.

◌

Chapter Eight /

"I THINK, THEREFORE (MAYBE) I AM "

If you can't call yourself a sociologist in Paris, your next-best bet to wow the gullible salon-and-media crowd is to call yourself a philosopher. Thinking about thinking is a badge of intelligence honored by long French tradition. But not all *philosophes* are philosophers; in France, the term itself is debased currency. When Parisian *poseurs* announce they're brooding on deep thoughts, prepare for a barrage of fog, clichés, name-dropping and pretension. The touchstones for everyday French 'philosophy,' at least the run-of-the-mill, op-ed kind, are dogmatism and fake complexity. You can never quite tell if the commentator or analyst (as we Anglos would call them), are superficially profound or profoundly superficial.

Did you read Tom Wolfe's mountebank-tripping book *The Painted Word?* Hanging *New York Times* art critic Hilton Kramer with his own words ("to lack a persuasive theory [of art] is to lack something crucial"), Wolfe shows how modern art has degenerated – not always into bad art, but into tarted-up theories.

Theory-mongering is an endemic temptation corrupting French intellectual life. Psychiatrist Jacques Lacan's structuralism, and literary spoil-sport Jacques Derrida's deconstructionism, for example, may still find a few fans at home. But only American academics take them seriously: These Frenchmen, goes the argument, are so incomprehensible they must be smart. Pierre Bourdieu, who theorized on social hierarchies and action, lasted longer in France. When he died in 2002 – an updated anti-liberal, anti-globalization Mr. Fixit – *Le Monde* gave him its main page one headline *two* days in a row.

In almost any French cultural or political field, you hear incessant talk of theory, ideas, schools of thought, cliques, clans, clubs, "chapels" and "currents." These satisfy a deep French need to exclude a lot of fellow-citizens, while including a few. They also build mystique around would-be leaders, providing vehicles for their ambitions. In politics, "Join my club" means "join my cabal and get me elected."

A less jaded comment: A country where the whole population thrills to read the main question on the final-year high-school philosophy exam can't be dull – or without an opinion. Still other reasons to go to Paris? Argue vehemently there about life's higher meanings. Dispute Michael Ignatieff's "narcissism of minor differences." And maybe, *en passant*, improve your mind.

Coffee, philosophy and a little flirting

Parisians in cafés are not just writing great novels or seducing their best friend's spouse. Nor are they necessarily sipping their Kir royal while devouring the Cahiers du Cinéma or ogling passersby. They may actually – mais oui! – be pondering cosmic questions of philosophy. They may be doing so nose in tome, or waxing disputatious with a friend. For more structured, liberating thought, they may even be sitting in on a "Café-Philo" – an informal group of mixed-background Parisians who drop in to discuss an issue proposed, and moderated, by a volunteer. Just for the fun of it. Or – philosophers do get lonely – to make new friends.

You know Socrates and Seneca. But what about Marc Sautet? What about the thousands of Frenchmen who un-blushingly term themselves *philosophes*? In English-speaking countries, sticking "philosopher" on a business card would get you guffaws. In France, parading as a philosopher wins you a tolerant, even respectful, smile – with just a touch of skepticism.

In this homeland of 17th-century genius René Descartes ("I think, therefore I am"), thinking is no smirking matter. Millions of French adults – all forced to study philosophy to graduate from high school – go through life philosophizing, and revelling in it: Applying "reason" is a national pastime. The best philosophy essays by graduating 18-year-olds appear in major newspapers. Mass-market magazines run cover-stories on philosophy and its wilder cousin, theology. A plethora of popular and academic periodicals entrenches the obsession: for thirty weeks in 2008, daily *Le Monde* offered a book-a-week collection called "The Great Philosophers."

Since 1992, a network of "*Cafés-Philo*" started by teacher Marc Sautet has brought together hundreds every week to ponder riddles like "How far should we go?" or "What is morality?" Or another actual topic: "The fantasy of the self-made man." A trained philosopher or layman moderates free-wheeling discussions, illuminating themes and suggesting solutions. At the original venue, the *Café des Phares* in Place de la Bastille, Sunday-morning meetings still draw scores of disciples (150 is routine, with maybe 15 moderators). Many participants are atheists or agnostics: clergymen claim those high-school *philo* courses killed their faith.

The *Café-Philo* idea of self-running groups has spread to 24 countries. It continues in Paris among students, expatriates and retirees, all eager to play Jean-Paul Sartre. Co-founder Michel Turrini told me that *Cafés-Philo* fill many needs – social (fighting loneliness), intellectual (stimulation lacking in media), even 'spiritual' (filling the gap left by loss of faith). "Many atheists come to make sense of the world."

I once attended a *Café-Philo* in a Latin Quarter brasserie. Ten people, all seniors, discussed "Is equality possible?"guided by brush-cut moderator Claude Bonnen-fant, a sixtyish former auto-worker. First-names-only de-bate was passionate, pointed and respectful, with plenty of laughter. "People come here for connection in a lonely world," Claude confided. "They want to learn, exchange, make friends."

Another café-culture trend formalizes book discussions. One group flaunts the playful label of *Les obsédés textuels* (parodying *les obsédés sexuels)*. But the idea's the same: good talk to stir brain cells, new perspectives, laughter, coffee, friends, and – why not? – a little flirting.

A newer trend is the *Ciné-Philo*. Fifteen Paris cinemas once featured live teachers analyzing images or films in re-lation to famous philosophers. "What's the relationship be-tween *The Titanic* and Lucretius, *Soldier Ryan* and Aristotle, Chaplin and Schopenhauer, Lars von Trier and Descartes?" asked host Ollivier Pourriol. The promise: "a new look" at familiar pictures –"to give movie-goers philosophical tools to decode images and find their meaning." Then-current topics: "The spiral of love" and "Desire as a clear object."

If your love-life is spiralling downward, or desire is not clear enough, you can go way upscale to the free public philosophy lectures of the *Collège de France*, citadel of the greatest minds in France. You can fall asleep there in the most comfortable chairs in Paris.

You find echoes of "philo" everywhere in daily life. I once asked my hardware-store man what kind of tape I needed for packing. "*A priori*," he assured me, "there is no perfect tape. But let's analyze: logically you need this one." To say somebody has a certain mindset, you say he is "in a certain *logique*." I emerged with tape, in a *logique* of packing.

The god of French logic is still old Descartes. Every school-child gets drilled in Cartesian logic, a doubt-rejecting system that elegantly strips away fuzzy thinking. "Cartesianism" threatens all ideologues and, as Pope John Paul II deplored, especially theologians. Poor Descartes died of pneumonia after Queen Christina of Sweden summoned him to her bedside for early-morning lessons. The official story blames a chill; unofficial ones whisper *une logique galante*.

With the French Revolution came theorists of people power, culminating in Marx's and Engels's1848 Communist Manifesto. German philosophers still befuddle plenty of French minds – Heidegger is a favorite. But you can't blame prolix Germans alone for hooking the French on intellectualizing the trivial and obvious with exotic obscurities. Auguste Comte and Émile Durkheim stand guilty of founding sociology. And Jacques Derrida's 20th-century cult "deconstructed" literature, squeezing every drop of joy from it.

France now harbors a cacophony of impenetrable new philosophers, few of whom ask that ideal *Café-Philo* question: "What good is philosophy?" The answer lurks in the bookstores. "People are buying simple books that teach you how to be happy," *La Procure*'s philo-man Pierre Collantier told me: Luc Ferry's down-to-earth *Learning to Live* sold

200,000 copies. "And year after year," he winked, "the classics beat everybody. People just love Socrates and Seneca. They're medicine for the soul."

Tony Blair (slowly) conquers France

The former UK prime minister, before he resigned and (openly) got religion, was the demon of French politics – a Thatcherite "traitor" to European socialism at a time when even France's nominally right-wing president Jacques Chirac denounced free enterprise. Ultimately, Blair became for the French an infuriating Man of the Middle. On his French left: about 36 varieties of share-the-wealth indignation; on his French right: limp-noodle apologies for freer wealth-creation.

Nobody, certainly not France's apoplectic, frozen-in-time Socialists, really trusted Blair: In a country of black-or-white truths, his tacking left and right on different issues confused and enraged. To muddy the waters: Both French left and right still revere the state. Both favor France's key industries as "national champions" deserving protection against evil foreign competition. Former Prime Minister Dominique de Villepin counted even Danone yogurt as such a "strategic industry." The ridicule greeting this news was just one of many signs that Blair, the empirical globalizer, was gradually winning French minds.

Cheery, helpful and peddling frightfully English common sense, Tony Blair stood before France's National Assembly on March 24, 1998 defining political success: "There is no right or left politics in economic management today," he told the 577 startled parliamentarians. "There is good and bad…There are no ideological preconditions, no pre-determined veto on means. What counts is what works." In left-right, dogma-split France, a provocation.

Blair was not a candidate in the bitterly fought May 2007 presidential runoff vote between neo-Gaullist Nicolas Sarkozy and Socialist Ségolène Royal. But both were his disciples – 'Sarko' a lot, 'Ségo' at least a little. So too was the now marginalized, but then wildly courted, centrist candidate François Bayrou. Together, these politicians won over three quarters of all votes in the first of 2007's two rounds, 100 percent in the run-off. With softening but still-radical left-right divisions, nearly everybody now leans to camping in Blair's "extreme centre." But without admitting it – and certainly not mentioning his radioactive name.

Other parties? Far-right Jean-Marie Le Pen's *Front National* has been chased by voters into virtual bankruptcy – selling both its headquarters building and Le Pen's armored limo. It sinks into colorful irrelevance. Diehard Marxists are now a music-hall joke, or they hide within a personality cult. Voters almost dissolved France's Communist Party, and condemned four smaller "left-of-left" parties to devising, like sherry-sipping Anglican prelates in a *Punch* cartoon, still more amusing little heresies. Only 34-year-old "revolutionary" Trotskyite postman Olivier Besancenot stays on the radar-screen – but as a likeable, baby-faced boy on TV talk-shows. That's enough to make him a left-nostalgic favorite as he launches in early 2009 his New Anti-Capitalist Party. But you won't soon see him holding court in the Élysée Palace.

For a decade of French politicians, Tony Blair was a (literally) unspeakable deviation. Irritatingly, his sold-out British workers got richer – as French ones, laggards in economic literacy, kept falling behind. The Third

Way he designed, in cahoots with U.S. president Bill Clinton, did more than build on Margaret Thatcher's icy-hearted capitalist revolution. It junked old-socialist dogmas to produce New Labour. Core ideas: make free enterprise work, while keeping safety-nets for the needy – but without sky-high Scandinavian taxes.

Economic dynamism with social solidarity. In France, most people think you can only have one or the other: the whole "left" package or the whole "right" package. Leaving entrepreneurs free to create wealth, claim leftists, means stealing from workers. Example: obscene golden parachutes for failed executives in huge companies (*Airbus, Carrefour, Alcatel*), even as big layoffs occur. But over-protecting workers, say rightists, strangles business. Example: laws against firing even incompetents discourage hiring, thus growth.

Over ten years after Blair offered his above advice, Britain's unemployment rate remains half of France's. Hundreds of thousands of job-seeking French youth have taken the Eurostar train to London. Thousands of French engineers flock to California. Intractable French unemployment and endless short-term jobs have blasted their hopes, costing France much of a generation's talent.

In the 2007 French presidential election, Sarkozy publicly cozied up to Blair. More bravely, presidential candidate Ségolène Royal risked excommunication from her ex-common-law husband François Hollande's Socialist Party by admitting she found some of Blair ideas discussable.

As of 2008, the Socialists are slowly sliding rightward. One of Royal's top leadership rivals, Paris mayor Bertrand Delanoë, even dares to label himself a "*libéral*" – a left-wing swear-word. Another, Dominique Strauss-Kahn, bides his time as managing director of the tough-love International

Monetary Fund. Sarkozy preaches results-based reforms. Spain's Blair-style innovations impress. Result: Blair's pragmatism now looks much less heretical.

Blair's formulas have gradually seeped into French public discourse. Many mainstream commentators, unionists and politicians (including, on a bad-humored day, Sarkozy), may still greet them with suspicion as alien, "brutal Anglo-Saxon" recipes. But that's for the gallery. A small, previously out-shouted group of intellectuals – Nicolas Baverez and Claude Imbert, most eloquently – is successfully defending *le blairisme* in the media.

Is France's old-Marxist glacier finally starting to crack? With Sarkozy's successful shift to the right, can France's ideological pendulum find uneasy peace in a pragmatic centre? Germany, even with Angela Merkel's awkward left-right governing coalition, achieved this. For France to follow, perhaps the Socialist rear-guard will have to grasp the absurdity of pleading: "Maybe Blairism works in practice, but can it work in theory?"

Horatio at freedom's bridge - Jean-François Revel

For decades a rare voice for liberty against France's intelligentsia, Revel in his way was a French Aleksandr Solzjenitsyn. Unlike the great Russian dissident, he did not risk prison, torture or death. But within Paris's intolerant, left-praising "microcosm" of establishment thinkers and media stars, he risked – and happily accepted – an ostracism from much of French cultural life. A banishment resembling ex-communication.

Only at Revel's death did many opponents realize they had chosen the wrong side (Moscow) in the Cold War. And the wrong sides of many other contests pitting democracy against totalitarianism. Their hard-learned lesson: Every generation needs a Revel to contest "la pensée unique" – its prevailing orthodoxy.

Bald, ruddy-faced and a mite creaky in the legs, he looked like a superannuated Telly Savalas. As he emerged from his favorite restaurant – his *cantine* – on the Île-Saint-Louis just behind Notre-Dame, he met a fan eager to thank him for his robust defense of freedom. Jean-François Revel, author of books on politics, history, philosophy, culture, cuisine and gardening, and one of the French Academy's forty *Immortels*, responded with exquisite courtesy – apologizing for carrying a two-thirds-finished bottle of Bordeaux to his nearby apartment.

On the eve of May Day, 2006, Revel died at 82 denouncing France's egalitarian and anti-American obsessions. He fought the good fight of liberty – and real fraternity – all his life. In a country where it is socially hazardous to admit even moderate right-wing beliefs, Revel got away with his libertarian, democratic heresies through passion, logic and wit. Journalist, polemicist, TV performer, and renowned *bon vivant*, Revel climbed out of a left-wing background to articulate disturbing truths. Disturbing, that is, to the orthodox French intelligentsia – the prophets of Orwellian *pensée unique*.

During the Cold War, Revel ran a one-man opposition to "Lenin's collaborators" – western intellectuals who shamelessly excused Moscow's crimes. He pricked the hot-air balloons of their knee-jerk anti-Americanism. For such a hell-raiser to end up as a member of the venerable French Academy was a charming anomaly. But he deserved it, as well as the dam-busting flow of praise that came out at his death.

Revel's books were scalding indictments of the smug, semi-official intellectuals who adored Karx Marx and fawned over his totalitarian children: Stalin, Mao, Castro. In *Without Marx or Jesus* (1970), Revel predicted the triumph of the American "revolutionary model," as opposed to left-wing models. In *The Totalitarian Temptation* (1976) and *How Democracies Perish* (1983) he crucified leftist apologists for romanticizing criminal dictators like Ethiopia's Mengistu Haile Mariam.

Given a choice between a free society and a totalitarian system, he said, many western intellectuals unerringly chose dictators. Because the "philosophers" craved symmetry and order, and saw themselves as a vanguard? Because they were bigoted and ignorant? Or just because any anti-Yankee was an ally? Such speculations won Revel cordial enemies.

Revel made social democrats squirm because they rarely equated Nazi and Communist murders – even after the opening of Soviet archives amply documented Communism's mass killings. Revel's last *livre à scandale* was *The Anti-American Obsession*. It dissected French envy and anger toward its messianic rival. It showed how Yankee-paranoia twists the minds and discourse of French politicians and commentators across the spectrum.

Facing French presumptions that anything labeled "liberal" or "free market" was evil, Revel didn't win his war while alive. State-worship by authoritarian "public service" élites still infects French politics and society from top to bottom. Eighty percent of parliamentarians come from public sector backgrounds, so they favor outrageous privileges for those already enjoying lifetime jobs. Three quarters of young people, as we saw, dream of a civil-service job. Paradoxically, three quarters of French voters also claim that the left is no more capable of governing them than the right.

Basically, Revel defended western civilization – the dignity and worth of individual vs. collectivity. He was a French John Stuart Mill – father of English liberalism – wielding pen as rapier. While anything but a nationalist (he worked in English and Spanish as well as French), he despised western guilt-trippers and hand-wringers who thought they should apologize for everything western nations had built. "Clearly," he said, "a civilization that feels guilty for everything it is and does will lack the energy and conviction to defend itself." While himself a sharp-tongued social critic, he warned that sapping the self-respect of true democracies served only totalitarians trying to destroy them.

Is it clutching at straws to glimpse victories for Revel now that he's gone? The outpouring of grief at his death shocked many left-wing detractors whose hypocrisies he unmasked. His books continue to sell and provoke. In the great sand-box where politicians preen, more and more leftists edge rightward to center. Some famous left-wing thinkers (see below) even veer to conservative religion. Under Nicolas Sarkozy, the word freedom is no longer anathema. And Washington, in spite of the fiasco of a blundering, war-mongering, dumbed-down U.S. under George W. Bush, no longer gets a Gaullist finger in the eye from Paris, but an outstretched hand.

With irony, iconoclasm and Bordeaux firmly in hand, Revel would have loved the spectacle.

Gallant view of 1968 upheavals

For decades a prized New Yorker short-story writer, Mavis Gallant has made Paris her hometown for almost sixty years.

With sharp eye, ear and wit, she looks at the French with a mixture of admiration and (like many Francophiles) amused dismay. An expert on exile as well as French society, she was a feminist before the word existed – defying newspaper bosses at least twice her age to cover stories they dismissed as unimportant, but that she thought mattered.

She still has her own ideas on everything, as a good reporter should. A lunch with her will get you a quick-witted argument over anything you want – including 'small topics' she still insists matter.

Appraising her white asparagus with lifted eyebrow, Mavis Gallant is living proof of playwright-wit Sacha Guitry's dictum that no woman in Paris is over forty. So when she chronicled France's student-worker May madness of forty years before, she was very young. Surprisingly, and Guitry aside, she landed in Paris from Montreal in 1950 at age twenty-eight.

Her eyewitness classic, *Paris Notebooks*, remains one of the most vivid perspectives on how students occupied the Sorbonne in May 1968 and ten million strikers paralyzed the nation. A year later, their earthquake finally drove President Charles de Gaulle from office.

Its aftershocks still ripple through France today. Graying rebels of '68 – many now in high office – tally their mixed accomplishments. Politically, these *soixante-huitards* ('sixty-eighters') failed: their mish-mash of Marxism, Maoism, posturing, partying and poetic nonsense changed little in France's power structure or economy. But socially and culturally, they won. Sexual freedom (a central motivation), women's lib, divorce, academic democracy, human rights and cocky irreverence ("It is forbidden to forbid") blew the roof off de Gaulle's repressive, ossified society.

Over lunch near her *6th-arrondissement* apartment, Mme. Gallant didn't let good grub fuzzy her recollections of May 1968. Why did Paris students occupy the Sorbonne and start spouting a dog's breakfast of leftist slogans?

"First, because after the campus explosions at Berkeley and Columbia [set off by America's Vietnam War and the assassinations of Martin Luther King Jr. and Robert Kennedy], student protest became a worldwide phenomenon. And, of course, because this is France, students immediately started wrapping it all in philosophy. Intellectuals [like Jean-Paul Sartre] typically leapt on this opportunity to feel *useful.*"

"Remember that this was a time of great prosperity in France – the 'Thirty Glorious Years' of 1945-75. These kids were not destitute, but well-dressed. They had time on their hands – and many decided to march against whatever was wrong in their own lives. As always, youth love demonstrating – it's exhilarating."

Why did millions of workers pile on? "Wealth then as now was very unevenly distributed. Workers were not getting their fair share of post-war prosperity. They were seething to demand fairer wages, and the student revolt just set them off. Students, intellectuals and workers all had different agendas. But their common demand was change – literally toward more liberty, equality and fraternity."

Did they succeed? "It depends whom you ask. And a lot of change would have happened anyway. But France became more democratic – too much so, say many. Authority and dogmas of all kinds came under attack in ways that still shape society. Many claim education has become far too lax, and that children learn less than before. The pendulum is clearly swinging back now to core subjects and firmer discipline."

What about the revolt's student leaders? "The only one anybody remembers is 'Dany le Rouge' [red-haired Franco-German student Daniel Cohn-Bendit.] He quickly rose because he was intelligent, eloquent, and knew France well. A Green Party politician, he has made a real career. Many still admire him."

That's quite a change from other 1968 student leaders, then media demi-gods. Although a few have made decent livings as journalists and teachers, several have abandoned Marxist dogmas to seek new absolutes in religion – Christianity, Judaism, Islam. "They have just gone from one structure to another. There are people – perhaps a majority – who like having barriers, or systems with rules."

After reading Gallant's *Paris Notebooks*, your best bet to understand why and how France went crazy forty years ago is to rent Louis Malle's charming 1990 satirical film *May Fools* (*Milou en mai*). Pomposity, cobwebby cant, class, cultural rituals and straight-faced farce add an irresistible counterpoint to Gallant.

Grande dame of Canadian letters, along with fellow *New Yorker* writer Alice Munro, Madame Gallant still tosses off memorable short stories and articles at a pace lifelong freelancers would envy. Proud of earning her way and never applying for grants, she has spent her life meeting deadlines, a woman determined to stay free.

Mavis Gallant has anchored Canada in France for fifty-nine years. She's a no-nonsense patriot who "can't stand that lot in Buckingham Palace" and doesn't see "why we can't grow up and have our own head of state." Like many Canadian expatriates, she rarely consorts with other

Canadians overseas, preferring to learn from locals. But she loves Canada from afar, and unconditionally: "Have you noticed? I even keep my Canadian 'eh?'"

Ignoring medical mishaps, she relaxes by rereading Tolstoy. And by singing for her supper with wicked anecdotes from a memory like a vacuum-cleaner.

But "in the fine flower of age," as the French saying goes, she finds joy mainly in work, friends, a glass of splendid red wine, and – am I imagining this? – a little girlish flirting with males of any age. Still carrying on like a forty-year-old *Parisienne*.

✒

PEOPLE, PLACES, DELIGHTS

Photo: Paddy Sherman

Chocolatier Christian Constant, ally for your love-life

Photo: Paddy Sherman

Fred Chevallier and cook Siva run la cantine

Photo: Keith Spicer

Philippe Tailleur bakes bread, smells roses

Photo: Paddy Sherman

***Sikh, and Ye shall find lamb curry at
La Coupole***

Photo: Keith Spicer

Rue Mouffetard: dancing nose to nose

Photo: Keith Spicer

Jardin du Luxembourg: magic and mystery

Photo: Paddy Sherman

Saint-Germain-des-Prés: philosophy and foie gras

Photo: Keith Spicer

Mating rituals in the Place des Vosges

Photo: Francs Arquebusiers

Call me a Taliban, and I'll chop your head off

Photo: Drapeau Rouge

Communist chief Buffet: I'm so happy Karl Marx lives

Photo: Daylife

I'm the mayor, and this thing will rent you a bike

Photo: La Poste

Don't I look cute delivering the mail?

Photo: Wordpress

I'll star in countless French movies

Photo: Bloggino

Anti-car crusade: cyclists reveal strategy

Photo: REUTERS/© Robert Pratta / Reuters

Students say: The minister's a tightwad (polite version)

Photo: French Government

Republican Guard rides to the rescue of whatever

Photo: Paddy Sherman

George Sand liked Chopin's mazurkas

Photo: L'Internaute

Olympe de Gouges lost her head for good causes

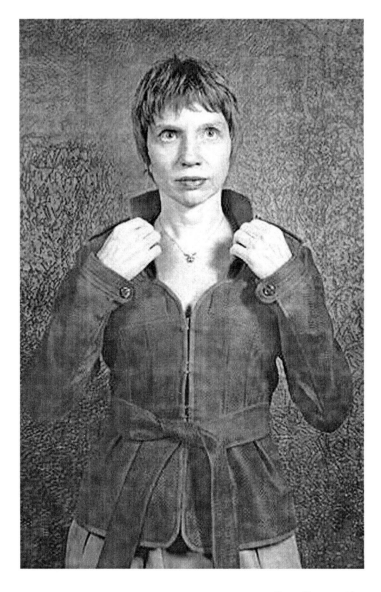

Photo: Idata.over-blog

Laurence Parisot is in charge of capitalism

Photo: Keith Spicer

Swinging Paris – maybe I'll be a ballerina

Photo: Nouvel Ordre Mondial

Sarko charms Angela: I'll tell Carla it's only diplomacy

Photo: Académie Française

Jean-François Revel: My sword's for defending freedom

༒

PART III

A COUNTRY IN FAST-FORWARD

Chapter Nine /

GARDENS OF THE MIND

Snobbery is hazardous to your reputation. In culture-Mecca Paris, whether through permanent cultural "installations" (museums, churches, theatres, orchestras) or fleeting concerts, festivals or exhibitions, you can find both sublime and vulgar, gold and dross – and sometimes the line between them seems slim. Partly, that's the nature of culture: akin to kissing, ahem, a thousand frogs to find a prince. Besides, as the French proverb goes, beauty is in the eye (or ear) of the beholder: "Taste and color are beyond argument." They are, broadly, mere personal preferences.

A more reliable saying, from the world of computers, is "garbage in, garbage out." This highlights the decisive role of schools in a nation's culture. Exploring the mindscapes of today's hip-hop, 'metalhead' graduates tells you most of what you need to know about culture tomorrow. What standards will prevail? What works of music, art and writing will survive? Can Nigel Kennedy's hedgehog haircut and indisputable violin skills rescue centuries of classical music for audiences now told that all music is just (hello iPod!) "songs?" Who will create what? Who will appreciate what new forms of expression – how, and why?

Guessing the answers will not likely reveal tomorrow's reality. We can at best imagine that the audio-visual media will continue dominating minds to the detriment of print: As bookstores close all over Paris, keep an eye on Amazon's hand-held electronic reader Kindle. Still more new media will emerge: Will holographic TV bring the Bolshoi Ballet into your living-room in three-dimensional, razor-sharp splendor?

To get a feel for where France is moving in education, let's take note of a deep-water current in favor of sounder teaching and learning. Following the eternal pendulum-swing, 1968's anything-goes French education system is painfully finding its way back to basics.

One seductive cultural medium will remain, in whatever forms (cinema, TV-on-demand, hand-held devices): movies, that great French passion. Along with evening cultural and drama series, this "Seventh Art" will remain one of few flowers in the great game-show, reality-show, talk-show and "moto-cross" wasteland of French television. A final hope is the grand buffet of French culture-promoting organizations. These range from the ground-breaking *Admical* cultural philanthropy launched by France's Monsieur Culture, Jacques Rigaud, to the innovative, grant-giving *Fondation de France,* to thousands of one-issue groups such as *Les Amis du Louvre.*

Finally, a word about politicians and the arts. In recent years, we have seen single-specialty presidents: books for François Mitterrand; Asian, African and aboriginal art for Jacques Chirac. Now we have a low-brow, show-biz prez gingerly embracing the tutelage of his highly cultured new wife, Carla Bruni. A second Transalpine Renaissance? The jury is still out. But thank God for Italy!

"Good old Golden Rule days"

"School days, School days," began the song before that nostalgic second line above. Throughout the western world's public

education systems, recent years have sung the bring-back-the-basics song in many accents. In France, not only angry parents have demanded a stop to stealing their children's right to a decent education. TV, movies and media have piled on. Ministers, their audacity calibrated to courage as they face down a reactionary education establishment, have dawdled along behind. But they're catching up – and setting the stage for dramatic changes.

Grey uniforms, *La Marseillaise*, respect for teachers, instant obedience, memorizing facts and poems, mental arithmetic, dictations, essays, punishment for misbehavior, good and bad marks read in front of the class. That was school in 1950s France.

Will it become French school again? Not exactly as in the 1950s, for society isn't there anymore. But moderate-right-wing ministers of education, starting with François Fillon in 2004-05 and going on to 2008-09 education minister Xavier Darcos, like much about the old regime and its bedrock values. So, we shall see, does "rupture"-and-reform President Nicolas Sarkozy.

Most French parents – even many children – agree a bit of back-to-yesterday is not a bad idea. France is awash in nostalgia for schools that taught knowledge and skills. Citizens are fed up with schools that don't teach, but pretend to "facilitate learning." That let standards, discipline and dress codes go to hell.

Parents and teachers are chucking "modern" textbooks. They're buying old-favorite manuals of thirty years ago, now being widely republished. Some such textbooks may reinforce recommendations of a government commission to refocus on fundamentals.

A 2004 runaway-hit TV series hammered home what education used to be, and what's been lost. The show – *Le Pensionnat de Chavagnes* – was a weekly flashback putting a class of mid-2004 twelve-year-olds into an imaginary 1950s boarding school. The final episode put them through yesteryear's rigorous primary-school-leaving *Certificat d'études*, abolished in 1989. Some questions (basically, the three Rs) came mainly from fifty years ago. Today's kids had big trouble with spelling, grammar and problem-solving. Not to mention with the Good Old Days' discipline, obedience, hard work, perfectionism and chores.

Other signs of education nostalgia: *Les Choristes*, a touching 2004 movie that broke attendance records, was about a tough-love 1950s school-master shaping twenty wild young boys into a choir, against the sabotage of a stupid principal. Another film that year (the year the nostalgia-dam broke): *Les Fautes d'orthographe* (The Spelling Mistakes). It showed the sometimes terrifying, but fruitful, discipline in a 1970s boarding-school against the tensions of adolescent sexuality and then-trendy political revolt.

What's at the core of retro-education? Well-known pediatrician Aldo Nauri, in *Le Nouvel Observateur* magazine, said the vogue for strictness proved children need more structure, less freedom. Too much liberty, he argued, abandons a child to unmanageable anguishes. "He feels lost on a suspension bridge above a gorge."

Give kids certainties, Nauri urged. To discuss, even explain, a decision undermines the teacher's legitimate authority and makes judgments, including marks, contestable. Most students crave rules to escape the "chaos" wrecking their education.

Author of France's back-to-basics Bible is veteran teacher Marc Le Bris. It's no accident he's from Britanny, the region of France where tradition, discipline and rigorous studies most easily thrive. His fiery pamphlet alleging French children soon won't be able to read or count set public anger aflame.

Lots of teachers, sick of being humiliated by students and betrayed by their politically correct ministry, share this anger. The ministry, dominated by ideologues from the 1968 society-challenging barricades, has practically made common sense, allege some, a synonym of fascism. Bureaucrats' "child-centered" approach sometimes seems almost to let kids run schools.

Hence, the pendulum-swing back to discipline, "values" and core subjects. In many French schools – and not only in immigrant ghettos - petty crime, violence, slovenly dress, rudeness, even physical attacks on teachers, are common. The government has assigned an on-call policeman to many secondary schools.

Standards of literacy and knowledge, claim critics, seem in free-fall. Softer marking lets far too many undeserving kids pass – then flunk first-year university. All in the name of democratic access to higher learning.

Well-off parents can still use influence to get their children into élite *lycées* – though even these come under attack for laxity. Money, as everywhere, can put kids into more disciplined, results-oriented private schools. Caving in to widespread parental demands, the government in 2008 hopes to abolish the *carte scolaire* forcing kids to attend a school in their home district.

In France's vaunted public school system – a glory of the Republic – change may come through a handful of "retro-visionaries" like Le Bris, a determined minister like Darcos, and a media-aroused public. France's identity crisis – fading international status, painful Muslim integration – will complicate debate.

Those back-to-the-fifties TV series, so-called "sepia-toned" movies, plus angry pro-and-con interviews, have opened up a countrywide French debate – passionate, dogmatic, fearful. Many French parents still worry their children are being robbed of their education. Often adolescents and first-year university students agree. They see themselves as victims of mushy, anything-goes pedagogical theories. Sound familiar?

Le Bris's native Britanny offers hope. Breton culture, notes Le Bris in newsmagazine *Le Point*, is rooted in conservative Catholicism. It believes in teacher-directed "instruction," not student-directed "education."

The *Collège des Hautes-Ourmes* in Britanny's city of Rennes thrives in a low-income area with 650 students of twenty nationalities. Yet even with underprivileged immigrant kids, reported newsmagazine *Le Point*, *Hautes-Ourmes*'s academic scores are six percent *higher* than the French average, rich-and-poor together. Teachers don't crack rulers on knuckles. They just demand respect for themselves and the rules, plus hard work.

Naturally, the education ministry hates such examples of old-school success. These threaten the ministry's parodied-but-powerful "Red Army" of civil servants with retreat, maybe defeat. Even four years after the nostalgia explosion, the war has just begun. But watch next how Sarkozy intends to win it.

A new French Revolution

If the French public suddenly began in 2004 to express its fury at bad education, the 2007 presidential and legislative elections put in place a Nicolas Sarkozy government determined to listen – and to change almost everything. It has a long way to go. But top-to-bottom changes are in the works, and even if unions and bureaucrats howl, in the end the public will join Sarkozy's education revolution. As it succeeds, France's society and economy will gain unhoped-for oxygen. A stunning development.

Eight-kilo backpacks sagging with books, millions of little kids trudge to France's schools to become informed, clever and French – not necessarily in that order. Most start classes at age three (some at two) in *l'école maternelle*. There they learn to get along with others, read, count, respect teachers, and sort of sit still. But the world has not sat still for France.

No longer is French education, as national legend long claimed, the "envy of the world." Though often superb for early ages, it is wildly uneven at the top, and troubled in mid-years.

In the widely recognized Shanghai *Jiao Tong* University ratings of the world's best universities, the 82 public French universities (there are another 100 of all types) have fared dismally. The top-ranked French university in 2008, Paris's science-and-medicine *Université Pierre et Marie Curie,* came 42nd; heavily nuclear-science *Université de Paris Sud 11* (France's largest campus) came 49th; and Paris's Nobel-Prize factory *École Normale Supérieure* came 73rd.

These numbers, contested by universities minister Valérie Pécresse, mislead. "Universities" in France – just the ones with this formal status – are rarely the cream of higher education. The top institutions for teaching and research are the famous *Grandes Écoles* (the above *Normale Supérieure* being Everest). These still churn out some of the world's best mathematicians, scientists and engineers.

Relatively small élite institutions with wide autonomy, the *Grandes Écoles* recruit by competition. Unlike universities, they're not obliged to admit anybody with a high-school graduation diploma (*baccalauréat* or *bac*). They tend to specialize in engineering, science and management – fields leading to top jobs, both government and private-sector.

But state universities are in dire shape. Until 2008 their duty to admit any and all high-school grads (who pay almost nothing to attend) guaranteed tens of thousands of first- and second-year drop-outs – an up-to-52 percent drop-out rate in first year alone. Over 90,000 still quit university each year without a degree. Universities dump on the labor market armies of youths with useless diplomas, shattered to realize they know little that employers want. Self-reliance is crushed by "anti-capitalist" ideology and suffocating small-business rules.

Low investment in universities has left many facilities shabby, even dysfunctional. Amphitheaters' historical décors are often glorious, but offices and equipment are ramshackle. Vital courses lack enough benches to accommodate students. Now you find computers – but getting them, and any change, is still guerrilla war.

Rigid rules prevent the best profs from moving around – or, if brilliant and young – moving up. At age 65, even world-class researchers have to retire – Dr. Luc Montagnier,

Pasteur Institute discoverer of the HIV-AIDS virus, was forced to find work in the U.S.

Suddenly in 2008, President Nicolas Sarkozy, Prime Minister François Fillon and Madame Pécresse have provoked an earthquake in higher education. This includes a massive budget increase: five billion euros for campus renovation alone. Startlingly, this will not go to every campus – only, by competition, to the top ten 'bidding' universities. Competition in French academia is heretical enough. But the government has also set up incentives for private companies to invest in universities, U.S.-style, promising matching grants.

Reforming elementary and secondary education too, President Nicolas Sarkozy sent a 32-page letter to every teacher in France to launch a new educational culture. Lucid, eloquent and daring, as are many of Sarkozy's reforms, this constitutes a bottom-to-top reform manifesto. It has already – an excellent sign – upset old-guard teachers' unions. And it has outraged officials of the foot-dragging Education Ministry.

Sarkozy's letter-manifesto dissects the purposes of education, its history in France, what has worked, and what has not. Its central focus: transmitting values, especially respect. Looking at the despair of French youth – whose unemployment runs at double older workers' rates – Sarkozy sees not only ill-adapted teaching and rigid administration. He sees a vacuum of values, a desert of hope.

Hundreds of thousands of French graduates find work only in Britain, Ireland and North America. Younger ones who fail, especially French-born children of immigrants, face lives of double rejection – from ancestral culture, and from France's job market. Drugs, riots and car-burning are not far behind.

Under the violence lies anger against authority – of teachers, parents, police. And against France itself: second-generation North African youth booed the *Marseillaise* at a stadium in the presence of a livid former President Jacques Chirac. Rap music calls France a "whore."

Sarkozy lays out tried-and-true school guidelines: "Rewarding merit, punishing wrongdoing, cultivating admiration for what is right, just, beautiful, great, true and profound, and detestation of what is wrong, unjust, ugly, small-minded, deceitful, superficial and mediocre…"

Sarkozy once wrote that childhood humiliation was the key to understanding the short, foreign-sounding boy still inside him. Hence, "…respect [must] underpin all education. The teacher's respect for the pupil, that of parents for their children, of pupils for their teachers, and children for their parents; respect for others and self-respect…"

Napoleon famously said every soldier carried a marshal's baton in his knapsack. As you watch little French kids hauling their heavy knapsacks to school, you wonder which new little Sarko (who, like Napoleon, never mastered sitting still) holds in his knapsack another education-changing key to the Élysée Palace.

Pssst! – Wanna see a French movie?

Painting, sculpture and music are the glories of France. But of all the arts, cinema seems the quintessential French one. Of course, as for all peoples, its powerful visual appeal draws minds to familiar or faraway places and ideas. And to emotions often below the surface. But the French recognize in film a people's art – an art of universal access that demands little or no effort to follow, yet can reveal humanity in uncommon richness. They sense it can reach, still better than literature, into inquisitive minds and troubled souls, in search of truth, feeling, mystery, humor, even illuminating ambiguity. In search of understanding life, love and death: as the philosophy-loving French know well, the only things that matter.

When Auguste and Louis Lumière showed the world's first movies at Paris's *Grand Café* on Dec. 28, 1895, spectators famously ducked under their seats as an oncoming train seemed to plunge into the audience. The Lumières' *"cinématographe"* – "an invention with no future," thought Louis, became a big-bucks talent-magnet for Hollywood. For France, it became the revered "seventh art" and, today, a "cultural industry" in splendid renaissance.

Like photography – another French invention (Niépce, Daguerre) – film enjoys inordinate respect in France. On a given day, you can see over a hundred different movies in Paris. Apart from still-dominant American ones, you can catch Iranian, Korean, Palestinian, Israeli, Bosnian, Russian, Pakistani, Indian, Peruvian, Albanian, Mexican or Chinese movies. Ordinary cultured people know 'exotic' directors: China's Chen Kaige, Zhang Yimou and Shi Runjiu, or Canada's Atom Egoyan, Denys Arcand and David Cronenberg. All get full-page write-ups in mainstream papers.

French movie magazines are not just fan mags. They dissect movies with an authority, historical depth and sureness rare in other countries. Paris critics tend to be incestuous and bitchy, slamming enemies and hyping friends. But their writing is often worth the price of admission. They know their stuff, and deepen columns with encyclopedic learning – from Hitchcock's dread-inducing camera angles to Eisenstein's eye for individuals in a crowd.

Apart from adoring Hollywood – and finding genius in Jerry Lewis – French film-goers take pride in their country's own rich celluloid traditions. They can rattle off names and styles of famous directors from the past nearly ninety years. Legends Abel Gance, Jean Renoir, Louis Malle, François Truffaut, Jean-Luc Godard and Claude Chabrol gave way to Luc Besson, François Ozon, Mathieu Kassovitz and many others. Movie stars? Behind Gérard Depardieu (who seems to star in 80% of all French movies), Catherine Deneuve and Juliette Binoche, toil scores of beloved French actors, and hundreds less known.

Film is a French obsession. A massive archive of French – as well as foreign – movies finds refuge at the famous *Cinémathèque Française*. Here, among the over 40,000 movies stored, you can call up almost any decent movie ever made, anywhere. The annual Cannes Film Festival remains the world's most glamorous movie meet. Terms like *film noir* and *auteur* long ago became English words. Subsidies abound. The minister of Culture – tending cinema's Vatican? – confers medals on the world's filmmakers. France fights trade battles to defend film and TV as a "cultural exception."

Until a few years ago, a "French film" often meant all talk, no action – just character-driven (almost word-driven) stories. Typical slow-lane mind-ticklers: Louis Malle's *My Dinner with André* or Eric Rohmer's *My Night at Maude's*. Hollywood does "remakes" of French movies. Some of these work: *Three Men and a Baby*, *The Birdcage*.

Others betray originals by telegraphing outcomes and/or adding a French-despised *le happy end* (or just a meaningless 'climax:' America's second-hand *Diabolique,* which ruined the French-original *Les Diaboliques.* Now, with handier technology, French film-makers can do action – even special effects – Yankee-style (*Fifth Element, Chevaliers du Ciel*).

In recent years, French cinema has found an easier balance between art and business. Before, making a movie that audiences liked meant "pandering to commerce" (Money for the French is like sex for Victorians: they love it, but hate discussing it). For many, *Amélie,* with Audrey Tautou as a magic Montmartre do-gooder, was an audience-pleasing breakthrough. Predictably, Paris critics ridiculed it.

Now they are mellowing. Any night of the week, you can see several popular French movies in cinemas – and more on TV. Not all the 258 theatrical-release movies France made in 2007 (counting co-productions) were brilliant. But enough were to take back France's screens from Hollywood: uniquely in the western world, about forty percent of all movies shown in French cinemas are French-made. Mayors, seeking prestige and economic pump-priming, often subsidize movie tickets. No need to subsidize Dany Boon's 2008 monster hit *Bienvenue chez les Chti's*: it drew a record-breaking 20 million viewers. Naturally, Hollywood asked Boon to direct a remake.

France holds more film festivals each year (166) than all the other 26 nations of the European Union combined. Not a week goes by without a festival somewhere in France, and no significant town is without one. France even holds a festival in Deauville each year just for American movies. The Americans reciprocate with a yearly festival of French film in Sarasota, Florida – happy hunting-ground for still more Tinsel-town remakes.

The French sometimes turn up their noses at the U.S. movie "business." But it's big business for them too. Not just for employment, investment and spending to keep their economy spinning. But because it's fabulous advertising for the world's most popular tourist destination.

Fine movies, commercial or not, will continue to pour out of France. Is it time for another terrifying Lumière-style flick to make you dive under your seat? That new 575 km.-per-hour (357 mph.) French TGV train could be just the ticket.

Carla leads Sarko to culture…and back to priorities

Nicolas Sarkozy may never match his third wife's standards of taste, formed in a wealthy family that gave her a broad education in culture, languages, music and comportment. He comes from elsewhere: a bootstrap land of ambition, obsession, hard work and survival. His only real culture is politics – hanging out with trashy "entertainment" stars replacing sophistication. In that, he is both impulsive and compulsive: visiting Pope Benedict XVI, he took along and introduced to His Holiness a foul-mouthed comic, then, while standing next to the Pope, text-messaged during the audience. Carla will strive to civilize her political animal. But his nature is largely untamable. Madame's true mission – vital for Sarko's reforming success – may be to remain his loyal counterpoint, his redeeming foil, his island of peace, his "warrior's rest." But also, with luck, his cultural guide and mentor.

The 'old' President Nicolas Sarkozy in a January 2008 photo: cell-phone glued to his ear, dashing *away* from the Taj Mahal, back turned to the jewel-encrusted masterpiece that Mughal emperor Shah Jahan built as mausoleum for his beloved third wife Mumtaz Mahal. The 'new' April 2008 Sarkozy: squiring *his* third wife, classy Franco-Italian Carla Bruni, to the high-brow *Comédie Française* – attending a play for the first time in memory. No word about his cell-phoning during the performance.

"Sarko:" insensitive lout or culture-vulture? Essentially the first, but let's salute a modest start on the second. Behind his fragile interest in high culture whispers highly cultured Carla, wrongly dismissed as a mere fashion-model pop-singer.

The president's savor-the-finer-things outing was just part of Sarkozy's makeover after a year in power. Months of his restless, whirling-dervish reformism had left the French people reeling and dubious: a poll then ranked him as the worst of France's seven presidents since 1958. Disgust at his flashy taste, love of money and chaotic love life left voters angry that he seemed to care more for fun than for people's needs.

Political honeymoons, like romantic ones, do end. Sarkozy's dazzling start quickly seemed like eons ago. Elected on May 6, 2007 by 53 percent of voters, Sarkozy fell to 32 percent 12 months later. Setting aside his off-putting personal soap-opera (twice-decamping spouse, borrowed billionaires' planes and yachts, Disneyland visit with new lover, then remarriage three-plus months after divorce), the deep reason for Sarko's doldrums was…the lack of doldrums. From the second he became president, he didn't

stop sprinting – that very day he hopped a plane to Berlin
to embrace Chancellor Angela Merkel.

He promised a break ("*la rupture*") from the stagnation
of earlier decades. And within days, he launched a non-stop
series of reforms – on taxes, social programs, political institutions, foreign policy. Sarkozy's trademarks: acting before
thinking, leaping on media opportunities, extrapolating
from anecdotes. He never set priorities, for *everything* –
from nuclear policy to fisheries to taxi-rates to tear-jerking
human-interest stories – was a priority whenever his restless gaze fell upon it.

Sarkozy harped on how his reforms were carefully in-
terwoven. But logic, coherence and relative importance
rarely guided his actions. He tried to overwhelm voters
with a blur of actual or proposed reforms. A few numbers
supposed to amaze the crowd: a dozen reforms in an ini-
tial "tax package" (which saddled an already disastrous state
budget with over eight-billion euros in mainly please-the-
rich loopholes); 490 "campaign promises;" 316 proposals
of the Attali reform commission (quickly ignored); 116
measures on "public policy" (sometimes expanded as "the
166 revisions"); 141 changes to "save money;" and 55 reforms tying education to employment. Finally, confused
Sarko allies evoked "the 13 reforms that matter." Who was
really counting? Nobody.

Not even Sarkozy – never mind citizens – could rattle all
this off. Even worse, when Sarkozy did reform, he too often
dabbled in half-measures. Not for him Margaret Thatcher's
damn-the-unions revolution or Jean Chrétien's draconian
Canadian budget-axing (wistfully praised in Paris). Sarkozy's words were always tough. But once a group threatened a demonstration – civil servants, educators, fishermen,

tobacco-sellers – he either backed off or came up with another costly fix. Result: a year later, the big-picture showed half of Sarkozy's reforms launched, but little fundamental change. He even deepened France's financial crisis.

But Sarkozy's dizzying energy conveyed reformist urgency and pulled off some striking benefits abroad. He rescued the European constitutional treaty from oblivion (before Ireland tried to send it back there); he patched up relations with the U.S.; he is bringing France back into NATO's unified military command and helping it in Afghanistan. In mid-summer 2008, as rotational president of the European Union, he midwifed a remarkable Union for the Mediterranean, and crafted a ceasefire between warring Russia and Georgia.

Some of Sarkozy's bad press comes from his unwillingness to impose cabinet discipline. He has the appalling habit of insulting his closest colleagues, including his loyal, popular prime minister, François Fillon. He bullies them all – except his four young female ministers in justice, suburban affairs, human rights and the environment. They've gotten away with attacking fellow-ministers, even government policy.

Sarko often says he will rein them in. But can he? Temperamentally, he has always had women problems – notoriously with his volatile second wife Cécilia. He tends to coddle younger female ministers, dragging them along on foreign trips like trophies. All good fun – but not if they keep embarrassing him.

Both critics and supporters regularly demand a more focused, "presidential" Sarkozy. But tactful, astute Carla is now the decisive influence for this trickiest of reforms: Sarko himself.

Pessimists recall her pre-marital confessions that she found monogamy "boring," calling "marriage another trap [because] … you have to swear to fidelity." But optimists can also quote her: "Love lasts a long time, but burning desire – two to three weeks."

For a speed-demon like Sarko, even three weeks might seem a fair price for a lifetime of love. With luck, gentle Carla will become his Mumtaz Mahal, cultural mentor or not. But maybe minus Mumtaz's thirteen children.

〜

Chapter Ten /

TINKERING WITH TRADITION

The French, in case you hadn't noticed, are not Americans. Patriotic, yes. Sure of a unique world mission, yes. But no grinning Yankee optimism lights Paris, no audacity of hope. Caution rooted in painful memories dims the lights. Subconsciously, Parisians peer west from the point of the *Île de la Cité* beneath the Pont Neuf, half-expecting to glimpse a new flotilla of terrifying, dragon-headed vessels bringing rape-kill-and-pillage Vikings to sack the town once more. Like most Europeans, though more so, French fear the new. It usually brings bad news, like an invasion – of land, ideas, culture or customs. Seen-it-all fatalistic, the French prefer to remember the past. And with their cult of *l'Histoire de France,* how they do! It's their anchor, explanation and justification for almost everything today – and why not tomorrow?

Partly this is in-the-gut realism. Old countries recall centuries of wars and disasters, and long ago stopped expecting utopias. Partly it's pride: France knows it can bounce back from catastrophe, soaring higher if not growing wiser. But recovery can be tricky to analyze. Happily, if the facts don't accommodate a therapeutic story, propaganda can. Charles de Gaulle managed to convince generations of French that his skimpy forces freed France in World War II – oh, maybe with a little help from some nameless friends. Rose-colored glasses firmly plunked on nose, he embellished his facts with brio. No surprise: He began his memoirs by confessing he saw France as "the princess in the fairy-tales, the Madonna in the frescoes." He told many fairy-tales, all to boost *Wehrmacht*-and-Vichy-demolished French pride. But bird-of-a-feather Winston Churchill played that game too, boosting "Britons and their Empire" and England's Finest Hour. He chuckled that "history will be kind to me, for I intend to write it."

France's staggeringly rich history tells one tale over and over. The story of how organization helps talent flow, and makes destinies happen. The French are a wildly talented, passionate people. To contain their restless energy, they need structure and safety-railings – eloquently-called *garde-fous* or madmen's balustrades. By instinct, and because of France's long occupation by Rome, the French crave and create, then venerate, institutions to channel their passions.

By temperament, the French are not quite democrats. They are anarchist-monarchists. The relative emphasis on anarchy or monarchy depends on time, situation, mood – and leaders. But the contradiction divides every Frenchman's soul. You see it easily in a long tradition of popular, authoritarian leaders with dedicated opponents: The Bourbon kings, Napoleon I, Napoleon III, Marshal Pétain and de Gaulle all enjoyed abundant enemies. *Le Grand Charles*, to be fair, was no dictator. He just decorated his democracy with naughty embroideries: bully-boys (*barbouzes*), spy-saboteurs (run mainly in Africa by the shadowy Jacques Foccart), fawning state radio and TV.

De Gaulle fashioned today's Fifth Republic constitution to keep the ship of state on a steady course – toward his and future presidents' power. How have French history and tradition shaped so many lasting institutions? First, a tip of the cocked-hat to a truly ambitious institutional architect: Napoleon I. Then a squirm at that most powerful tradition of all, sex, followed by the next most exciting thing in France, the Foreign Legion. A final rumination on two imperishable French institutions: God and cows.

Napoleon lays down the law

The great Corsican artilleryman did more than kill millions of people while occupying and pillaging most of Europe. He had an impressive civic imagination. His Expedition to Egypt opened that land's ancient civilization to Europe: he took 167 scientists there to document its art, monuments and history. Never mind that his real goal was anti-English trade and imperial ambition. His encyclopedic "Description de l'Égypte" became a pillar of world culture. But Bonaparte's most lasting accomplishment was at home. Presiding over teams of legal experts and drafters, he promulgated the "Code Civil des Français" – even now the basis of most law in France and the scores of nations it influenced. Does this compensate for Napoleon's bloody exploits? Possibly, if you were not one of his many victims.

So what if French vandals burn over 40,000 cars in a quiet year? This is not anarchy, just a little naughtiness. To understand how stable and law-abiding France really is, read Napoleon's *Code Civil des Français* – now, with many revisions, 204 years young. From kids to contracts, from wives to wills, it's the French Bible. But far clearer than Scripture.

Napoleon had plenty of blood on his hands, but also lots of ink. He personally guided an army of legal experts to compile a single national legal code. He hoped to settle all arguments in advance. A military man, he wanted order, not quibbling.

Why did France need to codify its laws? Pierre Briançon, in *France Magazine*, summed it up. Until 1804, citizens grappled with a thicket of overlapping, often contradictory, legal traditions. Roman law (strong in the south); Germanic customary law (north of Paris); church law (faith and morals); and royal law (the king's whim). Voltaire said crossing France, a man changed laws as often as he changed horses.

Napoleon wanted a single, overriding system anchoring the 1789 Revolution's ideals of liberty, equality, fraternity. Rejecting kingly, aristocratic and churchly privilege, he wanted all Frenchmen equal before the law.

Many argue that his deeper goal was, as ever, to entrench his personal power. His model was Byzantine emperor Justinian's 6th-century *Corpus Juris Civilis.* Cynics also claim he tinkered with the Code's family law to load the dice for later showdowns with wife Josephine. A field-marshal of the heart, she had outflanked the poor man all too often.

Napoleon attended 36 of 87 experts' meetings to define and refine French law. He intervened often, directed, even (as dictators do) dictated. If you visit Napoleon's tomb at Paris's gold-domed *Église St-Louis des Invalides,* you can read his words carved in stone all around you.

Apart from marrying the four basic traditions, his lawyers had to organize some 14,000 laws just passed by the revolutionaries. The result was 2,281 remarkably coherent, comprehensive – and intrusive –

articles that regulated almost everything a Frenchman touched except wine and mistresses. In spite of numerous updates to fit a changing society, the Code's architecture still stands.

Its range was astounding at the time: business deals, family, laws on freedom of religion and occupation, separation of church and state, abolition of privilege. Typically, Napoleon was liberal in financial affairs, and conservative in family law. But always the state won. Nearly every clause sustained public order, even when it protected the individual. Property was sacred.

In family law, Bonaparte's rules would outrage today's feminists. Laws confirmed husbands as uncontested heads of family, and tossed women into a (literal) no-man's-land with children and the insane. Few women complained: earlier law had allowed husbands to lock up naughty wives for life in a convent.

Adultery remained risky. It could jail a woman for up to two years. In *flagrante delicto*, she could even get killed, with hubby going free. A straying husband might get a knuckle-rapping fine of 2,000 francs. This aimed to back patriarchy. And, obviously, in those pre-DNA days with chancy birth control, to calibrate the relative impacts on lineage of men's and women's dalliances.

All this has changed. Today's most offensive family laws restrict only how you can dispose of your estate (most of it, but equally to each child), and make family gifts.

Napoleon wanted a code so simple and clear that there would not be a single superfluous word. Master-stylist Stendhal (Marie-Henri Beyle), author of that 19th-century classic of illicit love, *Le Rouge et le Noir,* claimed that, to inspire clarity and discipline, he started each day with a page of the male-pleasing *Code Civil*. (No wonder he dwelt on adultery). It's still a model of precision, though updates have rarely matched the original's lucidity. Culture writer Jacques Rigaud told me: "It combines Roman concision and French clarity." Another friend, law professor and editor Henri Pigeat, likewise praises its "brevity and clarity."

The *Code Napoléon*'s extraordinary impact comes also from its worldwide spread. Bonaparte imposed it on all his conquered European nations. Later French empire-builders exported it to Africa, Indochina and many other territories. Quebec adopted a version of it (now much changed), as briefly did Louisiana. Latin America borrowed massively. By 1960, over seventy nations had drawn inspiration, even texts, from the Code.

The Napoleonic Code was the modern world's first national "book" of laws. It helped re-unify France after the Revolution's anarchy; it restored the family to its central role in society after years of licentiousness; and it underpinned a rising middle class that would anchor France's stability. By a quirk of history, the Little Corsican's Bible ended up modernizing a multitude of other countries. Revisions and updates will keep it fresh forever.

Bonaparte thought the *Code Civil* his finest monument. But it left one self-defeating gap. Shakespeare, in Henry VI, wanted first to "kill all the lawyers." Surely Napoleon could at least have outlawed them.

No sex please, were French

Controversies over sex come and go in France, often tracking elections. Most of the time, politicians leave this topic alone, for many of them live in glass houses. It's only when sex meets other issues – especially violence or blatant defiance of society's standards – that politicians cry alarm. Carnal passions inside and outside politics continue to make France's world go round. Sex magazines, books and websites, after-hours TV shows, partner-swapping parties, online meet-a-fellow-pervert services, and frisky specialized clubs make for a free-wheeling scene. But the unstated rule is: Do what you like, but do it discreetly.

What's going on? Cops arresting nude cyclists? Even provocatively-dressed women? Is the homeland of Rabelais and Baudelaire, erotic sophistication, the *ménage à trois*, the Latin lover, official and unofficial mistresses, and a bedroom lexicon to rival the twenty-volume *Oxford English Dictionary* really upset by sex? Yes, if politics or indiscretion come into it.

Every few years, a politician tries to make hay from people's rolling in the hay. Just after World War II, the demagogue came from the *demi-monde* – entering at age sixteen the floating world of prostitutes or *horizontales.* Her name was Marthe Richard. Mistress, wife, aviatrix and spy in three-nation combinations over two world wars, Madame Richard amply deserved the Legion of Honor that her then-current lover, Prime Minister Édouard Herriot, gave her for – what else? – "foreign affairs."

Madame Richard got virtue as Jimmy Swaggart got religion. A main-chancer, she spotted her opening after 1945 when the Christian Democrats (MRP) offered her a seat in the Paris city council. She parlayed this into a campaign to close not only the brothels in her 4th *arrondissement*, but in all France. She managed to close 1,400 brothels throughout

France, including 180 in Paris. The *horizontales* simply moved *horizontalement* to hotels or the street.

Political opportunism again embraced virtue in the 2003 run-up to Sarkozy's long law-and-order campaign for the presidency. Backed by crusading Catholic legislator Christine Boutin, he defined a new crime: *raccolage passif* – "passive enticement" to paid sex. A risky business even for respectable women with a slightly racy fashion sense.

For Christine Boutin, TV was and is a perennial target. She hates increasingly crass "reality shows" displaying infidelity and promiscuity. But porno films offend her most, and she lobbies media and regulators to ban them. On half a dozen cable channels, skin-flicks appear after midnight, especially on weekends. Most exude all the charm of a training film for apprentice plumbers.

Polls say two thirds of all French people would be happy to get rid of these films. But they don't really mind. Deep down, they see blue movies, however pathetic, as visual Viagra for couples. Maybe even as a harmless way for teenagers to gain clues they'll never get from ever-shy mom and dad.

Boutin's anti-porn lobby deliberately confuses sex and violence – a revealing reflex. This way they can piggy-back on the searing election issue of "insecurity," suggesting a breakdown in law and order. Most feminists despise Madame Boutin for her old-fashioned, religion-tainted conservatism. But objectively, they are allies on many topics: They oppose a society of sex-drenched advertising and macho sexism in the workplace.

Madame Richard's early trade still booms in France – but much more quietly. (She herself left this world quietly at 92, still writing erotic novels). And discretion allows as much sex (paid or unpaid) as you wish, even while political opportunism may occasionally condemn it. Downscale prostitution thrives in seedy hotels, especially in northern Paris, as well as in some suburban forests. It exploits impoverished, often lied-to and beaten girls and women from Africa and Eastern Europe. The government could, and should, do much more to protect them.

High-end prostitution flourishes wherever big money sloshes around. Periodically, well-known and well-frequented "rings" are 'unmasked' in chic hotels or mansions. In 1998 film-actor Robert De Niro was questioned for nine hours by police about an élite 40-woman ring allegedly operating from his hotel. He denied all, and no charges were laid. De Niro sued publicity-hound investigators for smearing him in the media. He won $13,400 in damages from a French newspaper, *France Soir*. Meanwhile, he had threatened to boycott the Cannes Film Festival and give back his Legion of Honor. All the while, film-mad Parisians stood by him, considering the incident was not embarrassing to De Niro – only to France.

In 2007, Russian oligarch Mikhail Prokhorov got nailed for allegedly running a ring of girls in Alpine ski-resort Courchevel. He quickly explained that his Moscow girls were just friends, there for a party. The police understood. And the politicians saw no votes. For both innocent movie-star and Russian, insistence on privacy won the day.

What about the invasive indiscretion of "passive enticement?" Many women argue that one cop's view of passive soliciting may collide with an innocent woman's fashion sense. 'Traditional' (i.e. French) prostitutes, alarmed by cut-rate foreign competition, say Sarkozy's bill is outrageously vague, thus an assault on honest working girls who

also want to work in the shadows. In brilliant street theater, these *Irmas la Douce* demonstrated outside the Senate,
threatening to 'out' distinguished senators who "sleep with
us, but vote against us."

Politicians' public virtue and private vices got eye-
popping treatment in the 2006 book *Sexus Politicus*. Citing names, times and places, it ran readers through most
of the French political and media establishment. It gave
details of former President François Mitterrand's parallel
family and of Jacques Chirac's almost nightly scrapes. Also
of his productive interviews with enthusiastic female visitors. Joked Chirac's female staff: "Three minutes, including
the shower." Top ministers going to public sex-clubs also
earned dishonorable mention. A world-famous couturier's
organizing site-appropriate *fêtes* for politicians and trendies
in the Marquis de Sade's castle passed for, so to speak, artistic license. None of this made headlines. It just confirmed
that French politicians understood Henry Kissinger's famous dictum that power is the ultimate aphrodisiac.

Sex is safe in France, its alleged eclipse no smirking matter. Tales to the contrary are irresistible, but dead wrong.
The political reality, as often with sex itself, is simply that
power-games and hypocrisy seem to make it all a little more
fun. Hypocrisy? Winked 17th-century Court connoisseur,
the Duc de La Rochefoucauld: It is simply "the homage
that vice pays to virtue."

Dying for excitement – the Foreign Legion

*An institution that pays homage to fantasies of a different
sort is France's mythical Foreign Legion. It fascinates popular
imaginations worldwide. For slightly bad guys on the lam, it's*

a desperate escape to respectability. For lost souls, the unemployed or refugees, it's a chance to regain their footing. For restless young men, it offers a bracing chance to grow up – and to impress women. It's a last, life-risking stop in what can become a meaningful journey.

Tough, disciplined, well-equipped, the Legion can take on almost any military task from real fighting to truce supervision to reconstruction. It could offer a perfect model for a professional, fully integrated United Nations force, free of the notorious incompetence and corruption dogging several national UN units. Will that ever happen? Not likely. More than effectiveness, the UN seems to prize 'inclusiveness' (including, argue its 'gender advisers,' women in combat). Besides, the five veto-wielding permanent Security Council members may not all really want to see a force able to save lives by overriding state sovereignty: today Darfur, tomorrow Tibet?

Gentlemen: Is your image too bland? Looking for profile and panache? Just watch jaws drop when you tell your friends you're running off to join the French Foreign Legion.

First, rent the 1939 classic movie *Beau Geste*, swagger to the mirror and wink at its star, Gary Cooper. Maybe pick up the 1926 original with Ronald Coleman. Or the 1966 second remake with Telly Savalas. Even Marty Feldman's 1977 *The Last Remake of Beau Geste*. As heart-tugging heroism, the Legion has shelf-life.

Then Google your way onto the seven-language Legion website, and marvel at your future. In its mythic overseas force, France has 7,662 well-trained, ever-ready legionnaires from 136 countries. The Legion fuses these nationalities into a potent, élite force. It's one of the world's toughest, most reliable outfits – in Afghanistan, Kosovo, Chad, Ivory Coast and any other hotspots France likes.

The deal? Between age eighteen and forty, you need to be sane (applying may be *prima facie* evidence to the contrary); be able to do thirty push-ups, fifty sit-ups and eight chin-ups; climb a seven-meter rope without using feet; and run eight kilometers with a twelve-kilo rucksack in under one hour. A modest criminal record is OK, but nothing awful, please.

A rich anthology of legends, sayings and songs commits men to "honor," "fidelity" and "courage"– indeed to death for France. Legionnaires' religion is comradeship, their identity whatever they say on the way in, and their homeland the Legion itself. It's an awesome ethos for young men hungry for ideals and adventure.

The "brotherhood" guarantees them lifelong pals, even special holiday spas to meet them. Every man going in, whether married or not, is declared a bachelor. When you hear their ribald songs and jokes, you realize this is a heartfelt truth.

The Legion is more about mates than misogyny. Women, in Legion culture, are not warriors; they're the "warrior's rest" – soothing, off-the-field girl-friends. Frenchwomen, always practical, seem content to let the men do those thirty push-ups and die for France. "Surreal," sniffs a woman I know about possible female Legionnaires. "We are not interested in last-stand grandstanding."

Every year on Bastille Day, you sense the Legion's cachet. Legionnaires march slowly down the Champs-Élysées among faster-moving traditional units, thrilling the crowds with their stern, manly style. Their beards, white *képis* (short, stove-pipe hats), leather aprons, red *épaulettes* on crisp white jackets, and axes on shoulders make them a commanding sight.

The Legion bristles at suggestions it's a "mercenary" force. Interviewed in mid-2008, Lt-Col. Christian Rascle insisted that it is "a regular unit of the French army, commanded by the same officers and subject to the same discipline. It uses the same uniforms and equipment. And, unlike gun-for-hire mercenaries, recruits sign up to a permanent force."

But let's look further. France has devised a magnificently trained, all-volunteer force with passionate ideals of service. A small, fast-moving standing army that can do almost anything from stopping massacres and insurrections to managing evacuations and humanitarian relief. All in the most lethal conditions.

Isn't there another place where such a standing international force might prove useful: the United Nations? Instead of begging repeatedly in crises for often ill-prepared national contingents, why wouldn't the UN recruit only individuals – as "soldiers of fortune for peace?"

From the UN's founding in 1946, experts have fantasized about a permanent 'world army' to defend peace and security. Great Power disagreements always torpedoed such dreams. With few exceptions, sending UN troops has remained messy, panicky, and/or agonizingly slow. Waste in lives (through delay) and UN money (through perpetual improvisation) is staggering.

As of March 2008, 113 countries were contributing a total of 88,862 soldiers and police to sixteen UN peacekeeping or peace-building situations. Over fifty-seven years, about a million have served under the UN flag. Each time, the UN had to reinvent the wheel. It went out to individual states with begging-bowl for soldiers and equipment.

Over and over, the UN has had to race to patch together a plausible, tailored-to-fight force. National units struggle to mesh. Troops offered may be the wrong kind, or lack training and suitable equipment – one group had neither guns nor boots. Officers may lack experience in separating combatants, in anti-guerrilla tactics, or even in providing food.

Reforms based on the excellent 2000 Brahimi Report have improved things. But not enough to make the UN all it could be. Increasingly, and self-damningly, it is subcontracting missions to NATO, 'coalitions of the willing,' and regional-power mandates (UK in Sierra Leone, Australia in East Timor).

Something like the French Foreign Legion might meet a multitude of UN needs: speed, specialization, commitment, professionalism, economy. And political convenience: even the go-it-alone U.S. might find a "UN Legion" a handy rescue brigade, perhaps a fig-leaf for Iraq-style failure.

Such a force, with a powerful peace-and-security ethos, decent pay and a clear career path, could attract the world's best soldiers. Motivated, skilled professionals who wouldn't run from danger, as at Srebrenica, but would put themselves on the line for the UN, for peace, for innocent victims. Pride and prestige could save many lives.

Joining the Foreign Legion, as former Canadian member Evan McGorman put it, confers "an unmistakable celebrity status." There's a fellow who doesn't need the celebrity, but who's already famous for UN humanitarian causes. In the next remake of *Beau Geste*, wouldn't George Clooney look splendid in a blue helmet?

God creeps back into France

It's not easy to be God in France, though many have tried to play Him. Germans use Him as a metaphor for tourist joy; other foreigners see His churchly architecture as a tourist lure. Only the French see Him as a local deity – though also as a tricky legal problem. Never mind Voltaire's view that "If God did not exist, it would be necessary to invent Him." He's not just invented in this "godless" secular nation; with Sarkozy in power, He's turning up at every street-corner for the first time in a century.

Germans, expressing ecstasy, purr that they are "as happy as God in France." But – *Mein Gott!* – France passed a law in 1905 kicking God out of France. Well, of French public life. That includes state schools, government, and political discourse, with only a few anomalies: Many official holidays reflect the Catholic calendar; and, while believers pay clergy, the state pays for upkeep of church buildings pre-dating 1905.

The 1905 law separating church and state introduced the French particularity of *la laïcité*. This is too-narrowly translatable as 'secularism.' It means much more: The state must avoid any link, reference or deference to religion.

La laïcité has seeped into Frenchmen's marrow. Even fervent Catholics uphold it. No French president – Charles de Gaulle, Valéry Giscard d'Estaing or Jacques Chirac, for example – ever invoked God in a speech. If attending a funeral in Notre-Dame Cathedral, officially a national monument, they would not take Holy Communion. Chirac fought to banish any reference to Christianity in the preamble to the European constitution. He banned

Muslim veils and other ostentatious religious symbols in state schools.

All presidents honor Catholic, Protestant, Jewish and Muslim leaders. With the Dalai Lama becoming a demigod in France defending Tibet during the 2008 Olympics, they will also henceforth greet Buddhist ones (if only, not to offend Beijing, by the back-door). But curiously, they also regularly meet the Grand Master of the main, vigilantly *laïque* Masonic Lodge – the politically influential *Grand Orient de France.* Such meetings are close to a state ritual of agnosticism – of confirming freedom *not* to believe, as well as *to* believe.

Dramatically and on several fronts, President Nicolas Sarkozy has got religion – including "morality." He's not exactly known as a passionate church-goer – a *grenouille de bénitier* (sorry: frog in a baptismal font). A self-described "cultural Catholic," he has now been married three times and, claims ex-wife Cécilia, is a champion skirt-chaser. Money also sticks to him. When he won the presidency, he quickly increased his presidential salary by 140 percent. And investigators pursuing him in a housing scandal from his mayoral days in suburban Neuilly somehow suddenly found more pressing priorities.

But in a book barely noticed three years before he became president, and in later spectacular speeches to Catholic, Muslim and Jewish audiences, Sarkozy dragged God back into public debate. In his 2004 book called (in French) *Republic, Religions, Hope,* he revealed an affinity for issues of faith remarkable for a French politician steeped in *laïcité.* He showed fascination with religion as interior minister, a job embracing government dealings with organized religion and forbidden, brain-washing "sects." He united scattered Muslim groups into a single interlocutor for the state.

After that, he hyped faith-related morality and values at every turn. During the 2007 presidential campaign, he praised "Christian values" embedded in Europe's and France's identities. His opposition to Turkey's someday joining the European Union seems rooted in Islam's alleged 'foreignness' to the continent's Judeo-Christian values. When he slyly says: "If Turkey were part of Europe, somebody would have noticed," he's not just talking geography.

In a December 2007 Rome visit, Sarkozy thrilled Pope Benedict XVI by praising Europe's Christian roots and values: "In transmitting and learning the difference between Good and Evil," he lyricized, "the [state] schoolteacher can never replace the priest or pastor." In Riyadh soon after, he extolled to devout Saudi hosts *the transcendent God who is in the thoughts and hearts of every person*" – another astounding phrase for a president legally bound to defend state secularism. Weeks later in Paris, he told a Jewish audience that faith-based morality reflected "a transcendence all the more credible that it is declining in [our] radical society." He added that 20th-century wars happened not because of too much God, but because of the "absence of God" (Wait a minute: Wasn't Hitler an altar-boy and Stalin a seminarian?)

Why Sarkozy's new push for God? Where will it lead?

Several presidential associates – especially adviser Emmanuelle Mignon, a committed Catholic – are known as strong pro-religion advocates. Madame Mignon pressed hard for a revision of the totemic 1905 *laïcité* law. Like Sarkozy, she promotes "positive secularism" - one that "does not consider religions as a danger, but as an asset." During the September 2008 visit to Paris of Pope Benedict XVI, Sarkozy picked up and amplified this theme – to the delight of his guest.

Sarkozy – a pragmatist, not a mystic – doesn't present the "asset" of religion as a way of sneaking God back into a godless society. He ties it to national identity and unity. But few in this aggressively secular country will buy that. Legends of priest-ridden 19th-century France still buttress 1905 – making it, so to speak, gospel.

Sarkozy, an immigrant's son obsessed with belonging, will press on with his cultural-religious "symbols of memory." But instead of lighting candles, he may be playing with matches in a gas factory. Like many of his impetuous initiatives lacking public consultation, reuniting God and State risks reigniting a long-buried civil war between democrats and theocrats.

French secularists warn that Sarkozy's potential 1905 heresy hasn't a prayer of succeeding. Francophile Germans notwithstanding, might not God be happier wherever He is?

Milking cows and consumers – France's farm lobby

Parisians love their city, but yearn for the countryside. It's their weekend refuge from noise, stress and pollution. It's their annual holiday nirvana. But it's also a dream, a fantasy, a delicious fiction: that France is a country of farms and rubber-booted peasants.

In terms of exports, that's partly true. And in terms of wonderful home-grown food, absolutely true. The cost of the fantasy is, however, horrendous – in subsidies, middlemen's rake-offs, and especially the crippling of world trade talks.

*France's blocking of European Union agricultural concessions
to export-desperate developing nations flatters Parisians' visions
of a domestic rural paradise. But it kills the hopes of Third
World countries for a better life. French politicians bleat about
the fate of "poor" countries. Yet they deny the latter's low-cost
crops to French consumers – all the while bewailing the high
cost of food in Paris supermarkets.*

Barnyard fragrances: fresh sawdust, sweat, droppings of 3,000 animals in an exhibition hall the size of Brazil. The buzz and shouts of 750,000 visitors from thirty countries as they swarm 1,030 stands. Inaudible loud-speaker exhortations fight on-and-off music you just might term rock-pastoral. Slow-flowing rivers of faces convey pleasure, curiosity, wonder, a strange solemnity. For this is every French person's return to roots, a pilgrimage to ancestors, land and household gods. It's the High Mass of French civilization: Paris's annual *Salon de l'Agriculture.*

You may have heard about this thanks to an eavesdropping 2008 *YouTube* video. In it, France's perpetual-motion President, Nicolas Sarkozy, dismissed a man insulting him, letting fly: "Bugger off, you jerk!" Armies of Sarkophobes leapt on this "new gaffe" in a month where Sarko was tripping up once a day, if not twice. The next day's *YouTube* showed Sarko's nemesis, former President Jacques Chirac. A legendary friend of farmers, Chirac glided in glory through attendees' applause. Soaring in the polls as Sarko sank to 20,000 leagues under the sea, he proffered this Chesire-cat comment: "The *Salon* is the high point of the year." High, wink-wink, as in Sarko's low.

Third day, third *Salon YouTube*: Prime Minister François Fillon. France's likeable, low-key PM, ridiculed for months as invisible, floated 20 polling points above his president-boss – leading touchy Sarko to mutter about appointing a new PM. At one stand, Fillon faced a devilish choice: refuse the plump hen a farmer offered him, thus offending farmers; or accept her – even though the farmer slyly said the chicken's name was Carla, like Sarko's new instant-wife. Fillon took Carla (the chicken) home, risking Sarko's fury for inviting her to lay eggs in his rural riding.

All good fun, but froth. For the stage eclipses the actors. *Le Salon* is the setting for France's enduring self-image as a nation of peasants, indeed a people that thinks it invented eating.

Forty years ago, 20 percent of Frenchmen worked on farms. Now barely 3.5 percent do. But three factors weld even urban French to their countryside. First, they seek roots in a fast-changing, now-multicultural society: Snotty Parisians will proudly trot out muddy (in both senses) attachments to Normandy or Brittany. Amid big cities' chaos, noise and pollution, the clean air, rolling hills and long, straight vineyards of *la France profonde* seem a magic refuge.

Second, the French – while typically affecting disdain for money – adore the gigantic transfers of cash Paris siphons out of the European Union's Common Agricultural Policy (CAP). The CAP, a whopping 44 percent of the EU budget, pumps billions of euros into French agriculture every year – much of it to rich industrial farmers, not the disappearing small farmers whom unions and government like to depict in berets and clogs.

Finally, the French believe good food starts with fresh, thus home-grown, products. This ties into France's conservatism about many things new. Irrational terror of genetically modified organisms (GMOs) has led to reluctance to allow experiments proving they can be safe: vandals have even yanked up GMO test-fields. France, as the world's second largest agricultural exporter, brands itself as the homeland of authenticity – part of France's overall export brand of quality, whether for planes, trains, rockets, fashion, wine or perfume.

Backing *Salon* farmers, Sarkozy praised home-guaranteed quality. He promised France will defend preferences for European Union products. Bizarrely (he's low-brow in both cuisine and culture), he said he would ask UNESCO to declare French gastronomy part of "world heritage" – like the Taj Mahal. The Italians, who in the 16th century taught the French to cook, may demur. Chinese and others too. Soon the gastronomic Olympics?

Farm, food, wine and fine cuisine fuel a fervent national will to cherish something vital to the French soul. Much is already lost to fast food: some schools now offer courses on how to eat French-style. But France's nightmare is freer trade in agriculture. For seven years, France, driven by its tiny-but-powerful farm lobby, led Europe to scuttle trade talks (the Doha Round) aimed at cutting agricultural tariffs worldwide. In mid-2008 it did so again.

Failure's results? Selfish rejection of poor countries' exports. But ironically for France and Sarkozy, also sky-high French food prices. Elected as the "purchasing power president," Sarko then faced vilification as supermarket prices rocketed in a few months by up to 40 percent. To please 3.5 percent of the population, he makes 96.5 percent suffer. But so unquestioned is Frenchmen's support for farmers (indeed for almost any workers over consumers) that few see the link.

Want to sniff out how far the French will go to defend their string-pulling farm lobby? Come to the *Salon*. Sample the free pâtés, Camemberts and Bordeaux, maybe a tad of *foie gras*. And when your nostrils fill with barnyard aromas, remember you're scenting perfumes that seduce more French men – and women – than *Arpège* or *Ange ou Démon*. Next, will they bottle a whiff of the *Salon*? Maybe *Soupçon de Vache*?

❧

Chapter Eleven /

BURNING CARS AND DREAMS

"Is Paris burning?" November 2005 recalled Hitler's angry August 1944 query to his Paris military governor, General Dietrich von Choltitz. The general's brave refusal, for sixteen days, to obey Hitler's direct orders to reduce Paris to rubble saved the city from destruction. And it left irresistible shorthand for the flaming havoc caused sixty years later by thousands of black and Arab youth in Paris's suburban ghettos. Until then, "immigrant-origin" vandalism in Paris tended to bullying and minor theft on the *Champs-Élysées* and in the busy *Gare du Nord*. Paris itself didn't burn in 2005. But many of the often soulless, surrounding immigrant *banlieues* did. Especially in the angry, alienated, heartland *département* of Seine-Saint-Denis – 236-square-kilometer home of 1.4 million people half an hour north of Paris.

Unlike a dozen other heavily-immigrant towns of the *Île-de-France* (Paris) region, the actual *city* of Saint-Denis boasted a distinguished history and lively center. Reaching back to the year 250, its cathedral became France's royal burial-place. Resting there are 42 kings, 32 queens, 63 princes and princesses. Also unusual for the popularly-called "9-3" (not no. 93) Seine-Saint-Denis *département*: a Saint-Denis city council that, to some extent at least, resembled its multi-colored people. Along with an enlightened Communist mayor, this representation ensured that relatively few car-burning thugs came from their town.

The big problems were elsewhere in the "9-3:" in the less well governed *cités* (ghettos) around Paris. High unemployment, poor education, under-investment and racism (official and private) mixed a Molotov cocktail of fury. The accidental electrocution in Clichy-sous-Bois of two young immigrant-origin boys fleeing police lit the match. Three weeks of flaming anarchy ensued. Quickly, young black and Arab rioters played copy-cat all over France, burning cars and public facilities, and attacking police.

Book-ending the crisis, though this is after-the-fact musing, were two remarkable "9-3" Muslim women – one originally Senegalese, the other of Algerian background. Saint-Denis city councilor Rose Gomis watched with dismay as the violence started. And ghetto women's activist Fadela Amara, co-opted by President Sarkozy in 2007 to make radical changes in the *banlieues*, used her streetsmarts and rude street-slang to shake the government into adopting a wide reform agenda. Healthy changes of attitudes slowly appeared. But, as all too often in France, budgets tended to resemble a mirage.

The ghetto explodes - Rose Gomis warns

TV broke the story, including accusations that police drove two young boys to their deaths as they hid terrified, then burned alive, inside a huge Électricité de France transformer. Police, often themselves terrified at entering the immigrant ghettos, were again the symbol of a brutal, uncaring France. Within hours, fire and violence ravaged immigrant "cités" all over the country, especially around Paris. Measure the horror, the politicians' delinquency, then the wise words of a local elected official – black, Socialist, and a woman.

Cars burned in Saint-Denis, and so did anger. In this largely poor-immigrant Paris suburb where France's kings lie buried, flames lit up deep causes of France's dangerous malaise.

Every night, gangs of youths, often only fifteen to seventeen years old, set fire to hundreds of vehicles. They burned down buildings housing the very services their communities begged for: children's and mothers' clinics, old folks' and youth centers, gymnasiums. They fired real bullets at firemen struggling to extinguish hundreds of fires. They hurled Molotov cocktails at policemen, and dropped five-kilogram *pétanque* balls on them from upper stories. They murdered a middle-aged man in front of his wife and daughter. They doused a bus driver and a handicapped woman on crutches with gasoline, then threw flaming cloths on them.

The above was just a week of crisis. In an ordinary week in such dysfunctional communities, barely 15 kilometers from central Paris, only a few dozen cars burn. But street terror from Arab and African youth gangs was rampant. Young women feared gang rapes, drugs were everywhere, theft and violent crime endemic. Several million good people of modest means lived in permanent dread.

How could this be France – a civilized, modern country with its passionate motto of liberty, equality, fraternity?

Two things explained the scandal. First, the astounding disconnection of politicians from French voters. Even more than elsewhere, French politicians play in a little sand-box of their own, with their own games, their own ambitions, their own vague, impenetrable vocabulary: "social growth," "social fracture," "solidarity," damnable "ultra-liberalism." The entire French political establishment was mired in fuzzy, leftist language. But in spite of countless "plans," this rarely translated into concrete, plain-French reforms.

Law-and-order President Sarkozy made a career as interior minister of cozying up to cops and attacking anybody even looking 'anti-social.' He talked of "steam-cleaning" poor neighborhoods of thugs, denouncing "rabble" that made everybody's life hell. He had a point, but poor districts often took this as a collective insult.

Many Arab and African French were born in France, but suffer a doubly alienating identity crisis: rejection both by the French, and by their ancestral people whose culture many have lost. Confirming this, I spoke with Rose Gomis, a handsome, fortyish deputy mayor of the City of Saint-Denis. Born in Senegal of Muslim family, Ms. Gomis was a rare exception to the rule of political "exclusion." She understood well the devilishly difficult balance of "firmness and justice" that national politicians proclaimed as their goal.

She rejected violence as "completely unacceptable. Islam preaches peace," she insisted, "and respect for others." But she deplored Sarkozy's provocative language. As a street-level local politician with five children, she saw what kids saw. "Young people here cannot get an education or a job. They suffer daily humiliations – including constant identity checks. Even though born in France and loyal to France, they are rejected at every turn. They are totally without hope. So they turn even against their own communities."

Meeting then-Prime Minister Dominique de Villepin with other suburban mayors, Madame Gomis's boss, Saint-Denis mayor Didier Paillard, bluntly confronted the prime minister. Paris talked of better education, he said, but it shut schools and left one in three kids with no diploma. Paris increased minimum wages, but more people needed them. Paris promised a gimmicky "Marshall Plan" for the suburbs, but offered no money. Paris bragged about reducing violence, but police oppression only increased it. "The reality is," he argued, "that all the steps the government has taken in the past three years have mainly made life even harsher for those who already suffer most."

Rose Gomis, like Didier Paillard, believed in Saint-Denis. She believed in France and its *République*. Rising fast to deputy mayor in 2008, she was aiming higher – to national politics. Wish her luck.

Fires spread…and politicians tune their violins

As "burning Paris" became the "French Intifada," the media outdid themselves to explain why the roof blew off France's proud model of immigrant integration. So did the politicians. One far-sighted statesman warned as long ago as 1976, and several times since, that ghetto-generated violence demanded broad, brave reforms. Yet plan after suburb plan, budget after budget, these all failed. This wise and still-worried man: 2005 President Jacques Chirac. Give him high marks for perception and consistency, if not action.

As the suburbs' fiery madness spread to Paris and thirty other cities, and live bullets started to fly, President Jacques Chirac and his Prime Minister Dominique de Villepin played bad-cop-good-cop. Chirac called restoring security and public order his "absolute priority," and threatened dire sanctions for violence. A firm but conciliatory de

Villepin spelled out his emergency plan for creating opportunity, thus hope, for the hopeless young rioters. Did the two leaders' carefully measured two-step calm the "French Intifada?"

Three years later, long-term peace looks elusive. The shapeless, mercurial 2005 uprising followed a centuries-old French tradition of regime-shaking street rebellion. But it was new in nature, weapons and configuration.

First, it didn't pit 'white' French against 'white' French. Legalities aside – and the young African and Arab firebrands were mostly French-born, thus French nationals – we saw a post-colonial revolt against a former colonizer. This crisis of identity, culture and psychology remains unfinished business.

Second, weapons – Molotov cocktails, then shotguns – became ready tools of protest. But they may augur still worse: a few hotheads talked about attacking Paris with Kalashnikovs. Most novel of all, the hoodlums' key tool was the cell phone. Knowing their home *cités* inch by inch, they ran rings around terrified young police who, even in normal times, avoided their high-rise hells. Big groups broke up into elusive little bands that, minute by minute, chose new targets by phone and warned of coming police. Even France's toughest riot police, the CRS, had never seen small, mobile, peek-a-boo mobs like this – that came from nowhere, set fires, then faded before flames filled the sky.

Into the 2005 chaos stepped Prime Minister de Villepin with a mandate to define exciting new opportunities for angry youth. Assuming that restoring law and order had to come first, how convincing were his proposals? Broadly, the PM hit all the right topics. But people had heard them all before, and saw a familiar check-list, not a well-funded program commitment :

- education: new steps to prevent dropping out, and new opportunities for work-favoring apprenticeships;
- employment: streamlined efforts to match jobs to unemployed;
- housing: replacement of crime-fostering high-rises by "more human residences;"
- community-strengthening citizens' groups: a promise to restore the aid de Villepin's party had cancelled;
- discrimination: rallying the entire nation to fight it.

Fuzzy and plainly improvised, many of these ideas recycled old promises never kept. They offered neither the deep-reforming substance (especially for job creation) nor thoughtful detail – not even coherent packaging to hint at a real strategy.

Years later, of all the realities faced by the French government, the most dangerous was still France's unresolved post-colonial relationship with the peoples it used to govern. For such immigrants, France bravely chose assimilation – into a civic nationality based on citizenship, and ignoring color, culture and religion.

This model has many merits, especially its intrinsic denial of racism. But unofficial racism remains rampant in French society – in jobs, apartment rentals, even business. And as countless Arabs and blacks allege, in dealings with police. (I was once congratulated by a senior police supervisor for having "the right color."). Since interracial dating and marriage were never the taboo the U.S. knew, the French believed that racism was only for awful Anglo-Saxons.

Even Azouz Begag, author of forty books and the French-born Arab that de Villepin hand-picked as his minister for equality of opportunity, bewailed in *Le Monde* the conde-scending treatment he got in the French cabinet. A devastat-ing photo showed de Villepin patting him on the head.

Sadly, France remains paralyzed by its passionate self-image as the generous, non-racist "homeland of human rights." More than a century of gargling about its "civiliz-ing mission" left deep biases. Parliament in 2005 instructed the education ministry to highlight the "positive role" of France's colonial regime – this, even as Algerians commem-orated an infamous 1961 Paris police drowning of scores of Algerians in the Seine. Fortunately, President Chirac got the praise for colonialism killed.

France notes proudly that it gave French citizenship to many colonials, and does so also to its "overseas French" (e.g. Tahiti, Martinique).But today's suburban youth – jobless, living in run-down high-rises, and insulted by po-lice – wonder what good this is. When they refer to "the French," they don't mean themselves. They mean white Frenchmen.

Community leaders say France faces thirty years of pent-up ghetto humiliation and exclusion. Curing these will take just as long.

Familiar talk – and another hint – of reform

As television worldwide ran scenes of burning Paris suburbs, French media played back foreign reactions to aghast French audiences. Shock, shame and desperation to "do something" gripped French élites and people. For some months, and potentially longer, public-spirited French looked for ways to offer hope to alienated black and Arab youth. In 2006-07, Le Parisien daily ran a wildly popular series of immigrant-origin success stories: "parcours réussis" ("making their way"). Although ethno-cultural job-and-housing discrimination remained widespread in 2008, good-news stories began to surface: special job-fairs; big-company promises to recruit 'untraditional' candidates; encouragement for banlieues youth to start small businesses.

Three years after the chaos, what happened to France's car-burning African-and-Arab *banlieues*? A 2006 poll in the *Le Parisien* ran these "explosive" results: 86 percent of French citizens expected violence to return; barely 32 percent trusted the government to improve things; and only a dismal 17 percent believed proposed solutions would work.

All this sounded plausible. Politicians were still following their classic three-point crisis strategy: shout about suddenly discovered injustice; announce populist band-aids for which there is no money; go back to sleep. Oh yes, and go back to knifing each other with ideological stilettos first sharpened in the 18th- and 19th-centuries.

Early public pessimism was justified. Nearly all the problems behind the November youth revolt were indeed three decades old. And as often before, politicians' immediate reactions were slapdash and panicky – more save-the-ship PR than thought-out strategies.

Hope began to take hold. Promises to restore grants to voluntary associations helped ghettos take themselves in hand, even if money (as always) only trickled in. So, with 2,000 new police, did better local policing – many apartment blocks being no-go zones for police, and even firemen. So did more "merit" scholarships and privileged admissions to élite higher education: Paris's legendary *Sciences-Po* was a pioneer.

Thousands of new teaching assistants helped rescue failing high-school kids. Trial-jobs for youth wanting to consider army, police or community work tempted many. Unfortunately, a badly-explained Villepin first-job law for all youth went down in flames: unions and leftist politicians, backed by millions of misguided protesting students, torpedoed a chance to create more jobs by making hiring and firing more flexible.

Core issues still seethe: crucially, massive youth unemployment. The devil finding work for idle hands, this, unless corrected, will almost guarantee a future social explosion. Impractical education, prejudice against kids listing a Seine-Saint-Denis postal code, an immigrant mindset of defeatism, and dysfunctional families (not a few polygamous) all contribute to joblessness.

So does a sketchy regional public transportation system that makes getting to many suburban jobs a two-hour odyssey. Each time new violence erupts on trains or in stations, it revives employers' fears of dangerous young non-white males. Black and Arab girls find jobs far more readily, though still with difficulty.

Always rumbling through the *banlieues* is ethnic, cultural and post-colonial tension. Happily, some good news here. Post-riot polls all show three quarters of the French consider cultural diversity "enriching." Even so, they see achieving integration as a long, hard haul: anti-discrimination efforts for jobs and housing are roughly where they were in North America in the 1950s.

Integrating Arab and African ghetto-dwellers into mainstream France is a many-faceted puzzle. It's impossible to dismantle overnight the bleak high-rises that warehouse families and foster petty crime. Territorial segregation will continue to underpin ethnic, social and cultural segregation. Mayors of rich "white" municipalities laugh at a law obliging them to set aside 20 percent of city land for low-cost housing: ex-Neuilly mayor Nicolas Sarkozy, you may be sure, will never lean on his old springboard-town to obey the law he ignored. Unionized public schools fail ghetto kids even while next-door private ones educate them.

Some politicians realize that the November 2005 wake-up call may offer their last chance to reconcile Old and New French. Before he retired as president, Jacques Chirac declared May 10 an annual holiday to recall the "abomination" of France's slave-trade.

By shining light into France's shadows, Chirac sent to Arab and African youth – and to Old French – a powerful message of equal dignity. Eclipsing a divisive historical memory, he proposed South African-style truth and reconciliation. Might such a reframed 'integration' debate help gain time for hard reforms to bite?

All "just words" for now. But wasn't it words – like "steam-clean the scum," uttered by Interior Minister Nicolas Sarkozy – that helped set fire to 10,000 cars in three weeks?

A symbol, a voice, but where's the money? – Fadela Amara

From a poor North African Kabyle immigrant family of eleven children, 44-year-old Fadela (Fatiha) Amara witnessed outrageous prejudice all her life in France. Against North African men, but particularly (and often from their own men) against North African women. She reacted by fighting ferociously for justice within groups fighting racism, and violence against women. Her most influential achievement: creating "Ni Putes Ni Soumises" ("Neither Whores Nor Submissives") – a movement defending widely abused immigrant-origin women. This quickly seized public attention through mass marches, and by placing posters on the gates of the National Assembly. The spark for action was the burning-alive of still another young Arab girl by her ex-boy-friend – a 'custom' young Arab males (most with sisters) thought well-deserved. In the face of ridicule and every kind of opposition, Amara persevered.

President Sarkozy, to his great credit, plucked her from the political left that lionized her. He made her a junior minister for "city policy" – meaning the banlieues – with a limitless, if weakly funded, mandate. How long until her proposed reforms (assuming she keeps her job) can change things fundamentally? Start with two generations.

Both shocking and charming cabinet colleagues, rough-diamond Fadela Amara loves to rattle official teacups by trash-talking in *banlieue* slang. Of course, as a university-educated woman, she can talk high falutin' French at the drop of a subjunctive. But ghetto slang is her trademark, and her political battering-ram. It reminds everybody of why she holds her job, and of why they need to get behind her.

So too is her nose-thumbing independence. Though Sarkozy made her a minister, she loudly proclaimed that as a person "of the left" she wouldn't vote for him in the 2012 presidential election. Of course, there was an "unless"…but she made her point, and Sarkozy was the first to smile. Not because he saw her as court jester, but because he saw her as his best hope of winning back the *banlieues* he had offended with his tough-cop talk as interior minister.

Amara's *Espoir Banlieue* ("Suburb Hope") plan inevitably addresses all the issues turning up in previous reports: employment, housing, education, health, culture, sports, town-planning, transportation, security. When Sarkozy showcased her plan in a February 2008 Élysée Palace press conference before 1,000 people, he promised to find money for the plan – without saying how. The state is virtually bankrupt, says his Prime Minister François Fillon. Sarkozy only warned that youth – used to hanging around doing nothing – would have to "get up in the morning" and "take their own lives in hand." Failing that, the state would do "nothing" for them.

On the vital issue of housing, the plan promised to destroy crime-infested high-rises, replacing them with much lower-rise housing that people would be helped to buy. Where will people live during the transition? No one seems to have planned that – as with many other reforms.

Generally, Amara's *banlieue* people welcomed her plans. But they had seen plans come and go, and these all tended to resemble each other. Observed social critic Julien

Damon: "Over and over, we see 'new priorities' defining 'new priorities' previously defined."

Amara has many fans, and plenty of cordial critics. Regularly polling among the top five most popular ministers, she impresses a wide audience with her authenticity and commitment.

But if the people are on her side, her government allies aren't always. Governing-caucus colleagues went ballistic when Amara attacked as "disgusting" a government decision forcing DNA tests on immigrants. Her supervising minister, Christine Boutin, is plainly jealous of Amara's popularity and influence. An uptight, family-values Catholic, Boutin can't easily relate to a free-wheeling, tough-talking Muslim far more media-savvy than she. She even publicly contradicted Amara's entire strategy of a tailored-to-measure *banlieue* housing policy.

There are four keys to Amara's eventual success. First, will Sarkozy support her long enough – say, a few years – to allow her ideas to bite? Chances are good. Second, will the government keep its word to fund *banlieue* programs generously and long-term? With France's economy in late 2008 slowing dramatically, this is far from sure. Highly competent finance minister Christine Lagarde is not Snow White with a magic wand to produce cash. She is Old Mother Hubbard whose cupboard is bare. Yet failure to staff and fund government programs will destroy hope already stirred to high levels.

Third, can Sarkozy, Fillon and Amara keep bureaucrats from drowning reforms in their usual festival of paper? Power games, busy-body interventions and suffocating regulation have killed thousands of worthy programs. So has delay over timing and priorities. Rachid Kaci, a Sarkozy adviser, has already argued that "the money exists, but we need to spend it more wisely. Painting elevators when we know we're going to level the building makes no sense." But who knows if and when the building will get leveled?

The fourth key is public support for *banlieue* reform and rejuvenation. This means changing "white" Frenchmen's minds about the vast multicultural challenge underway. It means welcoming blacks and North Africans into mainstream society in all its dimensions.

The central issue – employment – conditions all the others. For jobs circulate wealth, anchor new businesses and, above all, give dignity and purpose to youth with neither. Good news: spontaneously in 2008, and surely awakened by the 2005 riots, large private businesses had begun systematic efforts to recruit young people from the ghettos. That year the national railway (SNCF), retail-chain *Carrefour*, construction firm *Eiffage*, car-makers *PSA-Citroën* and *Renault* made 12,000 such job offers. Amara aims for 100,000 new ghetto jobs in three years.

This last news is better than a dozen loudly-touted but under-funded government plans. For it means that French firms are no longer seeing suburban kids only as a crime problem. They are starting to see them as a business opportunity. Turning problems into opportunities: Just what Fadela Amara, in her rough, witty and perceptive language, has tried to do all her life.

Chapter Twelve /

WHO GOVERNS FRANCE?

Politics in France is an acquired taste. And an addictive one: issues and personalities seem both graver and more fun than elsewhere. Understanding what's going on is easy. You just need a thorough mastery of French and European history; a compulsion to read newspapers and newsmagazines (both 'serious' and satirical); willingness to digest a few polemical books every year; a love of gossip; and a healthy liver for attending lunches, dinners and receptions where politics is on the menu – as invariably it is, whatever the ostensible topic.

Before going far, you're reminded that politics – inverting von Clausewitz – is war by other means. And war is hell, *non*? It's lethal, dirty, slimy, sneaky, treacherous, furious, confusing, and rife with pathological vanities. The bug of ambition infects most often victims of early humiliation. So does the lust for lucre, though practitioners of politics' dark arts explain their larceny as public-spirited (e.g. financing their party instead of their holidays) or as a fair price to compensate "underpaid" servants of people and state.

In France, politicians' wish to serve both is so intense that most national parliamentarians simultaneously hold municipal – and even regional and/or European Parliament posts. Their beautiful rationale: To do a good job nationally, you need to stay "close to the people" (in a village, for example) or "close to the big issues" (as in Brussels). It would be rude to note that these multiple mandates provide multiple salaries, pensions, offices, staff and official cars. Rude also to observe that if a national parliamentarian loses his or her seat, another well-paid job sits handy to provide a financial cushion – and a launching pad for the next election. Once you crack the little world (*"le microcosme"*) of French politics, you're set for life. If that means you must bear living high on the hog, as the crass might say, no problem: the French, all monarchists in their guts, want their betters to live well. Especially with access, wherever they are, to a *bonne table*. In the end, it's only money. And it's just as things should be.

La rue – leading the people from behind

When you think of French democracy, perhaps you see demonstrations. "Taking to the street," for many history-obsessed French, passes for the normal way to get what you want. Dismiss the parliamentarians and ombudsmen in boring Anglo-Saxon and northern democracies. To defend your cause (or selfish interest), mobilize a mob. Give them slogans, signs and cheerleaders, then send them out to raise hell in front of TV cameras. When they pass the cameras, their festive faces will turn to snarls and fury: They must convey the impression they might break something, ideally, a minister's career. Marchers' numbers and threats are supposed to intimidate the government into backing down from whatever policy it plans. And traditionally, most of the time the government will swear "never" – then cave in. The idea: Convince the public (more potential mobs!) that agitators really decide things, elected 'leaders' being mere followers.

Nicolas Sarkozy believes he can cripple demo-mania, just as he will change everything in France, including the weather.

He bragged in mid-2008 that nobody paid attention to dem-onstrations or strikes anymore. The French, one surmises, would become Swedes. Ponder how likely that is from the 2006 misery of Jacques Chirac's then-Prime Minister Domi-nique de Villepin...a case where the mob won hands down, and thumbs-down on poor Villepin.

Laughing crowds, clowns, trumpets, whistles, drums, bullhorn-led chants, dancers, fireworks, banners demon-izing reform. A good-humored celebration for over a million youth, workers, old folks and children, led by linked-armed union and left-wing party leaders. Welcome to street democracy, French-style.

Teenage girls swarmed, then beaten up and robbed in downtown Paris. Boys on the ground kicked by hoodlums wielding baseball-bats. Small shopkeepers and news ven-dors assaulted and their livelihoods destroyed as politicians dither, policemen struggle, and judges suspend sentences. Schools, roads and railway stations blockaded, with stu-dents and unionists telling TV: "The street governs!" Weigh now the price France pays for romanticizing anarchy.

"The street" in healthy democracies means a road you cross. In dictatorships, it means the gossip of discontent, as in "Arab street." In France, it means 'mobocracy' – festi-vals of hyped-up anger, leftist sloganeering, fat-cat unions, coddled law-breakers, and a general belief that, in the end, a legally elected government should bow to the threat of violence. It's France's national sickness: *manifs*, or disrup-tive demonstrations. And it 'demonstrates' only one thing: the failure of representative democracy.

As so many times in its turbulent history, France in early 2006 again let mobs defeat elected leaders. First, President Jacques Chirac, to salvage his impetuous prime minister, Dominique de Villepin, said he would promulgate Villepin's "CPE" (first-job contract) youth employment law. This seemed to reject the street's demand that he withdraw the law. But in the next breath, he caved in to the street. He promised a new law to gut the CPE of the two clauses giving it a chance to create jobs: a two-year probation period (then one) and employers' right to dismiss underperforming kids without going through France's costly, kafkaesque labor tribunals. He simultaneously proclaimed the law... and suspended it.

This bizarre charade fooled no one. Villepin, disavowed, had lost his tough-guy gamble of defying the street. The new watered-down law echoed calls for "compromise" by his bitter rival for the 2007 presidency, Interior Minister Nicolas Sarkozy – now, humiliatingly, replacing the PM as point man on Villepin's signature CPE. Saving Villepin's face, Chirac avoided the hot-button word "withdrawal" opponents demanded. But this only further provoked the street. The leftist coalition of unions, students and politicians promised a fifth demonstration (The marches lasted from February to April).

The government feared youth agitation would draw in a broader, older public. Most dangerously, the chaos was rallying jobless youth from the boiling immigrant ghettos, scenes of the November 2005 car-burning violence. If new "contestation" united workers, general public, students and these immigrant *banlieues*, France would face hard-to-contain trouble.

Why does France allow street psychodramas to poison its democracy? First, as always, history. You can trace France's love of tumult to 14th –century pitchfork *jacqueries*, the 1789 storming of the Bastille, the 1830 revolt and 1848 "February Revolution," and the 1871 workers'

Commune – the latter updating class war with Marxist doctrine. The May 1968 student revolt drew ten million people into a general strike and eventually brought down De Gaulle. Strikers and mobs protesting welfare and pension reform also gutted Prime Minister Alain Juppé's plans in 1995.

Second, psychology. Intimately tied to "equality," street-sovereignty is the most powerful political idea in France. It is the threat-flaunting defense of hard-won privilege. Ordinary Frenchmen love to see people defying authority – as though elected politicians ("all crooks!") were elected by Martians. They tend to back marchers' privileges, hoping the street will back their own tomorrow.

Third, the élite's "autism." Villepin rammed his CPE through Parliament, consulting mainly, it seems, the ghosts of his heroes Bonaparte and De Gaulle. The CPE aimed to make it easier to hire young people. Impenetrable explanations (plus knee-jerk leftist disinformation), convinced most people it only aimed to ease *firing*.

Fourth, France's ambient leftist ideology. The CPE became a trampoline for every discontent tied to "precarity:" jobs, healthcare, pensions – especially bug-bear globalization. In all these fears seethed distrust of free enterprise – hated "ultra-liberalism." Roughly two-thirds of France's population questioned the market economy in which France lived.

Finally, culture. Demonstrations feed French people's love of drama, circuses and celebrations. "Everything ends with a song," as we noted earlier. But beneath the crowds' clowning, spoiled-child defiance of elective democracy, and Red Square-style sloganeering, lie values far from fun. Street bullying is not democracy. It is fascism of the Left.

Systematic contempt for elected politicians, and identification with the street, lead to fuzzy thinking. Beaten-up 2006 demonstrators deplored that "some people use violence to ruin our beautiful rebellion." They forgot that their beautiful rebellion was *rooted* in violence – including law-breaking blockades and frivolous transport strikes harming millions of travelers.

The sanest voice on street mobs in France in the early years of this 21st century: again the omnipresent Nicolas Sarkozy. As interior minister, then president, he has tirelessly and correctly judged street violence. Not as a romantic revolt. But as an assault on democracy. The French all want fraternity – but to get it, maybe they need to back "Sarko" on Liberty, Equality, Security.

Getting the 'drift' of French politics

It's all in their heads. But politicians' heads set policies, vote budgets, launch actions. Even if theories were born centuries before, some ideas still command legions of believers. And France's true political believers are almost all on the left, for as in many countries left-wingers adore splitting hairs, evoking icons, recalling great rebellions – and excommunicating heretics. Many would rather analyze than decide, argue than accomplish, be right than be in power.

The moderate-left Socialist Party follows the pattern. Forming circular execution squads firing inward, it has struggled with noxious rivalries – would-be leaders faking fealty to beloved ideological gods. Why change now? Just to get elected?

If you want practicality in politics, turn right. People right of center tend to downplay theory for reality. For graspable (in every sense), hands-on stuff like office, power and money.

While doing good (if necessary!), they hope to do well. And in doing well, they classically argue, others will do well too: trickle-down serendipity.

"She was as pure as the driven snow – too bad she drifted." That old groaner haunts Ségolène Royal, the mould-breaking politician fighting her party's old guard to win the Socialist Party's blessing as both chairman ("first secretary") and, for the second time, candidate in France's 2012 presidential election – in 2007, remember, she lost to Nicolas Sarkozy. The "drifting" jibe doesn't target Madame Royal's morals, though jealous enemies strain to dismiss her as a bimbo. It excoriates her alleged betrayal of socialist truth – the caviar-left's fast-crumbling citadel of shibboleths.

The accusation many nominal colleagues constantly fling at "Ségo" is that she commits the crime of *la dérive*, meaning drift. In France, where ideology often counts more than ideas or even facts, the notion of drift implies there's an orthodoxy to drift from. How so?

Beneath France's diverse society lie two rigidities. One is Catholicism, the other Marxism: in popular parlance, *les cathos et les cocos* (Communists). Both follow dogmatic systems proclaiming official truths and condemning *dérives*.

Both Catholicism and socialism take a good-vs.-bad view of society, of virtuous vs. sinners. The eggheads call that "Manichean" – a five-euro word for black-or-white. The resulting mindset – of received wisdom fighting free thought – defines France's public discourse in schools, universities, culture, media, trade unions and politics. Always leftward.

Some French do hold right-wing opinions. Fascists, monarchists, even a handful of free-market fans stir France's rich brew of marginal viewpoints. But *mainstream public discussion* glorifies worker-peasant revolt. It's the *pensée unique* – an all-pervasive, left-leaning worldview. It portrays state-imposed equality as virtuous, and individual initiative as inherently selfish.

The doctrine's foundation, we have seen, is the bloated, reactionary, 1.3-million-strong Ministry of Education. We saw earlier that even a mildly reformist Socialist minister, Claude Allègre, termed it the "Red Army" and the "Mammoth." Studies show over 75 percent of its employees voting Socialist, Communist or Trotskyite. A 2006 book by Éric Brunet called (in French) "Leaning Right: a French Taboo" documents chillingly how leftist (especially Communist Party) unions dictate curricula, make and break careers, even fire ministers. To kids from childhood through high-school, they teach their Economics 101: class war, with oppressed workers fighting greedy capitalists.

The bias damages universities too. Although the élite *Grandes Écoles* (for engineering, business and public administration) score well internationally, only two of France's 82 state universities – which allow high-school grads basically free, automatic entry – broke into Shanghai's *Jiao Tong University* top 100 in 2008. Curricula, hiring and promotion of profs, approval of theses – broadly toe the Marxist line. "Drifting" rightward equals excommunication.

Such one-sided schooling colors all society. Culture? Although private philanthropy is growing, the state dominates, despising freelance initiatives. Photographer Helmut Newton offered his lifetime collection of tastefully erotic photos to France; bureaucrats drove it to Berlin. Billionaire

François Pinault offered to build a Paris museum for his huge collection of modern art – sandbagged too long, he moved it to Venice.

Media? Ink-stained wretches worldwide tend to lean left. But in modern democracies, they can express a variety of political views. Not so easy in Paris. Unless you work for the financial press, moderate *Le Figaro*, or the exceptional newsmagazine *Le Point*, you might as well admit a small axe-murder as confess you're right-wing. Common advice to free-market believers: "Keep your opinions to yourself, and pretend you're *de gauche*."

With the above rare exceptions, media are overtly left-wing. When leftist sociologist Pierre Bourdieu died, we saw that revered daily *Le Monde* made him its main headline... *two days in a row*. Often the word "liberal" (meaning free-market) gets written "ultra-liberal." *Dérives,* in a black-or-white leftish universe, are by definition extreme.

Unions? Despite widespread belief, France is one of the least unionized countries in the world: about eight percent of workers hold union cards vs. a European average of thirty percent. But they dominate public services, where one in four active Frenchmen works. Result: their frequent strikes cause havoc: hundreds of rail strikes every year, several of them national. Air travel, subways, postal service, electricity and gas are all regular hostages. The unions running things are Marxist, hard- or soft-core. They protect retirement at 50 for some, fat pensions and exorbitant holidays – a minimum four weeks' paid annual vacation (many get six), plus eleven other days off – not to mention the virtually-dead 35-hour week (closer to 25 for some public servants).

Such is the country Madame Royal wants to lead. It has some of the world's smartest business bosses, but they are demonized, even as their world-beating firms (*Danone, L'Oréal*), are termed national "crown jewels." Nominally right-wing former President Jacques Chirac warned that "liberalism is as dangerous as communism." Royal promised to "frighten the capitalists."

Running up to the 2012 presidential election, almost everybody will play to the left-wing gallery. Even Sarkozy will continue rushing to defend enterprises judged "national champions" or "strategic," whether or not the state holds shares.

Chortling in the gallery, surrounded by graduates of the Education Ministry's "Red Army," camps Karl Marx. The Socialists try half-heartedly to dump him. But he'll likely stick around. He's too handy a bludgeon for cowing party enemies. He's why, for example, Royal got hammered for hinting that middle-of-the-road Tony Blair might have a few decent ideas. This was, as her doctrinaire colleagues growled, an unforgivable *dérive blairiste.* You get the drift.

Shaving in the Élysée Palace

Throughout much of this book, we've seen how the passionate personality and frenetic activity of Nicolas Sarkozy have touched France in countless ways. France has gone in a couple of years from "Sarkomania" to (say the shrinks) "Sarkosis." During the last lap of his ascension to the presidency, the French watched him with hope and horror, excitement and execration. An astonishingly complex man, "Sarko" is ambition incarnate. He plotted his rise since late teenage years, and did whatever it took to push, charm, seduce, maneuver and manipulate to reach his presidential goal. Many called him "unscrupulous" for tricking, betraying or shoving aside friends, mentors and allies. But he never made a secret of his goal. And he made his way as a textbook professional: a clear vision, tireless work, tactical agility, an uncanny ability to read the public, fearlessness, absolute self-confidence and awesome communication skills, especially for TV.

Sarkozy's restlessness and impulsiveness have cost him many fans. His too-advertised marital adventures dismayed his own social-conservative base. And foreign statesmen came both to admire and abhor him: his frantic hugging and mike-grabbing grated. Probably also they envied his stamina, that often-neglected ingredient of political success: During ten days in August 2008, after running briefly to Beijing for the Olympics opening, he raced to Tbilisi and Moscow to negotiate a ceasefire, then flew to Kabul for a few hours to console French troops who had just lost ten men to the Taliban. In between, he snagged a short holiday with his wife Carla…punctuated by endless phone calls as EU president and a Riviera visit by Condoleezza Rice.

Like him or loathe him, you must agree he earned his job. Let's recall how he looked the night of his presidential triumph. Then how, a few months later, he was already rocketing around France and the world like the Energizer Bunny – reforming this, that, and whatever else he stumbled upon.

Nouveau Napoleon with a law degree and five-centimeter platform shoes, Nicolas Sarkozy can now shave in the Élysée Palace. In 2003, in a protocol-defying answer for a sitting minister, he admitted he dreamt of being president of France – "and not only when I'm shaving." Over twenty years, "Sarko"'s white-hot ambition seared its way through conservative party ranks, burning up traditions, policies, loyalties and rivals. Brilliant, informed, tireless, a master of sound-bites, he's a political animal to the marrow. His lifelong hobby-horse, with France along for the ride: *moi.*

On the night of May 6, 2007, TV screens across France flashed his photo on the dot of 8 p.m., telling 64 million French that the "little guy from Neuilly" (a wealthy Paris suburb where he was raised) had finally made it. Decisively: an estimated 53 percent versus 47 percent for his remarkable Socialist rival, Ségolène Royal. The most colorful, ground-breaking presidential campaign in memory was over – its 85 percent-plus turnout testimony to French democracy's vigor.

Now France braces for Sarko's "rupture" – his term for hauling France into reform by the scruff of the neck.

Bring on the shrinks. They instantly spot how a little boy with a cruel, absent father found his passion to succeed. His dad, Pál Sárközy de Nagybocsa, came from Hungary's petty nobility. Dispossessed by the Soviets, Pál joined France's Foreign Legion. Dropping around to see his kids, he would tell little Nicolas that "with your name, France will never accept you." And "with your school marks, you'll never amount to anything." Add to that what every great man needs – a rock-strong mother – and Sarko was programmed to race to the top, trampling everybody in his path.

Raised by his struggling mother Andrée, Nicolas knew constant humiliation. He was short, 'foreign' and socially awkward. Unlike his richer classmates, he took odd jobs to earn spending money. As a teenager, he plotted revenge to 'show' everybody: he would become president of France.

Missing his diploma at Paris's prestigious *Institut d'Études Politiques*, Sarkozy graduated in law and set up a two-man real-estate business. Quickly bored, he gravitated to the neo-Gaullist party, wowing leader Jacques Chirac with a passionate speech. As Chirac's protégé, he had it made. Taking youthful charisma and precocious Machiavellism to the hustings, he elbowed aside another mentor to snag the Neuilly mayoralty at age 28. There he made his name by talking a maniac out of blowing up a kindergarten full of kids.

For the next twenty years, "Sarko" scampered up the ladder. His tools: a laser eye for popular issues, hard work, discipline, omni-directional networking, an obsession with self-promotion. He won powerful friends, while intimidating many others. His reputation for using his big-business and media pals to advance himself, and cow enemies, sticks to him like napalm.

He poached far-right voters, yet sickened many others with immigrant-bashing (meaning blacks and Arabs). Then – ever weaving, ever balancing – he tried to soften his tough-guy image. He deplored leftist campaigns to demonize him as a latter-day Hitler. He spoke of love and tolerance, actually portraying himself as a victim – to guffaws from his own self-perceived victims. Outraging Socialists, he even made a speech co-opting their historic heroes – Gambetta, Jaurès, Blum. As president, he seduced several Socialist stars with ministries, splitting an angry, confused Socialist Party.

Polls showed voters fully aware of Sarko's nasty side (he threatened to hang a mud-slinging enemy on a meat-hook) and volcanic angers – artfully hidden in the final Sarko-Ségo TV debate. But on competence, "solidity" and ability to deliver a coherent set of solutions to France's problems, he beat Royal handily. Eager for change even while fearing it, French voted for a strongman who knew exactly what he wanted and how to get it.

In a spectacular victory speech, Sarkozy called the environment France's "foremost combat." Internationally, he promised strong French commitment to Europe – desperately needed after French and Dutch referenda killed Europe's constitutional treaty two years before. (He succeeded with a new "mini-treaty" – shot down by Irish voters in June 2008). He swore to rebuild bridges to America. He proposed a new Mediterranean Union – hinting at an assist by France to Mideast peace-making. He vowed France's support for the world's brutalized women, children and hostages.

Eighteen months after winning, Sarkozy had delivered the goods on most of the above. And he had rammed through the most ambitious free-market economic reforms in French history. He had kept his word and produced a "rupture" with everything that had frozen France in amber.

On that ecstatic May 2007 election night, he spoke with the ferocious pride of a little "foreign" boy made good. And who knew, without a doubt, that he was about to take France on the ride of a generation.

Paris(h)-pump politics

National politics in France is the circus; the bread (and butter) of citizens' concerns is local politics. National media, especially TV, so invade voters' mind-space that it's easy to think the power-games of the Élysée Palace (president),

*Matignon (prime minister), the National Assembly and the
Senate constitute France's entire political life. Dip your toe into
municipal concerns and enjoy different, and just as illuminating, realities.*

"All politics is local," famously noted Tip O'Neill,
longtime speaker of the U.S. House of Representatives.
Even at the summit of politics, France's national figures
never forget it. For politicians know that being president
or prime minister, or just run-of-the-mill minister, you'll
never be more important than a mayor of one of France's
36,783 villages, towns or cities. Imagine: mattering every
day in people's lives, and daily eye-balling your masters the
"people."

Why does local life count so much for the French? Why
is a mayor a demigod in his or her domain? What might
befall you if you got closer to local power?

The French attach themselves to villages to reconnect
with an old, intimate France, a France that tells them things
never change. Refuges to know neighbors, revere absurd
local customs, and argue over down-to-earth problems.
Big cities, especially Paris, often uproot citizens from such
places. From places where a mayor, a teacher, a priest, a
doctor and a notary used to (and still often do) give society
structure and stability.

Familiar institutions also comfort. Travel anywhere in
France. In all but the smallest *commune*, you'll find rep-
licas of "republican" (national) life: a *mairie* (city hall),
a post office – and in larger towns a tax, social- security,
and/or *Gendarmerie* presence. If you're lucky: a *médi-
athèque* or multimedia library subsidized by Paris's culture
ministry.

Want to feel you're really running France? Become a village mayor. Get a French passport, live in your target-town, launch a populist party likely to win a majority – then talk of fixing everything that's not working. If your people win a majority or dominate a coalition, you win. Then you get to improve elementary schools, repair roads and sewers, marry people, fool the media – and, best if all, drape a *tricolore* "republican sash" across your tight little tummy. A vital accessory for civic ceremonies, solemn events and enthusiastic ribbon-cutting.

Mayors can simultaneously be a senator or member of the National Assembly. Nearly all national mandate-holders, we've seen, keep a local footing as mayor. Even if you're mayor of Sainte-Marie-des-Petites-Folies (pop. 83), you're a somebody. You're wielding hands-on power.

In the loose confederation of villages that is Paris, my village was until recently the Sixth *arrondissement*. Being an ambitious local patriot, I thought I should nudge the door ajar for a crack at the 6th's huge and influential *mairie*. (A fabulous trampoline for a shot at the 2012 French presidency!). As a long-term resident, I would need a couple of years to snag French nationality. Before the Élysée Palace, I could begin putting myself on the radar-screen for my *mairie du sixième*.

My first move: draw attention to myself as a public-spirited sort-of-citizen. For years, cars had illegally parked all along my sidewalk on rue d'Assas, forcing children, old ladies and me to step into the path of buses. I launched a campaign to have the Sixth's mayor, Jean-Pierre Lecoq, install car-blocking posts along the curb. He refused, citing a survey claiming my street neighbors didn't want them. My answer: "*Monsieur le Maire*, I am surprised that you give a slapdash poll precedence over the law. I suggest you choose one of three options: a) publicly admit you're incapable of upholding a simple, clear law; b) claim the law's an ass; or c) announce that if any old lady or child gets killed when forced off the curb, it's their own stupid fault."

I then organized a petition spelling all this out. In reserve, I had a plan to organize the *Front de Libération des Piétons (FLP or* Pedestrian Liberation Front*)*, a gray-panther cell of seniors who, at night, would let air out of the tires of illegally parked cars and stick view-blocking, hard-to-scrape-off FLP stickers on offenders' windshields. Meanwhile, the posts went up: I had cowed Lecoq.

On a roll, I applied to become (by lottery) a member of my official sub-district's *Conseil de Quartier*, a *Mairie*-sponsored advisory group to promote citizen participation in local democracy. I got lucky, and became a *conseiller de quartier*. I soon got a letter telling me to come to our first meeting – "to collect the flyers and posters" I was to distribute. And to bring my own sandwich.

Lecoq got another letter. "*Monsieur le Maire*, I signed up for bottom-to-top democracy. But I see you only want top-to-bottom democracy. As a result, I have the honor to resign. I am sure that with all the unemployment in our *arrondissement,* you will have no trouble hiring workers to do your PR."

Monsieur Lecoq was devastated, I know, to learn that his constituent from hell had moved to the Fifth *arrondissement.* Duly informing the police (who were surely on my tail), I was relieved to note that on my new residency paper they got my address wrong *twice,* and stamped it upside down. Just like Lecoq's local democracy.

Adam Smith's "invisible (political) hand"

France is no longer run by the mythical "Two Hundred Families" that Premier Édouard Daladier denounced in 1934 as masters of France's economy. But it does boast powerful companies whose owners and leaders are intimate with the highest political authorities. French capitalism, historically an incestuous affair, features a number of world stars. But behind its old-boy networks and traditional secrecy, it sometimes tolerates rather loose ethics —including a stunning lack of accountability. A politically worrisome trend is a vicious triangle of back-scratching: defense firms buy media companies to promote their weapons; their media support the defense industry's political friends; then the politicians buy new airplanes and ships, and around we go. That's oversimplifying, but not by much. Big business, including some of its wayward children, does indeed have a hand in politics. And it's not very invisible.

Bloated, top-hatted, puffing a big cigar. That's France's standard newspaper caricature of a successful businessman. The businessman's a woman? Drop the cigar, and load the lady down with a *Prada* mega-bag spilling euro-bills all over those stiletto heels – with detachable stilettos.

In France's always history-tinged society, money is not the root of all evil. It *is* evil – if possessed by somebody else. For many, great financial success is *prima facie* evidence of crookedness. Nineteenth-century French socialist-anarchist philosopher Pierre-Joseph Proudhon coined the famous phrase: "Property is theft." And today's envy-satisfying "fortune tax" (ISF) is all Proudhon: as we saw, it hits personal *assets* (not income) exceeding 770,000 euros.

Proudhon was briefly a friend of Karl Marx. Their hate-the-rich mindset infects much of French society to this day. They didn't invent this antagonism – thuggish kings and aristocrats did. But today's union leaders and socialist politicians – the "caviar left" – make a good living off it. In tones of outrage and resentment, they peddle a politics of envy: Anybody who leaps too far ahead of his turn or class is fishy – or unfairly connected.

Top capitalists in France have helped justify lefties' suspicions that the old nobility still runs France. Until 2005, chief spokesman for big business was a man with a red-flag moniker: Baron Ernest-Antoine Seillière de Laborde. Drawing on still-lively aristocratic presumptions, France's right-wingers love the *L'Oréal* ad: you are rich "because you deserve it."

And others don't. Historically, bitterest contempt for workers poisoned the coal and iron industries. France's 19th-century Industrial Revolution rested largely on coal, steel, armament and textiles. As in Charles Dickens's Britain, mine-owners brutalized workers, young and old. Zola's searing novel *Germinal* laid bare boss's greed and inhumanity.

The steel industry, grouped in a cabal called the *Comité des Forges* (run by a Seillière ancestor in the 1880s), rigged prices, formed an oligarchy, and notoriously influenced politics. Its name lives in infamy today. The corruption of its successor body, the *Union des industries et métiers de la métallurgie* (UIMM), is behind 2008's hottest scandal. Its boss, Denis Gautier-Sauvagnac, was caught misappropriating millions of euros for personal use. And, as he chastely put it, for "fluidifying social relations." Translation: secretly bribing union leaders to restrain their members.

Gautier-Sauvagnac's grand severance package (later trimmed) drew fury – feigned by in-the-know colleagues. Hand-in-till exits have tarnished executives in many countries. But in 2007 and 2008, France saw a long line of golden parachutes darken capitalism's already-dodgy image: at, for example, blue-chip companies *France Télécom, Carrefour, Alstom, Alcatel* and *Airbus*. In the U.S. and other western countries, anger at huge greed – if not leading to lawsuits – usually blows over as exceptional. In France, it feeds into centuries-old fury at abusive upper classes.

Further blackening free enterprise: a back-scratching culture of impunity for incompetent bosses. If not recycled elsewhere by fellow élite-school graduates, failed CEOs often just brazen it out. Remember the *Société Générale* banking scandal in early 2008 when a rogue trader lost nearly seven *billion* dollars? You'd think the top boss would have resigned. After half a year and more, Daniel Bouton saw no reason for *hara kiri*.

Another, more insidious, danger: some French arms manufacturers buy media companies. Cynics claim this allows arms merchants to use media to sell weapons, then gloss over sales to government at inflated prices. Without claiming that: *Groupe Lagardère* owns a chunk of *EADS* (European Aeronautics, Defence and Space). It also holds forty-seven magazines (including famous *Paris Match*) and a raft of influential newspapers. *Dassault Aviation* builds the jet-fighter *Rafale*. It also owns moderate right-wing Paris daily *Le Figaro*.

But forget stereotypes. What's positive? France fields some of the world's best global companies and sharpest executives. *Michelin* tires set world standards. *Danone* hooks new millions of people on yogurt. *Capgemini* (computer services), *Accor* (hotels), *Bouygues* (heavy construction), *Sanofi-Aventis* (pharmaceuticals) and *Air France* (absorbing *KLM)* are world leaders.

The *CAC 40* (Paris Bourse blue-chip stocks) lists a cornucopia of French brilliance. Anne Lauvergeon, a tough, daring leader, runs *Areva*, France's uniquely successful nuclear-energy company. Carlos Ghosn, miracle-making boss of *Renault*, saved *Nissan* from near-death and is now pioneering all-electric cars. At the top, France is outstanding at business. It remains an excellent place to invest.

Far down the ladder, sadly, French free enterprise still faces government and union hostility. Any small-business owner will tell you that getting started, and surviving, is guerrilla war. It means fighting against crushing bureaucracy, profit-eating taxes, and that 1,680-page Labor Code that exposes small-business bosses to the caprices of lazy employees and crusading inspectors. Recent progress promises change. But like a dash through molasses.

No top hats for heroic independent bakers, barbers, taxi-drivers, news-vendors or start-up risk-takers. And no cigars. But the smoke of history lingers, blinding enterprise's antagonists to where France's splendid *baguettes* and sweet butter really come from.

Bye-bye Lenin, hello Supertramp

Irretrievably identified with the horrors of Soviet Communism (not to mention Chinese, Cambodian and other blood-soaked regimes), the French Communist Party was for much of the 20th-century the most Stalinist of all Western Marxist parties. Yet when the Berlin Wall fell in 1989, it saw no reason to hide its name; just its shame. Overnight, it chose to forget the disgraceful parts of its history: blindly backing the Soviet empire and acting as a Cold War fifth column against France's democracy. Today, it prefers to remember only the good parts – the best one being its heroic role in the later years of anti-Nazi Resistance. Is it petty to recall that before Hitler invaded Russia on June 22, 1941 the Party loudly applauded the August 23, 1939 Molotov-Ribbentrop Pact (aka the "Nazi-Soviet Alliance") carving up Poland? Not at all.

No Stalin she, but a cuddly blonde 59-year-old granny. But Marie-George Buffet is boss of France's once-powerful Communist Party, now in possibly terminal decline.

Basics: for decades after World War II, the party (PCF) held roughly a fifth of all National Assembly seats. As Soviet archives later proved, Moscow dictated every significant twist and turn of PCF policy – even key personnel choices. President François Mitterrand's moderate left-wing governments (1980s–'90) crippled the PCF by putting Communist members in cabinet. As partners in an "exploitative" system, the PCF began a long, slow slide into irrelevancy.

As a May 2007 presidential candidate, Mme. Buffet won the lowest PCF popular vote in history: 1.93 percent. This stripped it of state funding, pushed its newspaper *L'Humanité* into near-bankruptcy, and forced the PCF to rent out part of its headquarters.

The huge annual Communist Party celebration I attended in September 2008 – *la Fête de l'Huma* – was your favorite country-fair multiplied by ten. Families, youth, old folks and handicapped of all races coursed through the crowded alleys. They were here as a family, and this was a cultural sharing as much as a political crusade. Most came for innocent fun: rides, rock-music, games, booths selling trinkets, toys, food, clothing and anything else to make a modest capitalist buck.

But there were differences. Many booths pleaded on behalf of unfortunates at home and abroad. Serious political debates drew rapt listeners, everybody preaching to the left-wing converted. An impressive book tent spread out volumes leaning to the political, social and economic. Volunteers stood ready to guide you, even to find you a ride home from the out-in-the-boonies fair-ground.

The "*Fête,*" attended even by political rivals, was also a quasi-religious get-together. But it was 'revivalist' mainly in the sense that a dying party needed reviving. Slogans everywhere reassured: "Onward to victory!" "Together to defeat the right!" "A troubled world needs change!"

The PCF, however, had trouble changing its own mind. Its basic ideas were frozen in time: free enterprise is evil, America is evil, globalization is evil ("See today's worldwide economic shocks?"), and pretty well everybody is evil, or at least profoundly misguided – except the left, and one is not even sure about certain comrades.

In an interview beside another buffet (superb), Madame Buffet gave me a brief update. She nailed New Labour Tony Blair as "essentially a Thatcherite, although we don't excommunicate as we used to." Tensing, she couldn't bring herself to say a fraternal word about Olivier Besancenot, the baby-faced, 34-year-old postman whose planned New Anti-Capitalist Party had the relatively tame-tabby Communist Party in a panic. "We will achieve unity of the left," she said, "but by negotiation, not grandstanding."

Asked whether hated globalization and capitalism had not lifted both China and India out of mass poverty, Mme. George sniffed: "Well, India was never socialist," even with fifty years of a planned economy. And China? "There were cultural reasons for that, plus a very disciplined government."

Remembering the hundred million or so murdered in the name of socialism, wouldn't she agree that revolutionary systems cause abuses? "Well," she laughed, "we certainly know all about that!"

The PCF was seeking space between socialism's moderates and far leftists. On one side brawled the Socialist Party, hopelessly divided on doctrine and personalities. On the other smirked Trotskyite Besancenot, young, media-smart leader of the Revolutionary Communist League. Snapping at Buffet's heels, "the postman" hoped to absorb the PCF Pac-Man-style – a little monster eating a bigger, but slower one.

Besancenot turned up at the *Fête* sneering he had been "uninvited to debate." Twisting the knife, he assured that "the PCF shouldn't worry," for his people would "only hand out [our] message to PCF members at our stand, not in the alleys." As he signed his book, the media mobbed him – to the teeth-gritting fury of PCF officials. They saw him seeking self-promoting publicity to make the nice-but-plodding Buffet and her party look old.

Old-Comrade Henri Malberg, member of the PCF's national executive council, didn't see Buffet or the party as old – but in process of radical rejuvenation. "This is a moment of starting anew," he told me. "I'm optimistic we will bounce back, with new ideas and people, as we always have."

Cheered on by some old rock-groups also trying to bounce back – *Supertamp, Babyshambles* – plenty of young *Huma* believers looked and sounded enthusiastic. "Our tradition of street protest goes back to the Middles Ages," recalled Malberg, "and it will go on."

After an excellent volunteer-served meal of *cassoulet* and wine as red as the Party used to be, I emerged from the restaurant-tent in search of H.G. Wells's "sunlit uplands." The PCF's possible destinies seemed contradictory: For Party pessimists, the *Internationale*'s hymn of "the final struggle." For its Malberg-school optimists, this huge, slogan-flaunting banner: "Communism – a New Idea!" Take your pick.

જી

PART IV

BEYOND THE SEINE: BUT HOW FAR?

Chapter Thirteen

FRANCE IN EUROPE, SOMETIMES

Forget Charlemagne, Stalin and Hitler. Uniting Europe was France's idea. Winston Churchill's 1945 plea for a "United States of Europe" (which he had first made in 1930) was mainly rhetorical. He was out of power and, in any case, made clear he would never put Europe above Britain's "special" relationship with the U.S. – or indeed above the British Empire and Commonwealth. The intellectual fathers of a united Europe were both Frenchmen: Jean Monnet and Robert Schuman. As French as they were, they were amazingly empirical. They wanted to build the new Europe brick by brick, industry by industry, solidarity by solidarity. Though brilliant persuaders in public and private, they were in practice 'stealth' unifiers.

A uniting Europe has always dealt with only one question: How united? That was the issue in the five exploratory years after 1945. It remains the core conflict among European governments to this day: how to divide powers between a central authority ("Brussels") and national governments? Deep disagreements have grown from history and geopolitics, indeed from personalities. On that point, how will history a hundred years hence judge the three Frenchmen incarnating Europe's federal/confederal/nation-states debate: the two 'federalists,' Monnet and Schuman; and chauvinist-sovereignist Charles de Gaulle? Who will be asterisk to the other(s)?

Europe at fifty: War? What war?

History must refresh its memories or repeat its follies. For people now over 65, the Second World War remains a lively memory. Even those under 50 may recall childhood talk of that war. And of the rationales and tools of collective security (United Nations, NATO) designed post-war to prevent new conflicts.

Soon after the war, Western Europe began looking for ways to make continental wars impossible – especially between "hereditary enemies" France and Germany. The year 2007 marked fifty years from the first concrete moves to marry these two nations' economies, the basis of their war-making potential. In January that year, a female German chancellor, governing a reunited Germany, took her six-month turn holding the European Union presidency. At age 52, Angela Merkel's relative youth underlined that a new generation of Europeans – not "feeling" their parents' or grand-parents' war – needed to remember that only unity guaranteed peace. They needed to mesh this awareness with new ideals and new goals, rooted in Europe's values and spirit.

Europe's anthem shouldn't be Beethoven-Schiller's *Ode to Joy* with its "All men will become brothers under thy gentle wing." It should be Joni Mitchell's *Big Yellow Taxi* with "You don't know what you've got till it's gone." Too many Europeans, aping shallow leaders, barely recognize Europe in their lives – much less bless it for their happiness. Amid scattered celebrations of a uniting Europe's 50th anniversary, were Europeans losing their great historic vision?

Not yet. Its power lay too deep. Charlemagne dreamt of Europe in the eighth century, France's Jean Monnet and Robert Schuman in the 20th. Angela Merkel, a small woman with big ideas, dreamt of consolidating its new reality in the 21st. Germany's first female chancellor was the most impressive statesman in Europe – gutsy, astute, resourceful. With Berlin holding the European Union's rotating presidency until June 30, 2007, she was determined to remind Europeans of their common destiny.

Sixty-two years after the Second World War, almost three generations had grown up with no personal experience of conflict. Most of the European Union's nearly half-billion people easily forgot this stunning truth: European unity, wisely backed by the United States, had delivered unprecedented decades of peace, freedom and prosperity.

Peace? Europe had known centuries of blood-letting, including three French-German wars (1870, 1914, 1939) that killed tens of millions. Europeans rarely thought of peace anymore; it was just there, and free like the air they breathed. Yet peace through unity had made war between Europe's nations inconceivable.

Making war impossible was paramount in the 1950s when Monnet and Schuman imagined building Europe brick by pragmatic brick: pooling coal, steel and atoms, building a customs union. When the original six nations founded the European Economic Community ("Common Market") and Euratom in 1957, they met in the shadows of Hitler's war and Stalin's threatened war.

Freedom was peace's twin aspiration. The Third Reich had snuffed out liberty in most of Europe. Moscow's Iron Curtain had done the same in Central and Eastern Europe. Prosperity, Europe's third contribution, anchored both peace and freedom. A generation before, Spain, Portugal and Ireland were impoverished, church-dominated backwaters. With Europe's massive financial aid and democratic demands, in 2007 they stood among Europe's freest, richest nations.

At Berlin's March 2007 European summit, Merkel brought a powerful personal reminder of how Europe had changed. The EU-founding Treaty of Rome was signed, she recalled, when she was three years old. The Berlin Wall went up when she was seven. At the summit, she added, "We are celebrating in Berlin. A city that, until 18 years ago, was divided by a wall, by barbed wire, by soldiers with orders to shoot – in which people paid with their lives for seeking to escape to freedom."

With a deft mixture of perspective, decisiveness and charm, Merkel used history to convince her twenty-six fellow European Union leaders to dream again. French and Dutch referenda in 2005 had killed a new European constitutional treaty, plunging Europe into a coma.

Since then, Europe's petty demons had begun crawling out again from under rocks. Many politicians – especially in France, Britain, Poland and the Czech Republic – almost daily denigrated Europe. They played parish-pump politics, blaming "Brussels" (the EU capital) for anything they couldn't fix at home. They ridiculed Europe by highlighting obscure EU regulations defining the shape of a banana. They mocked the euro which, for thirteen of them, was a life-saver (Cyprus and Malta joined nine months later, others were scheduled to join). They refused – preachy France being worst offender–to translate agreed EU decisions into national law.

They also ignored Europe as a nation-eclipsing ideal. In France's 2007 presidential campaign, "national identity" was no longer the monopoly of chauvinists. Moderate rightist Nicolas Sarkozy plunked it onto his agenda to steal votes from neo-fascist Jean-Marie Le Pen. And that celebrated renovator, Socialist Ségolène Royal, urged every French house to fly a French flag on holidays. At a youth meeting, she insisted the crowd sing *La Marseillaise*... twice.

Merkel knew that leaders needed to lift eyes to a Europe-defining horizon: sustained emphasis on shared values, on Europe's spirit instead of bureaucratic "plumbing." They needed a simple new constitution to better balance national and community roles, and to allow majority voting. She urged finding common causes that ordinary Europeans could identify with: the environment, energy, international peace-making, research, educational exchanges. But also – to help Europe play a credible role abroad – a common army.

Merkel's hand-crafted "Berlin Declaration" was a model of high thinking. In it, she invited Europeans to celebrate their civilization, not their treaties. She recalled that Europe existed centuries before its nations. She echoed Montesquieu's view that "anything useful to my country that hurts Europe...would be a crime."

Late French President François Mitterrand warned that "nationalism is war." His successor, Jacques Chirac (though an enthusiastic Brussels-basher), cautioned that unity's great gains could still be lost. Happily, that three-year-old girl of 1957, wryly admitting a few grey hairs, grew up to explain all this again. Lucky Europe.

Horsing around in the European Union

Thanks to Irish voters' June 2008 referendum veto of its rules-simplifying Lisbon Treaty, the European Union is still unable to make decisions through majority voting. So it continues handing a revolving six-month presidency to each of its twenty-seven members. In 2008, the lucky winners of this lottery were Slovenia (January-June) and France (July-December). Serious crises popped up to surprise both. But their differing national management styles remained characteristic.

What did white horses have to do with Europe in 2008? Plenty. For the first six months of that year, Slovenia – whose town of Lipica is stud-farm home of those dancing Lipizzaner steeds of Vienna's Spanish Riding School – held the rotating European presidency. In the second half, the presidency fell to France, home of cowboy-favored Camargue stallions that gallop wildly through waves on Mediterranean beaches.

Two white horses, two styles. And each horse portrays perfectly its homeland's diplomatic approach. Tiny Slovenia, with barely two million people and a delightful, unspellable capital (Ljubljana), launched its presidency with elegant restraint. It hoped to go with the flow of events – the scariest being, for this fellow-remnant of disintegrated Yugoslavia, Kosovo.

On Slovenia's watch, the 90-percent Albanian majority of the then-Serbian province declared its independence. This act drew official recognition by some, but far from all, western governments. Both Kosovo's declaration of independence and formal recognitions enraged Serbs. They also raised tensions between Russia and the West. Cautiously, most European nations joined the U.S. in recognizing Kosovo's sovereignty. Russia, eager to oppose Washington and fearing its own dissident republics, angrily backed its fellow-Slav Serb allies. Slovenia, an EU member only since 2004 and probably wishing it could go back to riding-school, had to try to coordinate Europe's uneven reaction. Low-key, it watched, waited and, as a devout Christian nation, prayed.

Slovenia's presidency inherited three EU mandates. First, it was to guide implementation of the Lisbon Treaty recently signed by the EU's twenty-seven members. "Lisbon" simplified EU voting, and replaced six-month presidency rotations with a two-and-a-half-year presidency. Ljubljana's light hand could do little after Ireland blocked the treaty in June, leaving this mess to France.

Second, Slovenia was to implement the "Lisbon Strategy." This, by contrast, was an unwieldy, indeed fanciful, grab-bag of EU goals "making growth and jobs the immediate target... hand in hand with promoting social or environmental objectives." This was Brussels EU fluff so vague that nobody noticed what Slovenia did: just a Lipizzaner prance or two – no more needed for applause.

Finally, there was in-the-trenches work where Slovenia might have shone: "police and judicial cooperation in criminal matters." This was part of the concerted EU "trio" of successive presidencies: Germany, Portugal, Slovenia. Ljubljana needed only to coast on its predecessors' priorities, discreetly highlighting its own taste for common foreign policy and intercultural dialogue. Excited yet?

Following Ljubljana's stately Lipizzaners raced the wild-charging ponies of the Camargue. Coincidentally, France's "hyper-president," Nicolas Sarkozy, had mounted one of these small horses to draw cameras during his spring 2007 election campaign (he would have looked more impressive on a merry-go-round). The second six months of 2008 saw Sarkozy mark his EU presidency in typical form – with a mad mini-Valkyrie ride riskily skirting Valhalla.

Ahead of time, France worked furiously to prepare its dash. Sarkozy hoped to cover the European waterfront: EU institutions, Balkan enlargement and energy-climate issues. He also wanted to stir debate on investment, trade, currency, immigration, terrorism, education, defence, research, his pet idea of a Mediterranean Union, and transatlantic relations.

Funny things happened, as with Caesar, on Sarko's way to the Forum. Ireland, instead of kick-starting the French agenda, derailed it. Reforming EU decision-making would have to wait a year or more. Quickly, other side-shows erupted. Sarkozy got into a weird face-losing spat with China just before the August Beijing Olympics – to which he flew for just a few kow-towing hours. This silly quarrel included tripping over his shoe-laces by inviting, then disinviting, the Dalai Lama to meet him. Providentially, if that is the word, wife Carla Bruni stood in for him with His Oceanic Holiness. She wore to the French Buddhist temple an outfit worthy of her old model-runway get-ups. But she certainly looked better in it than her husband would have.

Next, starting at his peek-a-boo Olympics visit, Georgia upended Sarko's plans by bombing and 'invading' its separatist-minded region of South Ossetia. This, we know, led to a well-planned Russian invasion of Georgia. Without consulting either American or European allies, Sarkozy dashed to Tbilisi and Moscow, negotiating a six-point ceasefire. The Americans discreetly co-opted this, correcting his inadvertent OK for Russia to keep troops in Georgia. Fellow Europeans, grinning through gritted teeth, went along with Sarkozy's ceasefire just to separate the warring parties – and because they were hopelessly divided on the whole question anyway..

The six-point plan would have been hard to pull off even if Sarkozy had built easy relations with his partners. But his idea-a-minute, damn-the-torpedoes approach frightened stodgier Europeans, as it did many status-quo-loving French. His personal relations with crucial allies German Chancellor Angela Merkel and Britain's Prime Minister Gordon Brown often suggested a Tasmanian Devil dancing with turtles. Sarko's touchy-feely mauling and mike-grabbing egotism deeply offended Frau Merkel. And Brown, the dour (or is it sour?) Scot, saw him as a wayward child who kept stealing the presbytery's collection-plate.

Another early distraction was the late-August death of ten French soldiers in southeast Afghanistan. This traumatized French opinion. Sarkozy's decision to put French soldiers at risk beside American, British, Canadian and Dutch troops in southeastern Afghanistan was already unpopular. Now he had to defend it against grieving relatives and anti-American leftists – or lose face at home, and influence within NATO.

As a result of his troubled relations with allies and bad luck elsewhere, France's EU presidency limped along to Dec. 31. Starting in September he tried to revive his European agenda. But extra-EU issues – mainly the Caucasus (meaning a resurgent Russia) and Afghanistan – eclipsed nearly everything. Merely trying to coordinate Europe's energy security was enough to curse France's presidency: Russia had already shown adroitness in splitting oil- and gas-hungry EU nations. Europe looked at sea, and France's hand on the tiller seemed flaccid.

But not for long. As the September-November 2008 financial tsunami swept the world, Sarkozy sprang into action on several fronts. He rallied Europe, giving it unaccustomed unity. He brought China into a more coordinated approach with the West. He sold George Bush on a world economic summit in mid-November. He helped focus a global approach to the drama. With all his colorful faults, Sarkozy became a heroic 'Mr. Europe.' His energy, strategic vision, tactical skill, imagination, media savvy and shrewd reading of public opinion steadied and inspired a rudderless European Union.

Just as expected, the EU's 2008 unfolded to fit its two presidents' unique styles. In all, it was a memorable year. From Lipica to Port Camargue.

Islam in Europe: immigration, opportunity, identity

Just beneath the surface of many European concerns – physical and social security, defense, diplomacy, even education and culture – lies Islam. It shapes France's and Europe's whole passionate debate on immigration, multiculturalism and national identity. Even unspoken, the threat of Islamic terrorism lingers, a shadow over inter-community relations. It frightens many, even Muslims embracing European values. The long-term challenge remains: How can Islam find the peaceful, positive role for which most of its faithful yearn? A role that "old Europeans" need to help them find.

From the cobblestones of Stockholm's Old Town to the dusty alleys of Palermo, twelve million faces of Islam are changing the face of Europe. Knapsacks packing clothes, Korans and hopes for a better life, two generations of Arabs, Africans and Asians have brought Allah to every corner of this continent. They challenge its peoples to reconsider identities – their own and their new compatriots'.

France's car-burning ghettos showed in 2005 that many Muslims actually 'immigrated' to Europe via European maternity wards. But culturally, Europe's Muslims present the broadest wave of non-European immigration in centuries. Neither Muslim nor non-Muslim Europeans have forgotten that Christians stopped Islamic invasions at Poitiers in 732 and Vienna in 1683.

Throughout Europe, Islam takes many forms. Recent arrivals, especially women, often cling to their religion as an anchor in Europe's troubled seas of sex, drugs (including alcohol) and materialism. A broad Muslim mainstream, imitating the godless, post-Christian societies they are joining, skip five-times-a-day prayers and become Friday-and-Ramadan Muslims – or just festive, end-of-Ramadan *Eid ul-Fitr* Muslims. Probably eighty percent of French Muslims never set foot in a mosque, or do so just a few times a year. Many, like my local Tunisian-French grocer, can offer knowledgeable advice on wine. A few girls wear head-scarves, yet plenty of tight-jeaned young "Fatimas" and "Abdullahs" embrace world youth culture.

A small, close-knit Muslim core tends the flame of Holy Islam with passionate introspection. They are the faithful of the faithful, the True Believers you find in any religion. Faith is their security, their whole identity. An even tinier core harbors paranoid reactionaries – successors of the "desert Muslims" denounced by Canadian Muslim critic Irshad Manji. Their fantasies feed murderous *Jihad* against the corrupting West.

In a remarkable 2005 interview in the Paris daily *Le Monde*, Pascal Mailhos, chief of France's internal intelligence service, explained how hard it was to monitor these few real terrorists. Of 1,700 French mosques studied in 2004, terrorists had tried to destabilize 75. France expelled 31 radical preachers, and 10 others remained under observation. Of about 1,000 Muslim preachers, only a third spoke French well. Most of their funding came from Arab governments with ideological strings attached.

Most Muslim actors of the burning *banlieues* were peace-loving local imams. Far from fanning the flames, they helped douse them. They sent rioters home, calling for action on causes of revolt: lack of jobs, of decent housing, and of acceptance by French society. What about violence-preaching Muslims? This tiny group rarely cruise mosques anymore. Extremist recruiters set up youth-clothing stores, after being unmasked running cyber-cafés and *halal* butcher-shops.

Models for accepting Muslims also vary. France, with over half of Europe's Muslims, has rhetorically if not in practice integrated its newcomers into a religiously and ethnically color-blind "*République*." Tolerant Italy's half-million Muslims freely practice ten kinds of Islam – their harshest persecutor being the late flame-throwing writer Oriana Fallaci. Germany until 2000 restricted new citizenship to blood-line Germans – including even distant-ancestor "Volga Germans" who spoke only Russian.

British, Dutch and Scandinavians have promoted multiculturalism – their tolerance importing cultures and religions into familiar ethno-cultural communities. All these models offer pros and cons. It's too soon to know which ones work best. For meshing immigrant and host-country identities is tricky and changeable. Strong anti-immigrant parties thrive – especially in Belgium, Denmark and (after the 2002 murder of Pim Fortuyn and 2004 assassination of Theo van Gogh) Holland.

In France, with the Sarkozy-engineered eclipse of the *Front National,* xenophobia bubbles mainly underground. Sarkozy is the first French leader to name Muslims to top jobs in his cabinet. But astutely, he contains anti-immigrant feeling by vigorously deporting illegal immigrants.

However they welcome immigrants, Europe's politicians are doing what their frightened voters ask: Assert host-country culture, tighten the flow of legal immigrants, crack down on illegals and fake refugees. Britain's Commission for Racial Equality, citadel of multiculturalism, now demands that all citizens absorb "a core of Britishness." France limits family reunification (especially in polygamous African families), as well as overseas marriages, even student visas.

Each European country must find its own style of integrating Muslims. That's increasingly difficult for both Muslims and their Judeo-Christian "hosts:" both sides feel their identities are fragile. Muslims ricochet between ancestral and new-country identities. Old Europeans, abandoning their churches to tourists, wince as they watch minarets piercing the sky.

Muslims, especially the young and jobless, crave acceptance as Europeans – in jobs, business opportunities, and political and media representation. Only if denied these, especially work, will most seek their core identity in religion. The deeper hosts' rejection, the more radical an answering Islam – Osama bin Laden loves unemployment.

Misunderstanding between Old and New (Muslim) Europeans focuses on clashes of identity. But beneath much anxiety lies competition for scarce jobs. French joblessness has crept down, but stays stuck at double Britain's.

Here's a sobering – and reconciling? – thought for all. Low Old-European birthrates (even in relatively high-birth France), plus early retirement and lengthening life-spans, guarantee that Europe's rich pension funds will go broke in a decade or two. To replenish them, Europe needs millions of new, young, ready-to-work immigrants *every year.* Most of these will inevitably be Muslim. Say wise Europeans: Forget Poitiers and Vienna. Let 'them' in. Save our pensions.

One small girl against the sea

Europe's true believers all bemoan that "Euroskepticism" grows from ignorance of Europe's history, values and ideals. Many wish for genuine popular heroes whom ordinary Europeans could admire and identify with. Music and sports are probably the handiest international languages for praising heroes. Sailing, with its allure of risk, bravery and confrontation with the sea's capricious power, is an exciting source of exemplars.

Two European women sailors lead the way: France's Isabelle Autissier, first woman to navigate the globe alone in competition; and a plucky young British sailor famous for her world-record, fastest-solo circumnavigation of the globe. Ellen MacArthur sailed so often to and from France's Atlantic coast, and spoke such fluent French, that the French claimed her as their own. When President Sarkozy visited Queen Elizabeth II in March 2008, he journeyed to the Old Royal Naval College in Greenwich (where Elizabeth I had knighted Sir Francis Drake) to award now-Dame Ellen MacArthur France's Legion of Honor. Racing for Britain, adopted by France, the "little sailor-girl" said something about Europe at its most inspiring.

All 1.56 meters (5.1 ft.) of rosy-cheeked, 28-year-old Ellen MacArthur stood on the deck of *HMS Ocean* in a spanking-fresh Royal Navy Lt. Commander's uniform. Saluted by senior officers, she was helping review 126 ships from 36 nations. The occasion: the bicentenary of Admiral Horatio Nelson's Trafalgar victory over France and Spain.

As France and Britain quarreled like fishwives over the future of Europe, MacArthur was something Britons and French could both feel good about. Her bilingual website welcomed each.

Self-made, modest, a fearless adventurer, MacArthur was a poster-girl for the centenary of the long-forgotten 1905 Franco-British *Entente Cordiale.* She was a gritty Brit to the core. But she started and ended many of her exploits among her French fans in Les Sables d'Olonne. From there, through awesome seamanship, she set a new record for round-the-world solo sailing in February 2005. Both British and French felt they owned her. Dame Ellen in the UK is "Queen Ellen" in France.

It was midsummer madness to suggest that MacArthur might bring British and French politicians together. They continued to snipe at each other over Europe (its budget, "social models," expansion), the U.S., the Olympics (just won by London in a bitter fight with Paris), language, goat's cheese vs. Stilton, and a thousand years of delectably remembered killin' and kissin'.

But in democracies, public moods help or hinder politicians. Conveying hope, potential or achievement, stars can incarnate optimism. They make great photo-ops for fading glories. MacArthur could still prove a dream symbol of British-French solidarity.

Pictures of her coasting victoriously into Les Sables, sails down, linger in everyone's imagination. She held aloft a spurting flare, and sipped champagne, as a night-time crowd of thousands cheered. She had beaten the world's best male sailors, and the world's worst storms, to become a cross-Channel heroine. Both French and British sponsors backed her.

Her story is fairy-tale inspiring. At four years of age, she went sailing with her aunt. As soon as she could read, she devoured every sailing book she could find. As an eight-year-old, she 'stole' part of her lunch money each day to save up for her first boat at thirteen. Then for fifteen years, she spent every free moment sailing. In time, her determination and hard-honed skills made her tough to beat.

Why is a soft story about a girl in a boat relevant to Europe today? Because setting goals and meeting them is not what's happening in Europe. After French and Dutch voters turned down the proposed constitutional treaty in 2005, and Irish voters killed a stripped-down substitute in 2008, the European Union has been floundering. Not only can member-states not agree on policies and budgets; they can't seem to remember why a united Europe was ever needed.

In case you missed this: 2005 was also the 60th anniversary of the end of the Second World War. Grand ceremonies in Moscow drew western leaders – even some (conceivably G.W. Bush?) who thought their troops had beaten the Nazis single-handedly. The postwar conclusion that six nations (France, Germany, Italy, the three Benelux countries) drew was: never again. They overcame hundreds of years of tribal wars to imagine, and start building, a Europe where war would be inconceivable. Since then,

European unification has been a spectacular success – even though, as Germany's Angela Merkel and many others have noted, European leaders have undercut it as much as 'sold' it to their peoples.

European institutions have set high moral standards, abolishing the death penalty and assuring basic human rights. Youth exchanges (the Erasmus program) and scientific cooperation (the Galileo project) have flourished. EU nations have made democracy, freedom, tolerance and peace incontestable. And contagious: by demanding all four as conditions of membership, the EU has exerted decisive positive influence on the policies of potential new members.

Tragically today, many Europeans – especially the young – forget why a united Europe exists. Not so, aspiring candidates for membership: the Balkans, Ukraine, Georgia, Moldova, Turkey. Sadly, MacArthur's home country is mired in Euro-skepticism. Its jingoistic press routinely ridicules and dismisses Europe. Tony Blair failed to use his six-month 2005 EU presidency to lead Europeans anywhere – merely promising, with absolutely no substance or follow-up, to "put Britain at the center of Europe."

Europeans ache for heroes – attractive, rallying models – in which to glimpse a Europe of daring and imagination. Maybe people like that brave, blingual, five-foot-one sailor.

∽

Chapter Fourteen /

AT HOME IN THE WORLD

The center of the world is wherever you are. But in everybody's world, there's a place called Paris. "Romantic," "beautiful," "historic" – through the ages, the clichés, all true, spell world capital of love and culture. In Paris, you quickly fall for the magic. It's easy to feel, and passionately so, that this is where you belong, where the world's center *really* is. Many other cities can stir such feelings: Rome, London, New York, Budapest, San Francisco, Vancouver, Rio de Janeiro, Mumbai, Shanghai, Johannesburg. But even in these great cities, the prospect of living in Paris causes eyes to mist.

A defining part of Paris's charm is its cosmopolitanism. Its ability to make all races and creeds feel at home. Its presumption that it is the logical place to contemplate, serenely and thoughtfully, the entire world. And – a touching vanity – its belief that the whole world is wondering what Paris is thinking and doing.

These past half-dozen centuries, France's place in the world has known dizzying ups and downs. It soared as 15th-16th-century pupil of Italy's Renaissance, then as Europe's superpower under Louis XIV and Napoleon. It knew singular humiliations in the 19th-century, even while Paris dazzled the world with its style and culture. The 20th-century – after France's triumph in one world war and defeat in a second – shrank France's world role to middle-power status. Now, Gaullist pretensions fading, France projects a constructive image magnified by unusable nuclear weapons and an occasionally usable UN Security Council veto. Thus armed, it tries to bridge antagonists in 'hopeless' conflicts: the 2007–08 European constitutional treaty crisis was bloodless but costly; the 2008 Russia-Georgia war was both bloody and costly. Paris remains an ecumenical diplomatic capital, its government willing to meet many leaders unwelcome elsewhere. It's still a choice venue for international conferences.

Paris plays many other roles in the world. Through its great couturiers and other arbiters of taste, Paris remains a universally admired fountain of youth and beauty. But luckily for its wicked satirical press, national politicians demonstrate a bottomless capacity to create world-class PR disasters.

More positively: The French people's deep well of idealism and generosity has repeatedly led the world to humanitarian action. Their non-governmental organizations often touch hearts throughout the globe, and rally to Paris volunteers from many nations. The city of *le Crazy Horse* and the *Folies Bergère*? Cheerfully so – but that's not the whole story.

Taking French leave…abroad

Every year, tens of thousands of talented, ambitious French youth leave France. Not just for adventure, but to find greener pastures. They see only this choice: Leave, or starve in a France of high unemployment, low wages, and few opportunities for advancement. If they come home, exiles will enrich their country with new skills and fresh ideas. But many stay abroad permanently. The loss of so many of its most dynamic youth, unless reversed, risks condemning France to slow decline.

"To leave is to die a little." To this well-known saying, 19th-century wit Alphonse Allais replied, "but to die is to leave a lot." Today, as for a generation, French youth (like the rich) are leaving France in droves, and France's economy is dying more than a little. Counting families, an estimated 2.5 million French citizens live abroad (1.3 million registered).

The rich flee to nearby lower-tax havens: Belgium, Britain and certain Swiss cantons. These places not only impose more reasonable marginal tax rates. They offer two interrelated benefits: a healthier attitude to money and enterprise, and a lack of France's infamous "envy" tax – its already-cited "Tax on Fortune." (ISF).

Attitudes toward money in France remain conflicted. Everybody secretly wants more, but to show it off – or worse, to brag about it – is thought not just vulgar, but suspicious. Today's media darlings in France are not dashing entrepreneurs. They are Trotskyites, peddling 1930s hate-the-rich nonsense but no practical solutions.

The best-known anti-capitalist cheerleaders – who, as we noted, see mere Communists as sell-outs to Big Business – are that postman-presidential candidate Olivier Besancenot and former bank employee Arlette Laguiller, a perennial presidential candidate. Both grace top magazine covers and star on prime-time TV. Both preach "revolution," whatever that may mean today in a wealthy, modern democracy. Otherwise sensible French people chuckle at 'plucky' Olivier and Arlette, egging them on as engaging icons.

But these estimable folk are not the main reason French youth leave their homeland. High unemployment (almost 20 percent for under-25s) and lack of opportunity at home are. Behind blocked advancement lies the oft-mentioned, massive *Code du Travail* (Labor Code) which ties entrepreneurs in knots and discourages them from hiring. Giving somebody a job, in spite of new, longer trial periods, is still tantamount to marrying them.

The second barrier to youth opportunity is cultural. In France, you get ahead essentially on diplomas – often dead ends, as with favored psychology and sociology courses. Proven workplace skills can't compete with sheepskins. Or with seniority. Young people rarely get a chance to prove themselves. Unless they start a business, and that's a bureaucratic nightmare.

Linking studies to the labor market is widely thought crass, except in business and professional training. For the average early-20s student, "insertion" in the economy means a series of nothing-jobs and endless unpaid internships. And *that* is if they are white-skinned. Arab and African youth, though getting better breaks than before, still face a steeper uphill climb against prejudice.

President Nicolas Sarkozy deserves much credit for fighting such discrimination. His cabinet stars spectacular black and Arab role-models. For the first time ever, serious ministries (four) have gone to "immigrant-origin" French citizens. This inspires hopeless ghetto youth – but opportunities for them will take years to become routine.

All these factors have led hundreds of thousands of young French to make their mark in Britain, Ireland and other European Union nations, Asia and North America. Britain alone hosts between 270,000 and 350,000 young French eager to make a mark, strut their stuff, learn new skills (including English), take chances, start a business, and leap-frog over diplomas and seniority.

Roughly 65,000 French citizens live in Canada. French under-25s coming to Canada don't always register as immigrants, but officials note a steady stream of about 5,000 French youth each year trying Canada for new opportunities. Popular daily *Le Parisien* urged French youth to go to booming Alberta and British Columbia – and, surprisingly, to skip Quebec, "where competition among French expatriates is tough."

Young French will continue moving abroad. France's economy in 2007-2008 showed somewhat better numbers. But 2008 and beyond are gloomy as Europe enters recession. The nation's crushing national debt, unmastered budget deficits and enterprise-punishing labor laws make creating jobs difficult. Sarkozy's backing off some contested economic reforms also discourages optimism. He may have blown his one, early-days chance to make brave reforms.

Sadly, billions of French-held euros (and revenues) will remain abroad. Adding to this waste, those hundreds of thousands of France's most enterprising youth will make their lives elsewhere. Losing hope as Sarkozy loses his nerve, both rich and young will continue voting with their feet. They will drain France of much-needed investment, taxes and skills.

Frenchmen identify intelligence as their nation's defining characteristic. Sarkozy and his team are indeed smart, daring people. They won the 2007 elections on a thrilling promise of "rupture" with the past's "immobilism." But while voters elected the Three Musketeers, continuing government missteps sometimes evoked the Three Stooges: ministers quarreled, policies flip-flopped, and MPs missed key votes.

Can Sarkozy find courage, even competence again? If not, in future elections he and his team, Allais-style, may "leave a lot." And so will France's best chance in a generation to reach its extraordinary, but long-self-sabotaged, potential.

Read on for a grand-scale example of self-sabotage. Of France shooting itself in the foot – or rather dropping an anchor on its foot.

'World tour' of the "Clemenceau"

"There is nothing – absolutely nothing – half so much worth doing as simply messing about in boats." The French have often applied with a vengeance Kenneth Grahame's words from his 1908 "The Wind in the Willows." Bordered by two great waters, the Atlantic and Mediterranean, they love and win sailing races – as we saw with Ellen MacArthur and Isabelle Autissier. They venerate, years after their heroes' deaths, highseas guru and boat-designer Éric Tabarly and undersea explorer Jacques Cousteau.

Naval tradition is another story. And a sore point for France's proud Bretons who even now refight ancient battles with perfidious Albion. The cowardly Brits, goes the tale, always feared to fight, so blocked French fleets in their home ports.

Some French naval vessels also evoke painful memories: submarines sinking themselves, frigates (for Taiwan) sparking huge financial-espionage scandals, and, above all, defective pride-of-fleet aircraft carriers. The "Charles de Gaulle," among other major faults, lost a propeller.

But the saddest tale is the 'endless ending' of the venerable carrier Clemenceau – condemned for scrap after a 36-year career. It bounced from scrap yard to scrap yard, its search for dismantlement seeming to last almost as long. This highlighted a genius for boondoggles that did not amuse Paris's red-faced landlubber-ministers. The saga started in 1997. Several countries, even business-hungry India, refused to risk dismantling the nomadic, asbestos-laden ship. Finally, in August 2008, the "Clem" took its cocktail of toxic chemicals for break-up in – sweet vengeance? – treacherous l'Angleterre. At the same time, a mythical French passenger-ship, the "France," knew a similar fate, though finally dying in India.

Gutted, rusting and forlorn, condemned to wander the high seas like the legendary ghost-ship *Flying Dutchman*, the retired aircraft carrier *Clemenceau* and *S.S. France* sailed Frenchmen for several years between pride and ridicule. These iconic but headed-for-scrap ships stirred lawyers' lusts and diplomats' martinis. And they launched an environmentalists' guerrilla war.

Why does France so romanticize great ships? Recall its sea-going travails. Admiral de Grasse defeated Britain's Royal Navy in 1781 at Chesapeake Bay, but France lost almost every other naval battle against Britain over hundreds of years. (Since Chesapeake Bay led straight to U.S. independence, it rather made up for the losses),

After France surrendered to a German-dictated "Armistice" on June 22, 1940, Britain ordered the French navy either to rejoin the fight against Hitler, scuttle its ships, or quit the war. Weeks later, Britain sank most of France's North African fleet at Mers-el-Kébir, killing 1,297 sailors. France's remaining fleet at Toulon scuttled itself that November, minutes before Germany could seize it.

On the civilian side too, tragedy struck. The S.S. *Normandie*, world's largest, fastest transatlantic ship in the late 1930s, was stuck in New York just as war broke out. Seized in December 1941 by a joining-the-war U.S., it caught fire in February 1942, ending the war as scrap. Once again, "Anglo-Saxons" had sunk France's sea-glory.

On May 11, 1960, Yvonne de Gaulle broke a magnum of champagne on the bow of the 57,000-ton *S.S France*. The ship, ultra-modern from anchor to ash-tray, immediately set transatlantic speed records. It became the floating grandeur that was France. Even on a young professor's salary, I pinched pennies to voyage on it with French wife and two small children.

Once again, fate killed French dreams. The 1974 oil crisis and cheap airfares priced the *France* off the Atlantic. It rusted in Brest with angry crew and weeping fans. All the usual scenarios came up and died – a hotel, a casino, a museum. Finally, Norwegian Cruise Lines bought it, renaming it the *Norway* – as a downscale cruise ship. A few years later, the Norwegians gave up, and French fans wept again. The old *France* now became – *ah, quelle décadence!* – the *Blue Lady*. She finally died, scrapped at India's Alang yards, in mid-2008.

The *Clemenceau*, like its sister-ship *Foch* (later sold to the Brazilian navy), made a similar claim on French emotions. State-of-the-art on entering service in 1961, this elegant ship participated in all major French naval operations over nearly four decades. With all-French aircraft and electronics, and a crew of 1,920, it was a showcase for French technology, an inspiration for patriots. The 2000 commissioning of aircraft-carrier *Charles de Gaulle* was to amplify this glory. But a lost propeller, dangerous radiation, inadequate flight decks and constant repairs made her a sad joke – though she did do valuable service for NATO in Afghanistan from the Indian Ocean.

Meanwhile, the *Clemenceau's* retirement in 1997 became a nightmare of confusion and incompetence. Sold for scrap in 2003, the ship was meant to earn taxpayers several million euros from scrap.

Again, the "Anglo-Saxons" intervened. Greenpeace, the Vancouver-founded environmental group, was still furious over two French attacks: the 1973 beating of a Canadian protesting French Pacific nuclear tests; and President François Mitterrand's 1985 bombing (with one death) of Greenpeace's protest-ship *Rainbow Warrior.*

Greenpeace learned that the French government was violating the Basle Convention forbidding export beyond European waters of "toxic" ships. Removing asbestos from hazardous hulks would poison scrap-yard workers in India and Bangladesh. Through French and foreign courts, Greenpeace dogged France at every turn, alerting to asbestos dangers Egypt (to block the shorter Suez Canal route to Asia), then Asian governments.

Result: an unbelievable fiasco involving both *Clemenceau* and *France.* In February 2006, India banished the arriving *Clemenceau* from Indian waters. President Jacques Chirac, on the eve of a state visit there, had to order the ship towed home. Total cost, including back-and-forth towing, already dwarfed scrap value. Worse, with Suez off-limits, the "*Clem*" had to chance South Africa's Cape of Good Hope – on the edge of the "Roaring Forties" where the *Flying Dutchman* allegedly sailed – in the monster-wave season.

All the way, widely-read satirical weekly *Le Canard enchaîné* ran a front-page, make-believe diary by the hapless captain marooned on the towed monument. Capping the *Clemenceau* humiliation, cash-poor Bangladesh then banned the asbestos-laden ex-*France* – already towed from port to unwelcoming port for three years.

Meanwhile, France's nemeses, those wretched Anglo-Saxons, continued to have fun in ships. In 1967, the original *Queen Mary* (1936–67) fled the scrap-yard to retire to Long Beach, California. You can stay, sleep and dine on it, for it's a quayside hotel. On Feb. 22, 2006, Cunard's spanking-new *Queen Mary 2* dropped by for a nostalgic salute. Jolly, wot?

But here's revenge for Paris: Britain didn't build the *QM 2*. France did. Maybe the French can't figure out how to 'bury' great ships. But most of the time – never mind the odd lost propeller – they still know how to build them.

Dressing the world – Yves Saint-Laurent

He wished he had invented blue jeans. Instead, he reinvented happier lives for millions of women. Though he worked among the most beautiful women in the world, from his friend Catherine Deneuve to all the supermodels, his great gift was to dress ordinary women in styles that made the dowdiest female chic. He democratized fashion by bringing runway to street, and street to runway. He empowered women by offering them close-to-unisex styles that gave them spunky confidence – but with a wink and a whirl. He guessed the spirit of changing times with uncanny instinct. Until he died in 2008, he was the megastar of French taste and luxury. He died a worldwide

*icon of one of France's signature industries: the art and business
of making people look good and feel good, of guiding them to
appreciate astonishing but simple beauty. Paris, passion, and
"YSL" – a trilogy that everywhere says "France."*

They carried his *tricolore*-draped coffin down the steps
of Paris's *Église Saint-Roch* – steps against which, on Oc-
tober 5, 1795, Napoleon had fired cannons to "clean off"
the young Republic's enemies. Now on June 5, 2008, the
whole world's fashion village had come to pay homage to
a man who hated guns and armies. A giant of the world of
esthetics, a decider of taste with no enemies, just devoted
admirers.

Among the 800 grieving Yves Saint-Laurent: President
of the Republic Nicolas Sarkozy and his former-super-
model wife, Carla Bruni. Almost all of today's great couturiers. Scores of Saint-Laurent's models and long-lost *petites
mains*, the meticulous women who sewed his creations.
Deneuve, with a sheaf of green wheat. His mother, his eternal feminine ideal. Finally, his shattered long-time lover,
then companion, Pierre Bergé.

All this for a "dress-maker?" Even Bergé, while wor-
shipping the man, dismissed his trade, saying his friend
Yves was "a man of exceptional intelligence practicing the
trade of an imbecile." A neurotic, fragile, drug-and-booze-
addled genius "born," as again Bergé noted, "as a nervous
breakdown."

On the strength of a 17-year-old Saint-Laurent's cock-
tail-dress design, New Look fashion-god Christian Dior
hired him as his assistant. Four years later, at the master's
sudden death, the boy-wonder took over Dior's "house."
His "trapeze" look became a sensation. But two years later,

the French Army conscripted him for Algerian war service: hazing quickly drove him to psychiatric care. The drugs given him then cursed his life for decades.

Dior management fired Saint-Laurent, but Bergé and he quickly founded a new Yves Saint-Laurent *haute-couture* house. Its first collection (1962) was a hit, and the new house zoomed to the top. It stayed there for forty years – long after Saint-Laurent had left.

Why did he succeed so naturally, year after year? Because he had an unerring flair for what women really wanted. Over the years: pants (day and night), but also trench coats, navy pea-jackets, safari jackets, "rich-peasant" clothing, "Paris beatnik" styles, even tuxedos.

Although the 1940s had put sexy Hollywood dames in pants, this Rosie-the-Riveter fad had only charmed wartime audiences. Fads fade. And postwar women went back to the frilly stuff. Then, in 1968, Saint-Laurent put women back into more stylish pants. *Scandale!* Suzy Menkes, fashion editor of Paris's *International Herald Tribune*, cites the case of a trouser-wearing woman denied entrance to a tony New York restaurant: She took off her pants, and marched back in, wearing just the pant-suit top.

Saint-Laurent could do the highest of *haute couture*. But his deep originality came from his ready-to-wear clothes. Dressing 'ordinary' women in extraordinary but simple clothes, his *Rive Gauche* boutiques made Everywoman a woman of style – in his view far more important than fashion. Bergé's business acumen spun off *Rive Gauche* boutiques around the world. This led to hundreds of licenses for scarves and jewelry, then shoes, even men's wear. Not to mention cosmetics and perfumes. "YSL" became a ubiquitous brand. It attracted billionaires and the Paris Bourse.

How to explain Saint-Laurent's timelessness? Simplicity, an eye to what lasts while "respecting our times," and a profound respect for, and love of, women. Women sensed this, and stayed with him. They cherished his inspirations, his textures, his cuts, his startling colors. They appreciated too that he respected their budgets. "A woman's wardrobe shouldn't change every six months," he insisted. "You should be able to use the pieces you already own and add to them. Because they are like timeless classics." If a woman wanted to stay fashionable, he added, all she needed was "a pair of pants, a sweater and a raincoat."

That raincoat, of course, should be a YSL trench coat, with cinched belt rakishly tied in front. The stylish day clothes underneath should convey energy, action, a woman going places. *Joie-de-vivre*, freedom, proportion, a sense of just being 'right.' "I am not a couturier," said Saint-Laurent, "I am an artisan, a manufacturer of happiness." And happiness is more than dressing for fancy balls. Though for these, said Menkes, he could bring down fashions from the sky as if "clouds had dropped from the heavens and onto the body."

While admitting that, for him, "fashion is an incurable disease," Saint-Laurent believed that "fashions pass, style is eternal." He clung to this credo through the drugs, the drink, the recurring depressions. And he always kept clothes in perspective: "The most beautiful clothing a woman can wear is the arms of a man she loves. But for those who haven't had the luck to find this happiness, I am here."

Could any man but a Frenchman speak such words? As Bergé said in his sobbing eulogy at *Saint-Roch*, Yves Saint-Laurent – world symbol of taste and beauty – was as French "as a verse by Ronsard, a flower-bed by Le Nôtre, a page by Ravel, a painting by Matisse."

Saving the world – Bernard Kouchner

Probably in no other country of the world would a president or prime minister name as foreign minister a hero of humanitarian action. But for almost a generation, France's Bernard Kouchner was voted most popular politician in France – even when, for years, he was not in politics. A medical doctor and sometime minister of health, he was co-founder of Doctors Without Borders and Doctors of the World. Whatever his job, he always went where people overseas were suffering, or in danger: Biafra, Somalia, Beirut, Myanmar, Kosovo, Darfur and many other tragic zones drew him in. Out of his experiences, he promoted a "duty to intervene" wherever bad men hurt innocent people – including their own countrymen.

With a Jewish father and Protestant mother, Kouchner represents a deep ethic of humanitarian service – perhaps the true greatness of the French people. Whatever their government's behavior, ordinary French men and women express, like Kouchner, an extraordinary "right and duty to intervene" abroad, as well as at home.

Bernard Kouchner carries an albatross: a sack of rice. In 1992, when civil war caused mass starvation in Somalia, he loaded a freighter with 15,000 tons of rice he had appealed to French children to fund. Keeping the food flowing demanded that he build support at home for more aid. So when French TV news asked him to carry a sack of rice up a hill in Mogadishu, he obliged.

Enemies accused him of showboating. Sixteen years later, Kouchner's puppet on the weekday TV satire show, *Les Guignols de l'Info*, constantly totes a sack of rice. In politics, you're always dancing on a tightrope between daring and ridicule.

Notoriously, Kouchner likes cameras and microphones. But using the media to awaken consciences is not absurd. Neither is a healthy ego. All Western nations claim traditions of international solidarity. France is just lucky to have a world-famous spokesman who inspires a multitude of good causes. The Kouchner "package" includes an unassailable humanitarian track-record, passion, eloquence, courage, determination and lantern-jawed integrity. He's the Frenchman that Frenchmen like to believe is the world's image of France.

Born-in-France international humanitarian groups multiply. The most established are Kouchner's old outfits: *Médecins Sans Frontières* (Doctors Without Borders) and *Médecins du Monde* (Doctors of the World). In 1999 MSF, active in almost a hundred countries, won the Nobel Peace Prize. Both bodies have international staffs, and attract thousands of volunteers from around the world.

At over a million members, the *Secours populaire français* (French People's Assistance), founded in 1945, is among the country's largest humanitarian groups. Its mission: helping the poor with food, shelter, health, jobs and summer camps. Running 149 "solidarity projects" in 45 countries, SPF mobilizes supporters throughout France: 86,610 *animateurs* work from 4,000 offices within 98 federations. Almost every public entity in France contributes money, as do millions of citizens.

Action contre la Faim (Action Against Hunger) was started in 1979 by a group of well-known Paris intellectuals, journalists, writers and doctors. Its single goal: fight hunger in all its forms, anywhere. Its employees and volunteers work in 20 countries to secure food and clean water for distressed populations, especially children. En 2007, it helped over 1.6-million people.

A similar Catholic Organization, the *Comité catholique contre la faim et pour le développement* claims 15,000 volunteers and 500 projects in 80 countries.

A different kind of French-originated international group is *Reporters Sans Frontières* (Reporters Without Borders). Run mainly by volunteers in Paris and many countries, it's one of the world's most respected press-freedom bodies. It also publicizes persecution of journalists in war zones and dictatorships.

These are only French-founded bodies that have become world centers of concern. French people also powerfully back all the world's best-known causes such as the Red Cross, UNICEF and many United Nations agencies.

The French people have always supported international humanitarian law. And their governments have reflected this. First, in the 1899 and 1907 Hague Conventions on the weapons and customs of war. Then, in the Four Geneva Conventions of 1863-2006 (protecting wounded and sick soldiers, sick and ship-wrecked sailors, prisoners, and civilians). To the extent that they are still discussed, these enjoy unquestioning popular support. So does the 1997 Ottawa anti-personnel land-mine treaty.

A strange but telling development: the French government's crusading, with wide public support, for freeing hostages. In 2007-08, President Sarkozy pressed the cases of Col. Kadhafi's outrageously imprisoned Bulgarian nurses. In colorful fashion – sending his then-wife Cécilia to charm the dictator, and letting the "Guide" set up a tent across from the Élysée Palace – he succeeded. Libya released the hostages. For several years too, French opinion mobilized to demand that Colombia's FARC rebels release Franco-Colombian hostage

Ingrid Betancourt. Although the Colombian president got her freed, Sarkozy, playing to the humanitarian gallery, let on that he played a key role too.

Doing good – not just being "bad," as foreigners often think – lies deep in France's domestic tradition. Placing just before or after Kouchner in popularity polls, the figure long voted "most admired personality" in France was for decades the Abbé Pierre, apostle of decent housing for the poor. In his footsteps briskly walked Soeur Emmanuelle – like both l'Abbé Pierre and Kouchner, a blunt-speaking, kick-'em-in-the-pants scold. In the same spirit are France's 2,100 *Restos du Coeur* (canteens of the heart). Founded in 1985, *les Restos* boast 470,000 donors, and their 48,000 volunteers each year serve over 75 million free meals to the poor.

Why does all the above matter? First, because outside the scheming, often dirty corridors of politics, French people are helping millions of unfortunate human beings stay alive and healthy. Second, because it tells you that these frothy, frivolous French – those "sex-obsessed" party animals, those effete, wine-swilling, perfumed *fashionistas* – are, at bottom, a profoundly decent and moral people.

That's the shocking secret of France. And that's why, to keep it, along with their sulfurous reputation, the cynics always portray Kouchner with a sack of rice. As in nice – instead of naughty.

⁓

P.S. Finding your own Paris

This book gives only one man's personal impressions of Paris and Parisians, of France and the French. You should form your own.

First, read a little. Find an engaging book or two on Paris and France, picking ones that take you beyond clichés. Consider a solid but vivid history of France. A primer on French culture. Buy a French phrase-book to help you break the ice (or cause sympathetic hysterics) at hotel, restaurant, train station, and so on. That's a courteous and sometimes useful gesture, though basic English now flourishes almost everywhere. Finally, buy a good guidebook and a pocket map.

If you're game to go a bit further, or plan a much longer stay: Acquire a book – there are scores – on "understanding French psychology," and getting along with the French. Maybe also get an anthology of French popular thinkers, from Montesquieu to Luc Ferry, for an inkling of how French people reason and look at the world. Add a translated novel or two by Flaubert and Balzac to climb inside typical French characters. In Chapter Two, I mentioned those gritty *Inspector Maigret* novels by (Belgian) Georges Simenon. They're fun, and exist in English. Stir all this, then marinate.

Next advice: Get lost. Put on your walking shoes and wear them out. Wander to new Paris districts, and admire what's different and/or beautiful about each. Watch how people live in each, and how they make their own special Parises. Go to bed early sometimes, then get up at 5 or 6 a.m. to stroll and study the streets before a car or even a cat turns up.

As the sun slowly rises, watch its light creep down the façades. Marvel at the detail of buildings, vistas, little squares and tiny parks. Slip over to the small park behind *Notre-Dame* – where you will definitely see cats, on playful, early-morning patrol. Then perhaps take a detour across the Seine to the *Église Saint-Gervais* to watch the 7 a.m. procession of Jerusalem Fraternity "sisters and brothers" as they file in to chant, and to adore the Virgin Mary. Atheist, heathen, heretic, agnostic or believer, you will find the peace and mystery of this ceremony will move you, and awaken fresh thinking for the day. Next, stroll freely through the Marais, stopping for coffee and croissants in the grand symmetry of the Place des Vosges. Revel in being in Paris.

You will quickly find your own itineraries. The point is, you must walk, not ride (unless on a bicycle), and not sleep in. You will never see Paris as naked, true, secret and peace-giving as it is in early morning.

Third: Don't wait to make friends – especially French ones, but "foreigners" too. As anywhere else, slipping into Paris like a warm bath requires seeking and offering human warmth. Gently joke and tastefully flirt wherever you can. It's not hard to make friends in France, even among those supposedly hard-to-meet Parisians. Just use the old universal formulas: Take the initiative, find shared interests or solidarities – then, to make a friend, *be* a friend. If friendship (or a little dutiful flirting) lands you in a romantic liaison, don't feel guilty: It's all research.

Fourth, remember why you came to Paris. Apart from a simple change of pace, a celebration or a search for "culture," you should come to change your life – to whatever extent, and in whatever direction, you want. Without abandoning your values or personality, set out to find people and situations to enrich, even reshape, your life – your outlook, your taste, your biases, your long-held beliefs.

In my case, Paris hauled me at age twenty – but for life – out of a cocoon of narrow-minded, little-traveled conviction. It gave me skepticism, a lifelong habit of questioning 'undeniable' home truths. It gave me a horror of tribalism in all its forms – national, linguistic, racial, ethnic, religious and, I suppose now, even gender. Because of Paris, I'm now a radical anti-tribalist, convinced that the world's only hope for peace is intermarriage (or something like it) among all races and religions. In my view, sticking to "one's own people" is, over time, a guarantee of stupidity, bigotry and conflict. I question all credos about 'exceptional' or 'superior' peoples, nations and religions. Sorry: If the shoe fits… Just come back, I say, and rejoin the human race – the only 'race' worth winning.

As a student in Paris, I also learned something about emotion. I came to Paris in 1954 as an appallingly serious-minded young scholar, though a wildly idealistic one. There and then, I learned that mankind is more than mind and matter. It's heart. Grafted onto clear ideas, heart is what moves individuals, crowds and nations. Needless to say, getting my nose out of the books to meet French and other (for me) 'exotic' girls deepened my exposure to emotion. It put me – good-bye books! – on the thrilling roller-coaster of love.

A fifth piece of advice, especially to younger pilgrims: Use your trip to seize your life and pursue it. For Paris and France are places to reinvent the way you live. To figure out what life could be and should be, and how to live it well. How you define 'well' doesn't matter; what matters is simply living life your way, within an ethics and worldview you're comfortable with. And which, if possible, serves some version of civilization.

A sixth counsel: Don't over-praise the French, just respect them. For sure, don't try to ape them. Their customs and historical memories are so distinctive that you will end up venerating things the French actually consider absurd. We foreigners will always be pale-copy Frenchmen. You may think you've perfectly mastered the social codes; then, at a sensitive moment, you will put your foot in it – a "Danube peasant" who tries hard, but blurts out a gross indelicacy at a wedding. Study French culture seriously, praise what you can, and criticize what you dislike – but with warmth, wit and complicity. The French, all experts in contradictions, won't take offence. They'll admire your perceptiveness and integrity.

Corollary: Never forget who you are. If you do, the French will quickly remind you of who you are – and just at the moment you think you pass for a real Frenchman or French woman. If you're a Kazakh sheep-herder or Hong Kong derivatives trader, live that role, without fanfare and without feigning. Whoever you are, or whatever you do, you can dine out on it. For the French are insatiably curious. The more authentic you are, the more they'll want to know you.

Final advice: Never say *Adieu* to Paris. Or to France. It's just not possible. That's why, in their own and in every language, the French invented not just *Bon voyage…* but *Au revoir!*